Germany—
Phoenix in Trouble?

GERMANY
Phoenix in Trouble ?

Edited by Matthias Zimmer

University of Alberta Press

Published by
 The University of Alberta Press
 141 Athabasca Hall
 Edmonton, Alberta, Canada T6G 2E8

Copyright © The University of Alberta Press 1997

ISBN 0–88864–305–5

Canadian Cataloguing in Publication Data

Main entry under title:
 Germany—phoenix in trouble?

ISBN 0–88865–305–5

 1. Germany—Politics and government—1945–1990. 2. Germany—Politics and government—1990–
3. Germany—Economic conditions—1945– 4. Germany—Social policy.
1. Zimmer, Matthias.
DD290.25.G47 1997   943.087'9   C97–910729–6

∞ Printed on acid-free paper.
Printed and bound in Canada by Quality Color Press, Edmonton, Alberta, Canada.

The University of Alberta Press gratefully acknowledges the support received for its publishing program
from The Canada Council for the Arts, The Department of Canadian Heritage, and The Alberta
Foundation for the Arts.

Contents

Contributors

Dieter Haselbach is Reader and Director of European Studies at Aston University, Birmingham (UK). He was DAAD German Studies Professor at the University of Victoria, 1992–1995. His publications include *Franz Oppenheimer* (1985), *Autoritärer Liberalismus und Soziale Marktwirtschaft* (1991), and *Multiculturalism: Germany and Canada in Comparison* (ed., forthcoming). He is also one of the coeditors of Ferdinand Tönnies's Collected Works.

Walter R. Heinz is Professor of Sociology and Social Psychology and Chair of the Special Research Centre "Status Passages and Risks in the Life Course" at the University of Bremen, Germany. He was Visiting Professor in Canada at the Universities of British Columbia, Alberta, and Toronto, and in the United States at the University of Minnesota. His main research areas include labour markets, transitions from school to work, comparative education and training, and vocational stabilization. Among his recent publications are *Arbeit, Beruf und Lebenslauf* (1995) and *Society and Biography* (1996, ed. with A. Weymann).

Thomas Hueglin is Professor in the Department of Political Science at Wilfrid Laurier University in Waterloo, Ontario. His main areas of research include problems of European governance, federalism, and political economy. Among his publications are *Tyrannei der Mehrheit* (1977), *Sozietaler Föderalismus. Die politische Theorie des Johannes Althusius* (1991), and, recently, *Have We Studied the Wrong Authors? On the Relevance of Johannes Althusius as a Political Theorist* (1997).

Gert-Joachim Glaeßner is Professor of Political Science at Humboldt University in Berlin. He has been Professor at the Free University of Berlin from 1986 to 1992, guest professor at the universities in Loughborough (1989) and Bath (1990) in Great Britain and the University of Connecticut (1989), and Visiting Scholar at the London School of Economics and Political Science in 1994. His recent publications include *The German Revolution of 1989: Causes and Consequences* (1992), *Der schwierige Weg zur Demokratie. Vom Ende der DDR zur deutschen Einheit* (1992, 2nd. ed.), *Demokratie nach dem Ende des Kommunismus* (1994) and *Germany After Unification: Coming to Terms with the Recent Past* (1996).

Stefan Immerfall is Assistant Professor in the Department of Sociology at the University of Passau. He was DAAD German Studies Professor at the University of North Carolina at Chapel Hill from 1994 to 1996. Among his publications are *Einführung in den europäischen Gesellschaftsvergleich* (2nd. ed., 1995), *Die westeuropäischen Gesellschaften im Vergleich* (with S. Hradil, 1997) and *Territoriality in the Global Society* (ed., 1997).

Hans J. Michelmann is Professor at the Department of Political Studies at the University of Saskatchewan. His publications include *Organisational Effectiveness in a Multinational Bureaucracy* (1978) and, as coeditor, *Federalism and International Relations* (1990, with P. Soldatos), *The Political Economy of Agricultural Policy and Trade: Toward a New World Agricultural Order* (1990, with J.C. Stabler and G.G. Storey), *Politik und Politikstile in Kanada: Gesundheits- und energiepolitische Entscheidungsprozesse im Provinzenvergleich* (1991, with U. Kempf and T. Schiller), and, most recently, *European Integration: Theories and Approaches* (1994, with P. Soldatos). He has been coeditor of the *Journal of European Integration* since 1983.

Katherine Nash is a doctoral candidate in Sociology at the University of Minnesota. Her research interests focus on gender, work/family issues, and social policy.

Andreas Sobisch is Assistant Professor at John Carroll University, Cleveland, Ohio. He has published on the German and British party system and European integration. His most recent publication is *Developing European Citizens* (1997, with I. Davies).

Christian Tuschhoff is DAAD Visiting German Studies Professor at the Political Science Department of Emory University. He was a Volkswagen-Fellow at the American Institute for Contemporary German Studies and the German Historial Institute in Washington, 1992/1993 and Senior Research Fellow at the Center of Transatlantic Foreign and Security Policy Studies at the Free University of Berlin, 1988–1992. His publications include *Einstellung und Entscheidung: Perzeptionen im sicherheitspolitischen Entscheidungsprozess der Reagan-Administration* (1990), *Die Grundsteinlegung deutscher Sicherheitspolitik, 1949–1955* (1994), and *Machtgewinn auf leisen Sohlen: Deutschland, Kernwaffen und die NATO* (forthcoming).

Thomas von Winter has been Deputy Professor of Political Science at the University of Marburg and the University of Hamburg. Among his publications are *Politische Orientierungen und Sozialstruktur. Ein Beitrag zur Theorie des Wählerverhaltens* (1987), *Politische Kultur im nördlichen Hessen* (1993, ed. with T. Schiller), and, most recently, *Sozialpolitische Interessen. Konstituierung, politische Repräsentation und Beteiligung an Entscheidungsprozessen* (1997).

Matthias Zimmer is DAAD German Studies Visiting Professor in the Departments of Political Science and History and Classics at the University of Alberta. His publications include *Nationales Interesse und Staatsräson: Zur Deutschlandpolitik der Regierung Kohl, 1982–1989* (1992), *Eigentum und Freiheit* (1993, with U. Margedant), and *A Chorus of Different Voices: German Canadian Identities* (forthcoming, ed. with A. Sauer).

Abbreviations

BDA   *Bundesvereinigung Deutscher Arbeitgeberverbände* (Association of German Employers)

BDI   *Bundesverband der Deutschen Industrie* (Association of German Industry)

BP   *Bayernpartei* (Bavarian Party)

BVP   *Bayerische Volkspartei* (Bavarian People's Party)

CAP   Common Agricultural Policy

CDU   *Christlich Demokratische Union Deutschlands* (Christian Democratic Union of Germany)

COCOM   Coordinating Committee for East-West Trade Policy

CSCE   Conference on Security and Cooperation in Europe

CSU   *Christlich Soziale Union* (Christian Social Union)

DAG   Deutsche Angestellten-Gewerkschaft (German Association of White Collar Workers)

DBB   *Deutscher Beamtenbund* (German Association of Civil Servants)

DDP   *Deutsche Demokratische Partei* (German Democratic Party)

DGB   *Deutscher Gewerkschaftsbund* (German Association of Unions)

DIHT   *Deutscher Industrie- und Handelstag* (German Chamber of Industry and Commerce)

DVP   *Deutsche Volkspartei* (German People's Party)

DVU   *Deutsche Volksunion* (German People's Union)

EC   European Community

ECSC   European Coal and Steel Community

ECU   European Currency Unit

EDC   European Defence Community

EEC   European Economic Community

EFTA	European Free Trade Association
EMS	European Monetary System
EPC	European Political Community
ERM	Exchange Rate Mechanism
EU	European Union
FDGB	*Freier Deutscher Gewerkschaftsbund* (Free German Association of Unions)
FDP	*Freie Demokratische Partei* (Free Democratic Party)
FPÖ	*Freiheitliche Partei Österreichs* (Freedom Party of Austria)
FRG	Federal Republic of Germany
GDR	German Democratic Republic
HBV	*Gewerkschaft Handel, Banken und Versicherungen* (Union of Workers in Commerce, Banking and Insurance)
IGC	Intergovernmental Conference
INF	Intermediate Range Nuclear Forces
KPD	*Kommunistische Partei Deutschlands* (Communist Party of Germany)
MLF	Multilateral Force
NAFTA	North American Free Trade Agreement
NATO	North Atlantic Treaty Organization
NÖS	*Neues Ökonomisches System* (New Economic System)
NPD	*Nationaldemokratische Partei Deutschlands* (National Democratic Party of Germany)
NPG	Nuclear Planning Group
NSDAP	*Nationalsozialistische Deutsche Arbeiterpartei* (National Socialist Workers Party of Germany)
OECD	Organization for Economic Co-operation and Development
OPEC	Organization of Petroleum Exporting Countries
ÖTV	*Gewerkschaft Öffentliche Dienste, Transport und Verkehr* (Public Services and Transport Worker Union)
PDS	*Partei des Demokratischen Sozialismus* (Party of Democratic Socialism)
REP	*Die Republikaner* (Republican Party)
SED	*Sozialistische Einheitspartei Deutschlands* (Socialist Unity Party of Germany)
SPD	*Sozialdemokratische Partei Deutschlands* (Social Democratic Party of Germany)
WEU	Western European Union

Introduction

Stability and Crisis:
The German Model Challenged

MATTHIAS ZIMMER

I As Germany approaches the twenty-first century, it is faced with a variety of political, economic, and social problems that put the only recently united country to the test. Some argue that the defining characteristics Germany inherited from the Federal Republic of Germany (FRG) and that have guaranteed West Germany's stability over four decades are being challenged in the unification process.[1] Others see the "German model" with its social stability and its continuous economic growth rates in a major crisis.[2] Whenever the question of the stability of Germany becomes prominent, there is also concern which is rooted in the historical record of Germany in the twentieth century. The historical experience suggests that Germany has a tendency to resort to authoritarian solutions when faced with political, economic, and social turmoil. In other words, Germany might not only be in trouble, but potentially be trouble herself. Is the democratic tradition in Germany already well established to the point that those specters of history are effectively banned? This question is certainly of paramount interest for Germany's neighbours who are already faced with Germany becoming the dominant power in the center of Europe again.[3] Will the twenty-first century be faced with the *incertitudes allemandes*, the German troubles, as was the twentieth century?

Indeed, there is rarely any other nation who has had such a discontinuous history in the twentieth century as the Germans did—a history that is disrupted and disjointed in various ways and seems to swing like a pendulum from weakness to strength, from hubris to humiliation, from destruction to miraculous re-emergence. Defeated in the First World War, the German Reich, founded only in 1871, was transformed from a monarchy to a republic in 1918. Yet the republic was ill fated from the outset. Burdened by economic crisis, the humiliating Versailles Peace Treaty, a lack of popular support, and a growing political discontent, the feeble republic gave way to the National Socialist regime in 1933. During the twelve-year reign of the National Socialists, Germany was transformed into a totalitarian dictatorship. A massive state intervention into the economy and a large scale rearmament program helped to overcome the effects of the economic crisis of the early 1930s. The Weimar Republic's covert revisionism of the Versailles Peace Treaty became overt. Germany again became a power to be reckoned with. But the Nazis had plans that went beyond the revision of Versailles. Their quest for dominance in Europe and living space (*Lebensraum*) in the East plunged the world into another World War. Their racial fanaticism led, at the same time, to the most heinous crime in recorded history—the Holocaust—the industrialized mass murder of millions of Jews.

Following the destruction and defeat of Germany in 1945, Germany was occupied by the Allies. Torn apart by the emerging East-West Conflict, two states emerged from the ruins of the German Reich: the German Democratic Republic (GDR) in the East, a communist regime under Soviet tutelage, and the Federal Republic of Germany in the West with a liberal democratic constitution. It did not take decades to overcome the material effects of the war, as pessimists argued. Both German states quickly recovered from the devastation of the Second World War. The FRG in particular recovered in an unprecedented and almost miraculous way. Within two decades after the end of the war, West Germany had become one of the strongest economies in Europe, a partner on (almost) equal footing with France and Great Britain, and an essential part of the common Western political, economic, and military institutions. It is particularly this success story of a rise from the ashes that parallels West Germany's postwar history to the myth of the Phoenix, the bird rising renewed from the ashes. It shaped the FRG's image as an exemplary model of economic success and social and political stability at home and abroad.

Ironically, the deep caesura of 1989, which brought democratic freedom to Eastern Europe and East Germany, has raised doubts about the future of this image of Germany as an exemplary model. Germany and Europe found themselves facing a new situation: coming to terms with the collapse of the communist bloc and the transformation of the countries formerly under Soviet tutelage and devising a new political structure for Europe. The Germans were faced with the additional task of reuniting two different societies and overcoming the social and economic effects of four decades of division and of communist rule in East Germany. Decision makers in the FRG have tried to emulate the postwar recipe of West Germany's recovery to remedy the situation. The swift introduction of the West German social market economy, combined with substantial financial transfers to improve the infrastructure were at the core of this strategy. Moreover, a personnel transfer to the East and the immediate integration of East Germany into the institutions of the West were additional steps taken to ensure a rapid recovery. The expectation was that the new, the unified Germany would overcome all problems and that East Germany would quickly recover from 40 years of socialism.[4]

Yet this optimism, which found one memorable expression in Chancellor Helmut Kohl's prediction in 1990 that East Germany would, within five years, be transformed into blooming landscapes, has abated. The public mood has become more somber. The economic burdens of unification are still as straining as the obvious alienation between Germans in East and West. Political, social, and economic problems are abound in the unified Germany. The Phoenix may have risen from the ashes, but he is in trouble: his wings are clipped, and he flies more clumsily than elegantly into the dawn of a new European order.

This poetic image can be substantiated by a diagnosis of Germany's troubles on at least three different levels and in three issue areas.

In East Germany, the impact of unification and the regime transformation has had effects into all wrinkles of public and privates lives. East Germans had to bear the brunt of the unification process, having to adopt to a new political, legal, social, and economical environment. Individual life experiences have been devaluated on a large scale. A persistent and protracted economic crisis, manifest in high unemployment rates, is an additional burden for the East Germans.

In West Germany, the unification certainly did not have the dramatic effects it had in East Germany. But the costs of unification have amplified an already lingering economic recession and increased doubts on the feasibility of the welfare state on the level West Germans had been used to. Sentiments of frustration with an seemingly insatiable financial need for the "Reconstruction East," and higher taxation, levied in the name of all German solidarity, have strained the initial reactions of joy and helpfulness that had accompanied the fall of the Berlin Wall and the unification process. Moreover, West Germans have to come to terms with the fact that unification has not just added something to the "old" Federal Republic, but has created something qualitatively new. The new Germany is not merely the continuation of the FRG by other means, but has a quality of its own that questions the premises and perspectives of the "old" West German identity.

Last but not least, Germany as a whole has not yet transcended the cleavages and divisions between East and West. Germans are not "one people" as political slogans sometimes euphorically suggest. The harmonization of rules and regulations does not automatically ensure a harmonization of identities and biographies: the disparaging terms *Wessi* and *Ossi* are but an example for an existing mutual uneasiness. Moreover, it is unclear what particular national identity the unified Germany is about to develop. Will Germany foster her roots in the tradition of western liberal democratic ideas or revive concepts of a German *Sonderweg*? Will Germany continue to define her identity in European terms or become more self-assertive, more oriented towards national interests? The answer to those questions is intertwined with Germany's status and role in the international environment: What will Germany's role and status be in the new Europe? How will its position in the center of Europe affect its foreign policy? Will the European integration of Germany and her long tradition of a civilian and multilateral foreign policy be sufficient barriers to prevent a relapse into foreign policy patterns that are exclusively determined by national interests?[5] In short, what "philosophy" of foreign policy is the unified Germany about to adopt?

For most of its history, the FRG was a model of political, economic, and social stability. For the united Germany, this stability seems to have become questionable. Most of the issues troubling the united Germany today are a issues inherited from the "old" Federal Republic. This is not surprising giving the character of the unification process: the political, economic, and social structures of the FRG were exported to East Germany and implemented with great celerity. Apart from the problems arising from the transfer of a whole legal system into a different society, this transfer also carries the structural problems and deficiencies of the exporting society. Three different issue areas emerge where Germany's stability is challenged. First, the integrative potential of the existing party system is being challenged. Second, the prolonged economic crisis in Germany raises doubts about the continuation of the German economic miracle. Third, the crisis of the welfare state may end the social peace Germany has been taken for granted.

Ever since its early years, the FRG has been concerned about political stability. The Weimar Republic and its abundance of political parties that fragmented the political spectrum (and thus left the Republic vulnerable to the assault of extremist forces) was a spectre haunting the postwar politicians in the FRG. During the 1950s, the party system in West Germany narrowed down to major parties—the Christian Democratic Union and the Social Democratic Party—and one minor party, the liberal Free Democratic Party. Two factors contributed to this development. First, the introduction of a required minimum of the popular vote to be represented in the parliaments on the national and state levels sealed the fate of the small and marginal parties. Second, both major parties became *Volksparteien* ("catch-all parties") with a broad appeal to voters transcending traditionally defined milieus. This structure guaranteed political stability and continuity. Starting in the 1980s, three developments started to upset the established party system. First, the emergence of new social movements brought about the formation of the Green Party, which has been a factor to be reckoned with since the early 1980s. Second, the emergence of right-wing political parties provided voters with an opportunity to voice their protest against the "established" parties, leading to an intermittent electoral success of those parties. Third, a general decline in the voter turnout and in the ties between the established parties and the electorate indicate a growing dealignment of voters and a higher electoral volatility.[6] The unification in 1990 has added another dimension to the already existing problems of the party system. The "established" parties are institutionally weaker in East Germany than they are in West Germany. Moreover, the former communist party in East Germany, the Party of Democratic Socialism remains a regionally confined and defined political force which is also represented in the German lower house, the *Bundestag*. This opens a whole range of questions: Can political discontent be absorbed by the existing structures? Will Germany remain a stable democratic system even though the structure of the party system is changing?

The economic stability of the FRG, as defined by the 1967 Stability Act, rests on four pillars: steady economic growth, full employment, price stability, and an external balance. Whereas price stability and external balance have not been a major concern during the 1980s, a declining growth rate and rising numbers of unemployed have. Indeed, the growth rates have steadily declined starting in the 1960s, averaging at only 2.1% in the 1980s. This "gradually fading miracle"[7] of economic growth was accompanied by an increase in the number of unemployed during the second part of the 1980s. After a short-lived economic boom in the wake of unification, the unemployment rates have soared to unprecedented heights. Debates about the *Standort Deutschland*—Germany as an (attractive) industrial location—abound. One of the main arguments is that Germany has lost its attractiveness due to prohibitively high costs of labour. The high unemployment rates and low growth rates have strained the traditionally cooperative industrial relations that have for four decades smoothed social friction. How will Germany cope with a prolonged economic recession, how will it cope with high structural levels of unemployment? How will it affect the industrial relations and what will the political ramifications be?

Finally, the social stability in the FRG rested on her ability to alleviate social friction by redistributing wealth. The resulting welfare state with its generous unemployment benefits, a system of universal health care, comprehensive social security, and indexed pensions was in turn dependent on a certain level of economic growth to finance existing programs. Already during the 1980s, reform bills had to be introduced to cut down the explosion of costs and the proliferation of entitlements and to bring the social programs in tune with an economic reality of slowing growth rates. The already difficult situation was dramatically intensified with the unification of Germany. First, the expansion of social programs and entitlements to East Germany were saddled on already strained social budgets, alienating West Germans and East Germans alike. West Germans had to pay more into the social budgets while at the same time entitlements were rolled back. For East Germans, the application of West German social legislation contrasted unfavourably with the much more comprehensive welfare system in the GDR. Women in East Germany were particularly hard hit by the transformation; the lack of adequate child care facilities became one symbol of the alleged gender bias of the West German social system. Second, the massive influx of ethnic Germans from the Soviet Union and Eastern Europe and of foreigners following the collapse of the communist regimes additionally drained public social budgets. Subdued feelings of xenophobia erupted in violent outbursts against foreigners.[8] Those strains in the social fabric of the society lead to other troubling questions: How will Germany in the future cope with cutbacks in social programs that have been taken for granted? How will a more divided society deal with foreigners—can it maintain its liberal policies or is it bound to fall for nationalist and exclusionary political rhetoric? Last, but not least, can Germany become a society that respects diversity?[9]

All those question indicate a sense of crisis that Germany finds herself in today. One has to keep in mind, though, that some of those problems Germany faces are also problems her European neighbours are faced with. High unemployment, the crisis of the welfare state, dissatisfaction with the political elites, xenophobia, are all not typically German, but typical in the larger European context, indeed typical of industrial societies in general in the process of transformation to postindustrial societies.[10] Germany is, in effect, facing the challenge of managing both the transformation to the postindustrial society and the effects of unification. Germany is experiencing a dual crisis that puts the German model to an unprecedented test.

The collection of articles in this book addresses the different aspects of the predicaments Germany finds herself in, and reflects concerns and questions that have been raised about the future of the German model in the broadest sense. Focusing on the women in divided and unified Germany, Katherine Nash argues that they have been hard hit by unification and a protracted economic crisis; women in East Germany in particular bear the brunt of those changes. Walter R. Heinz describes the crucial phase of the transition of youth from education to work in a comparative perspective; the stratified education system in Germany and its institutionalized passages from education to work seem to be able to absorb some of the youth unemployment problems that Canada and the United States are faced with.

The economic crisis in Germany is the backdrop of the contribution by Thomas von Winter. He argues that industrial relations in Germany, having long been regarded as exemplary and instrumental for the social stability in Germany, have come under pressure from high unemployment rates and the forces of globalization; yet, he argues, the social partnership has proven to be flexible to cope with the new challenges. Dieter Haselbach focuses on the role the "social market economy" has for Germany's identity. In the 1950s, with the economic miracle, the "social market economy" became an integral part of West German identity. The

introduction of the "social market economy" in East Germany did not bring
about the desired result of a second miracle and thus questions one of the
central myths of German identity.

Thomas Hueglin's essay is a reminder that some of the old specters of
German history may not have been banned, but may be on the rise again;
nationalism and extremism seem to flourish in a climate of desolidarization
and social polarization. In the wake of those tendencies, racism and xenophobia manifest themselves in violent attacks against foreigners. The rise
of right-wing extremism has also left its traces in the German party system
which is, as Stefan Immerfall and Andreas Sobisch point out, undergoing a
transformation, trying to cope with both the changes in the industrial
society and the impact of unification. They conclude that it would be
premature to dismiss the integrative potential of the German
Volksparteien. Gert Joachim Glaeßner looks into the legacies of the
German Democratic Republic. What is left after the demise of the second
German state? The GDR has been, for 40 years, the frame of reference for
the people; understanding their history is necessary to obtain a deeper
understanding of the social divisions between East and West that burdens
the process of internal unification.

The first three contributions primarily look at the foreign policy dimension. Matthias Zimmer sketches the differing approaches of the FRG's
policy towards the national question during the decades of division. The
down-to-earth strategies of dealing with the national question and their
foreign policy implications may not only have paved the way for a smooth
unification, but may also become a valuable tradition for the unified
Germany. Christian Tuschhoff explicates two contending approaches for
explaining German foreign policy since 1949. Those approaches not only
draw a different picture with regards to the history and the nature of
German foreign policy, but also open differing options and perspectives of
German foreign policy today. The collection starts with Hans W.
Michelmann's analysis of Germany's integration into Europe. This dimension is crucial not only because of the persistent commitment of German
foreign policy makers to the European integration since 1949, but also
because the German unification in 1990 gave an additional impetus to the
process of uniting Europe. It seems that in particular for the German
government, European integration has become a cornerstone of the political *raison d'être* of German politics, indeed, as Chancellor Helmut Kohl
once argued, a question of war and peace for the twenty-first century.[11]

Maybe it is here, in the ever closer European Union, that the German Phoenix finds a lasting stability. And maybe the European Union is indeed the answer to the *incertitudes allemandes*, the German troubles, guaranteeing for both Germany and Europe a twenty-first century conspicuously different from the "age of extremes"[12]—the twentieth century.

NOTES

1. Peter Pulzer, "Unified Germany: A Normal State?" *German Politics* 3, no. 1 (April 1994): 1–17.
2. Hans Georg Betz, "The German Model Reconsidered," *German Studies Review* 19, no. 2 (May 1996): 303–20. In a broader context Michel Albert and Rauf Gonenc, "The Future of Rhenish Capitalism," *The Political Quarterly* 67, no. 3 (July-September 1996): 184–93.
3. See Ines Lehmann, *Die deutsche Vereinigung von außen gesehen: Angst, Bedenken und Erwartungen in der ausländischen Presse* (Frankfurt/Main: Lang, 1996); see also *Internationale Politik* 52, no. 2 (February 1997), which focusses on external perspectives on the united Germany and its international role.
4. From the vast amount of literature dealing with the unification process and its consequences see *inter alia* Konrad H. Jarausch, *The Rush to German Unity* (New York and Oxford: Oxford University Press, 1994); M. Donald Hancock and Helga A. Welsh, eds., *German Unification. Process and Outcomes* (Boulder: Westview, 1994); Ralf Altenhof and Eckhard Jesse, eds., *Das wiedervereinigte Deutschland. Zwischenbilanz und Perspektiven* (Düsseldorf: Droste, 1995); Robert Hettlage and Karl Lenz, eds., *Deutschland nach der Wende. Eine Bilanz* (Munich: Beck, 1995).
5. On the "civilian" tradition of German foreign policy see Hanns W. Maull, "Zivilmacht Bundesrepublik Deutschland. Vierzehn Thesen für eine neue deutsche Außenpolitik," *Europa–Archiv* 47, no. 10 (1992): 269–78. For the tradition of the center Matthias Zimmer, "Return of the 'Mittellage'? The Discourse of the Center in German Foreign Policy," *German Politics* 6, no. 1 (April 1997): 23–38. On German foreign policy options Gunther Hellmann, "Goodbye Bismarck? The Foreign Policy of Contemporary Germany," *Mershon International Studies Review* 40 (1996): 1–39.
6. See in general: Carsten Zelle, *Der Wechselwähler. Politische und soziale Erklärungsansätze des Wählerverhaltens in Deutschland und den USA* (Opladen: Westdeutscher Verlag, 1995); Michael Eilfort, *Der Nichtwähler: Wahlenthaltung als Form des Wahlverhaltens* (Paderborn: Schöningh, 1994).
7. Herbert Giersch, Karl-Heinz Paqué, Holger Schmieding, *The Fading Miracle: Four Decades of Market Economy in Germany* (Cambridge: Cambridge University Press, 1992), p. 4.
8. On the problems of foreigners and xenophobia see Thomas Faist, "How to Define a Foreigner? The Symbolic Politics of Immigration in German Partisan Discourse," *West European Politics* 17 (1994): 50–71; Manfred Kuechler, "Germans and 'Others': Racism, Xenophobia, or 'Legitimate Conservatism'?" *German Politics* 3, no. 1 (April 1994): 47–74; Dietrich Thränhardt, "The Political Uses of Xenophobia in England, France and

Germany," *Party Politics* (July 1995): 323–45. On political extremism in Germany see Geoffrey K. Roberts, "Extremism in Germany: Sparrows or Avalanche?" *European Journal of Political Research* 25 (1994): 461–82.

9.   For the underlying issues of Germany's citizenship stipulations, foreigners, and the questions of multiculturalism see Klaus J. Bade, *Ausländer, Aussiedler, Asyl. Eine Bestandsaufnahme* (Munich: Beck, 1994); Klaus J. Bade, ed., *Die multikulturelle Herausforderung. Menschen über Grenzen—Grenzen über Menschen* (Munich: Beck, 1996); Sabine von Dirke, "Multikulti: The German Debate on Multiculturalism," *German Studies Review* 17, no. 3 (October 1994): 513–36; Stefan Senders, "Laws of Belonging: Legal Dimensions of National Inclusion in Germany," *New German Critique*, no. 67 (1996): 147–76.

10.   See Stefan Immerfall, *Einführung in den europäischen Gesellschaftsvergleich*, 2nd revised edition (Passau: Rothe, 1995).

11.   Speech at the University of Leuven, 2 February 1996, in *Bulletin* (8 February 1996), ed. Presse- und Informationsamt der Bundesregierung, pp. 129–31; 130.

12.   Eric Hobsbawm, *The Age of Extremes: A History of the World, 1914–1991* (New York: Pantheon, 1994).

1

Germany and
European Integration

HANS J. MICHELMANN

I Of all the political metamorphoses in Western Europe over the last half century, that of Germany is unquestionably among the most dramatic. The image of a phoenix rising from the ashes surely applies to a nation that transformed itself from an international pariah in 1945 to the economic powerhouse of Europe some 50 years later, prosperous and democratic, with her two formerly separate component states politically united if not fully socially and economically integrated. A good part of the explanation of how this transformation came about can be found in the examination of domestic factors having to do with political, economic, and broadly social institutions and practices. But another part of the explanation must be based on an exploration of the European context in which the Federal Republic of Germany (FRG) unfolded and which helped to determine the direction of her development in the early postwar years. An exploration of West Germany's role in the process of European integration and of the development in the 50 years following World War II of an ever closer union among the nation states of Western Europe is central for an understanding of modern Germany.

Germany as a political issue, then as a founding country, and, subsequently, as a powerful member state, has been at the heart of the political, economic, and social processes that constitute European integration.[1] At the same time, European integration and the forms it took as a number of different Communities, has been of central importance to Germany, both in terms of its self-definition and its role in the world during the second half of the twentieth century, and in terms of its impact on German domestic politics and policy. This chapter explores these themes, first, by giving a brief overview of Germany's role in European integration and the impact of the Communities on Germany's international role, and then by exploring what membership in the various Communities has meant for German domestic affairs.

The External Dimension

Germany was a main protagonist in the wars that have scarred European and world history in the twentieth century; indeed she was the precipitating actor in World War II and an international pariah at its close because of the horrors of the Holocaust and the suffering her armed forces had inflicted on the length and breadth of Europe and the world. She had experienced the thorough and utter defeat of her powerful military machine. Her cities lay in ruin as did large parts of her industries that had become the heart of her economic life. Many of her people had been uprooted and were refugees in those parts of Germany not destined for annexation to her neighbours. Weakened, and occupied by her former enemies, Germany was loathed because of what had occurred since 1933 and feared because of the potential of her military revival. The four major nations that had defeated her carved Germany's territory into zones of occupation. These became the basis of the division of Germany in 1949, after the commencement of the Cold War, into the Federal Republic of Germany, also known as West Germany, and the German Democratic Republic (GDR), or East Germany. East Germany was integrated into the Soviet Empire and played little or no independent role internationally. But, the Federal Republic of Germany had restored to her many of the instruments of national sovereignty on her founding. What role she was to play in the family of nations was one of the main questions on the international agenda of the postwar period.

A large part of the answer to that question came from among West European nations with the acquiescence, even active encouragement, of the United States of America (USA), the superpower anchoring the emerging Western alliance. It came in the form of the advocacy for uniting Europe to undermine the basis of the excessive nationalism that had helped lead Europe to chaos, and for engaging West Germany in a common European enterprise. One of the primary reasons, then, for the establishment of the first of a number of European integration schemes was the collective containment of Germany by her neighbours and the enmeshing of West Germany in a web of institutions and relationships which would help to ensure that she would develop along a liberal democratic trajectory domestically, and a peaceful one internationally.

The first such scheme in which West Germany became a member with France, Italy, and the Benelux countries in 1951–1952 was the European Coal and Steel Community (ECSC). Among its purposes was the establishment of joint, i.e., international, control over the strategic coal and iron/steel industries in participating member states. This was proposed in good part to ensure that in West Germany they would not be used to relaunch a strong military machine, but also to rationalize these industrial sectors in a larger economic space, and set up of the concomitant trading regime (a customs union) for their products.

But this scheme and others to follow could not function well if West Germany were to be a mere passive object of control and not an eventually equal and even enthusiastic participant. There were also reasons of *Realpolitik* to court West Germany's active cooperation in the creation of a European family of nations. As the Cold War began and then persisted, a reviving West Germany, the Germany of the *Wirtschaftswunder* (economic miracle), became the potential and then the actual centrepiece of a strengthening, integrated West European economy crucial for helping to sustain a collective North American-West European effort at containing the threat of what governments in the North Atlantic area were convinced was an expansionist Soviet Empire. Of course a rearming of West Germany was tremendously controversial. Thus was devised a plan for a European Defence Community (EDC) in which participating member states, including West Germany, were to pool their military forces under the command of non-German officers. This plan, proposed by France in 1952 and ratified by the Benelux countries, Italy, and West Germany, failed on its ratification vote in the French Parliament due to the combined votes of nationalist Gaullists and pro-Soviet Communists. With the demise of the EDC were also stillborn the plans for a radical European Political Community, that would have led to a rapid political integration of partici- pating states. In the meantime, however, the need to devise a system of burden sharing in West European defence had been unmet. In 1955, at the insistence of a United States wishing to harness growing West German resources in the interest of a collective defence effort that lay dispropor- tionately on America, the FRG reluctantly rearmed under the aegis of NATO and in return had restored to her most of the instruments of national sovereignty that had been held back at the founding of the Federal Republic of Germany in 1949.

These security considerations were very much in line with Chancellor Konrad Adenauer's efforts to anchor the FRG in the Western Alliance, though there is a sense in which, notwithstanding some strong domestic opposition to that policy from the ranks of the Social Democratic Party

(SPD), she had little choice but to go along with what the victorious Western allies prescribed. Equally important for FRG's anchoring in the West were the economic reasons for the creation of the various European communities. These transcended narrow security considerations. Such economic rationales could be supported by the West German government out of strong positive conviction and for reasons of national interest. West Germany's rapid economic recovery after 1948 was based theoretically on the economic principles of the Freiburg school, espoused most prominently by Ludwig Erhard, father of West Germany's postwar economic miracle as economics minister and then the Federal Republic's second chancellor. Pre-eminent among these principles was free trade. The abolition of barriers to trade among member states and the establishment of common foreign trade policies were key features of the successful European integration schemes, hence West Germany's interests as the strongest industrial power in Western Europe were well served by the ECSC and the European Economic Community (EEC). At least during the Adenauer era, which encompassed the formative years of the FRG and those of the European movement alike, the universalistic and humanistic principles of the European Christian Democratic parties and politicians, among them Konrad Adenauer, Italy's Alcide de Gasperi, France's Maurice Schuman and Belgium's Paul Henri Spaak, provided the ideological foundation for the European enterprise at a time when such ideological appeals were more powerful than they are now. West Germany's participation in the European communities, then, was consonant with post-World War II international realities including the interests and policies of the USA, France, and the United Kingdom (UK), the economic and social doctrines of Germany's strongest political movements, and her interests as Europe's foremost industrial state. This anchoring in the European Community (EC) has remained a keystone of Germany's foreign policy to the present day.

In the years following the inauguration of the ECSC in 1952, West Germany's governments and her people were among the most enthusiastic proponents of European integration. Because of the legacy of World War II, Bonn governments from the outset took a restrained and passive approach to foreign relations, an approach that soon gave her the reputation in world affairs (only now beginning to dissipate) of economic giant but political dwarf. In the EC's political affairs she was content to play a backstage role, letting others, particularly France, take the lead, even when the results of such leadership ran counter to her vision of a strong, federally united Community or at times her interests. Thus, for example, French President Charles de Gaulle opposed increasing the authority of Community institutions in 1966 and vetoed British requests for accession in the 1960s, both measures strongly supported by West Germany. De Gaulle's actions were in line with his vision of the Community as an inter-governmental regional organization led by France, the core of a Europe extending from the Atlantic to the Urals and acting as a third major power bloc, even to intervene between the two superpowers if necessary. Such a vision was contrary to West Germany's preferences for a strong, federal Europe operating as an ally and not a potential rival of the USA, whose nuclear umbrella protected West Germany in her exposed position adjoining the fault line that divided Europe into two great contending camps. But because reconciliation with France was also a *sine qua non* of West German foreign policy and a central rationale for her European policies, West Germany deferred the pursuit of Community organizing principles and membership policies more congenial to her until a change of government in France made their attainment more likely.

In the meantime, given her economic strength and the array of common policies that arose after the inauguration of the EEC in 1958, West Germany became the single largest financial contributor to Community coffers,[2] a role she continues to play currently and is sure to play for the foreseeable future, and one that gave and gives her great influence. West Germany's weight in the Community also increased inexorably over the years as her steady economic and financial policies, especially those dedicated to the fight against inflation, impelled the German mark from strength to strength against other major Community currencies. Thus it was not necessary for her to take a visibly political leadership role in the Community to have a strong influence among the Six, the Nine, the Ten, the Twelve and now the Fifteen,[3] a role that in the past would not have been welcomed by her EC partners.

The German mark became the central currency in various mechanisms established to stabilize Community exchange rates and thus to help foster intra-Community trade and economic stabilization, if initially not monetary integration. West German economic policy effectively determined much of the Community's conjunctural cycle. This was demonstrated most clearly in those instances when other member states attempted to undertake policies that were out of phase with West Germany's macroeconomic orientation. One striking example was the French Socialist government's reversal after two years of its reflationary policies initiated in the heady days following its 1981 electoral victories, when the franc, because French economic policies were out of phase with those pursued by West Germany and the countries in her monetary orbit, went into a near free-fall against the mark and other Community currencies. Though not visibly at the forefront of political leadership in Western Europe, West Germany, because of her economic might, had by the late 1980s become the Community's *de facto* powerhouse. This economic clout bestowed upon her the coleadership of the Community. When French and West German leaders saw eye to eye, the Community maintained a sense of direction and could undertake joint action; when there was discord between the two countries, the Community often appeared to lose its sense of direction.

The dramatic events leading to German unification in 1990 again demonstrated the centrality of the European Community to Germany and Germany to the European Community. They also initiated a new phase in Germany's European role. In the immediate aftermath of the fall of the Berlin Wall and during what seems in retrospect to be the inevitable progress towards unification of the two Germanys, it became clear that past suspicions and rivalries in the Community had not fully been laid to rest. This was made most evident by the actions of the French and British leadership. French President François Mitterrand demonstrated through a variety of statements and actions his reservations about unification and the strengthened Germany that would result. Before unification West Germany was the most populous Community member state; after unification she would, with 80 million people, have approximately one-and-one-half times the population of the next biggest member state and a similar if not greater edge in economic terms. Thus the uniting of the two Germanys had the potential to eclipse the role of France even more. Similar reservations about unification were expressed by Margaret Thatcher and members of her government.

In the event, such reservations about a united Germany were far from powerful enough to counteract the forces that impelled unification. The most important among them were: 1) the determination of the Kohl/Genscher government to push ahead with rapid unification; 2) the eagerness of the GDR government elected in March 1990 and that of a strong majority of citizens of the GDR to unite with the FRG; 3) the strong support of the American Bush administration and that of some other German allies for unification; 4) the acquiescence of the Soviet Union's President Mikhail Gorbachev to unification after a series of meetings with Chancellor Kohl that assuaged major Soviet security concerns; and, last but not least, 5) the determined support by European Commission President Jacques Delors for German unification and his successful lobbying of European leaders.[4]

The centrality of the EC to FRG's external relations once more became evident in Mr. Kohl's and Foreign Minister Genscher's explanations of a united Germany's place in the world. To reassure his European allies as well as his neighbours to the East that a unified Germany posed no risk to them, Mr. Kohl reiterated his strong support for a strongly federal EC with more powerful institutions, including a considerably strengthened Parliament, and increased responsibility for common policies. The corollary was a cession of powers to the Community. Sensitive matters over which the Kohl government was prepared to transfer power to Brussels came to include many aspects of foreign and security as well as immigration policies, border controls, and, most controversially in Germany, the creation of a common European currency, with all the reduction of member state sovereignty entailed in Community control over fiscal and monetary policies required for the establishment of an economic and monetary union.

In underlining the German government's strong support for increased powers, Mr. Kohl and Mr. Genscher wished to make it clear that these developments would lead to a Germany strongly enmeshed in a democratic EC, a Europeanized, nonthreatening united Germany that could be trusted to keep the peace and to work at the forefront of those states wishing to further advance European integration. The consistency of this theme with Germany's approach to the world 40 years before is striking (and the need to make such arguments says much about the persistence of outdated stereotypes even among her fellow member states). What had changed in the meantime was Germany's now central role in Europe and her need to assuage the status concerns of two of her two most powerful allies in the European enterprise, France and the UK.

That the arguments about a Europeanized Germany were not simply an expedient to gain acquiescence by two of the four states whose assent was required for the legal unification of the two Germanys has become evident in the German government's continued strongly pro-European policies through the 1990s. Mr. Kohl's commitment to closer integration has been made manifest by numerous actions and pronouncements: his government's strong support for the Maastricht Treaty;[5] for enlargement of the European Community/European Union (EC/EU) to include East European countries; for the implementation of the Schengen agreement to arrive at policies that would allow the removal of border controls among European Union (EU) member states and thus to facilitate the free flow of people across EU frontiers as well as a more uniform treatment of the influx, legal, quasi-legal or illegal of third country nationals into the Union; and, most recently, his continuing strong support for economic and monetary union in the face of persistent majority of a German public, of late loath to give up its cherished Deutschmark for a common European currency.

It might be added that many of these policies were and are in Germany's national interest. As the member state with the strongest economy, a very liberal policy towards refugees and asylum seekers (altered by legislation in 1993), and as the member state situated, until Austrian accession, closest to many of the regions that were actually or potentially the source of much of the flow of refugees into Europe in the turbulent post-Cold War era, it was in her interest to arrive at common measures at more effective influx control and to have other member states share the burden of supporting dislocated foreign nationals that had fallen disproportionately on Germany. Similarly, the accession of East European states to the EU would help to bring about a greater sharing of the obligation to aid these countries that, for historical reasons, fell to a large extent on German shoulders, provide a buffer between herself and a Russia which, together with her client states, still constitute a strikingly unstable region, and draw more closely into her economic orbit countries that have been traditional German trading partners.[6]

Similarly, in its relations with countries beyond Europe, Germany is able to profit from its European vocation. Her increasingly warm ties with Israel, the unlikeliest of friendly partners, have benefited from her propensity to channel her foreign policy through Europe.[7] What is more, Germany is beginning to chide her fellow member states about their fiscal rectitude and preparedness for economic and monetary union, even bully them, according to former Chancellor Helmut Schmidt.[8] And in concert with her European and North American allies she undertook what until recently seemed unthinkable, to send German troops onto foreign soil on a peace-keeping mission in the former Yugoslavia. What has happened, then, especially since unification in 1990, is the completion of the transformation of Germany's role in the world from a political dwarf to a player willing to exercise a degree of influence commensurate with her economic might. This transformation of Germany's international behaviour must rank with one of the most important features and greatest rewards of her membership in the EC/EU.

German Unification and European Integration

West German membership in the European Community was crucial for the foreign policy dimensions of German unification, one of the most momentous developments in German history since World War II. This was so because Germany's firm anchoring in the EC/EU helped to allay the suspicions and concerns of her European neighbours regarding a significantly strengthened Germany, even if they did not reduce the status anxieties of some politicians in such powers as France, the UK, and even Italy.[9] But this is not the whole story of the impact of EC membership on unification. This story began well before those dramatic weeks in 1989. It began at the time of West German membership in the Communities when West German negotiators ensured that intra-German trade (i.e., trade between the FRG and the GDR) would not be subject to the Community's trade regime, the GDR, for purposes of trade, being effectively included in the EC. This led some commentators to claim that the Community had always had a hidden additional member; for the FRG this provision facilitated the various trade and economic policies by which FRG sought to ease the life of GDR citizens in the years before 1989.

The accession of the GDR to the Communities could have taken one of two forms: either through an application for membership independently through a series of negotiations, or by way of integration into the FRG through the provisions of the Basic Law's original (unamended) Article 23 and then a simultaneous and automatic membership by virtue of the GDR having become an integral part of an existing member state. The second course of action was clearly more acceptable to the political leadership of the two Germanys in the rush toward unification during the days after the GDR election in 1990. It also had the support of a majority of Germans and citizens of Community member states early in that year. Opinion polls showed that the large majority of GDR citizens were aware of and favourably disposed toward European integration. Citizens of the FRG, for their part, when polled at the same time, demonstrated a striking support for their country's existing international commitments particularly those to her West European allies: while 77 percent were in favour of German unification, support for unification at the expense of continuing German membership in NATO dropped to 24 percent, and only four percent were willing to sacrifice membership in the EC for unification. Across the Community as a whole, fully 71 percent favoured German unification (though with variations of from 52 percent to 81 percent in individual member states), probably being convinced by the argument that a Europeanized united Germany was unlikely to undertake a *Sonderweg*.[10] East German accession as part of united Germany was officially sanctioned by the Community's special Dublin Summit of April 1990, whose concluding communiqué read in part:

> We are pleased that German unification is taking place under a European roof. The Community will ensure that the integration of the territory of the German Democratic Republic into the Community is accomplished in a smooth and harmonious way. The European Council is satisfied that this integration will contribute to faster economic growth in the Community and agrees that it will take place in conditions of economic balance and monetary stability.[11]

In the event, the consequences of German unification for the EC/EU were not as smooth as the Dublin Summit's communiqué had predicted. Indeed, financing the huge financial transfers to the five new *Länder* by the German government in the adjustment period after unification led to substantial government borrowing, inflationary pressures in the old *Länder* as the increased demand stimulated by spending in the former East Germany was met, and unprecedented increases in German interest rates mandated by the *Bundesbank*. These, in turn, put unbearable pressure on a number of other Community currencies, forcing the UK out of the European Monetary System shortly after that member state had entered at considerable domestic political cost to its government, and forcing devaluation in other currencies. Repeated calls from its monetarily weaker fellow member states for a decline in German interest rates were not heeded by the *Bundesbank*, whose resolve to fight inflationary pressures is legendary.

The resulting financial turmoil led to considerable discord in the Community.

Domestically, accession went more smoothly. The five new *Länder* were subject to some 80 percent of Community laws upon entry. The remaining provisions, especially in the sensitive areas of agricultural policy, the environment and regional policies became effective after two transitional periods terminating, respectively, in 1992 and 1995. Because the former East Germany is an economically underdeveloped region when compared to most of the Union, with a level of prosperity roughly equivalent to that in the Iberian member states, the five new *Länder* are entitled to regional aid from the EU in Brussels. This in a not unimportant aspect of Germany's membership in the European Union.

Germany, European Integration and the Domestic Constitutional Balance

An examination of the implications of German membership in the EC/EU for the constitutional relationship between Bonn and the *Länder* governments provides a useful transition as we shift our focus more closely to domestic politics. One of the classical questions about the external relations of federal states is the division of constitutional powers between the national and component unit governments on international matters and the actual apportionment of responsibilities for them, which may not reflect the actual wording of constitutional texts.[12] In Germany, given the centrality of federalism to the constitutional order, intergovernmental relations, both vertical and horizontal, permeate "all aspects of political life."[13] As is the case in practically all constitutions of federal states, powers over foreign relations were awarded the federal government in the Basic Law. The forgers of the Basic Law also made provisions for German participation in international organizations through its Article 24, which states that "(t)he Federation may by legislation transfer sovereign power to intergovernmental institutions." Federal politicians have traditionally argued that this article confers upon Bonn the right to transfer powers to the European level, whether or not these were in its jurisdictional domain.[14] These arguments were based not only on a literal interpretation of Article 24 and the normal propensity of politicians and public servants to protect and expand their turf, but also on what the *Auswärtige Amt* (foreign office) believed were practical necessities. Its officials thought that due to the complexity, importance, and intensity of relations with Brussels, it was essential that the FRG should speak with a single voice in the Community, and that the involvement of the *Länder*, if only on matters that were domestically under their jurisdiction, would not only significantly complicate the representation of German interests, but could tempt the other participants in European decision making to play off the various German actors, thus undermining the national interest.

It should come as no surprise that the *Länder* disagreed fundamentally. The strength of their feeling on this issue can be explained in part as resulting from frustration at the erosion of their legislative powers brought about by the federal government's increasing use of the Basic Law's concurrent powers over the years, which left the *Länder* powers to legislate in but a few areas, culture, education, and communications and broadcasting foremost among them. *Länder* governments argued that the domestic division of powers should not be altered by the process of European integration so that the federal government became responsible exclusively for representing in Brussels matters that domestically were in their jurisdiction. As Brussels became active in some of these areas, *Länder* governments saw their remaining modest jurisdictional base eroding further, with little participation by them in the decision-making process leading to the transfer of powers to the European institutions and no guarantee of influence in the implementation of the policies subsequently made in Brussels.

The pattern of federal dominance on European matters was set early on. Konrad Adenauer was reluctant to have the *Länder* participate in European matters. In the establishment of the ECSC and in its subsequent operation, the federal government did little but keep the *Bundesrat* informed about ongoing developments. When the Treaty of Rome inaugurating the EEC was ratified by the West German Parliament, the *Bundesrat*, whose assent was required, managed to extract from the federal government a commitment to provide information on a continuing basis about the legislative activities of the EEC's Council of Ministers, the Community's principal legislative institution. Relevant documentation was sent to the *Bundesrat*'s Committee for Questions of the European Community. The *Bundesrat*'s views were often taken into account by the *Bundestag* and the federal government because of the technical expertise that *Länder* administrators could bring to bear on the matters at hand. But this manner of bringing to bear *Länder* influence was not unambiguously effective because the upper chamber had no effective legal leverage over the federal executive on most matters treated in Brussels.

Because this was so, the *Länder* sought additional means of making their influence felt. They sought to have *Länder* representatives as part of the delegations to the EC or of the West German contingent on EC committees. They were allowed an alternate member on two committees dealing with vocational education and regional affairs, respectively. When *Länder* representatives accompanied the West German contingent, they did so subject to the instruction of the West German chief representative, always a federal official, and because the federal government insisted on its preeminence in German representation to the Communities. Since the inception of the EEC and European Atomic Energy Community (Euratom), the *Länder* have also had an observer in Brussels, whose status was regularized through agreement with the federal government. He has in recent years been nominated by the conference of *Länder* economics ministers. With his seat in Bonn and an office in Brussels, the observer attends meetings of the EU Council of Ministers as a member of the German delegation, and reports to the *Länder* the most important developments taking place in Brussels. Through the observer, the *Länder* have had an independent source of information about Council developments, but one person is unable to do much lobbying for the *Länder*, let alone provide a comprehensive intelligence gathering service for them individually or collectively.

Over the years, with unrelenting pressure from the *Länder*, the federal government conceded to the *Länder* additional means to influence the Community decision making process without, however, giving up its claim to represent Germany's interests, including those of the *Länder*, because it maintained its view that once jurisdiction over a matter was transferred to Brussels, the domestic division of powers was no longer of consequence. In 1979, the federal government committed itself to making serious attempts at coming to a common position with the *Länder* on matters either entirely or in part in their jurisdiction, and then representing that position in Brussels and deviating from it only for the most serious foreign or integration political reasons. It pledged to involve two *Länder* representatives in Council when matters under their exclusive jurisdiction were under consideration and on Commission committees insofar as such representation was feasible. In typical German fashion, an elaborate inter-*Länder* coordination mechanism was created to facilitate the increased paper flow required to sustain the new procedure.

This new procedure did not lay to rest all *Länder* concerns. It became clear that the federal government continued to give priority to its own views of West German interests, and thus a number of *Länder* persisted in pressing for the legalization of the 1979 agreements. The opportunity to do so in part came in 1986 with the passage of the Single European Act, an EC legislative initiative critical for completing the Community's internal market and one enhancing Community institutions' decision-making powers, for which *Bundesrat* approval was required in the ratification process. In essence, the *Länder* forced the federal government to entrench the consultation process on EC matters affecting their powers in the ratifying law of the Single European Act as a *quid pro quo* for their speedy assent to that measure. At about the same time, the *Länder* undertook to represent their interests toward the Community even more aggressively. Contrary to the wishes of the *Auswärtige Amt* and previous practice, which assigned German permanent representation abroad exclusively to the federal government, they established contact offices (*Länderbüros*) in Brussels to look after their particular concerns, though, in deference in part to federal sensibilities, as institutions of private, not public, law.[15] This practice reflected the growing importance of the Community for *Länder* concerns; it also demonstrated a new level of assertiveness by them in their dealings with the federal government on EC matters.

A final step in this progression of increasing the profile of the *Länder* in German interactions with the European institutions came at the time of the ratification of the Maastricht Treaty. The changes took the form of amendments to the Basic Law's Article 50, which previously stipulated that the *Bundesrat* participates in the legislation and administration of the Federation, to read that the *Bundesrat* now participates in legislation and administration of the Federation and in matters pertaining to the European Union.[16] Hence the *Länder* now constitutionally have the right to participate in making and implementing laws pertaining to Germany's membership in the EU.

A revised Article 23 of the Basic Law now fully constitutionalizes the relationship between federation and *Länder* on matters pertaining to EU legislation. In those areas in which the federation has powers to legislate but *Länder* interests are affected, the federation must take into account the opinion of the *Bundesrat* but is not bound by that institution's majority vote. But where the *Länder*'s legislative powers, their institutions, or their administrative procedures and powers are affected, the *Bundesrat*'s opinions must be given "due consideration" in federal decision making. If no agreement can be reached between the federal government and the *Bundesrat*, a decision taken in that institution by two-thirds majority is binding on the federal government. An amendment of the EEC Treaty's Article 146 allows a Land minister to represent Germany in the EU Council of Ministers, and regularizes the previously established practice of allowing *Länder* representation in German delegations when substantial *Länder* interests are involved in European negotiations. Most importantly, the Basic Law's revised Article 23 stipulates that when the exclusive legislative jurisdiction of the *Länder* is affected, Germany's rights as a member state of the EU "shall be transferred by the Federation to a representative of the *Länder* designated by the *Bundesrat*. Those rights shall be exercised with the participation of and in agreement with the Federal government; in this connection the responsibility of the Federation for the country as a whole shall be maintained."

The significance of these developments for German federalism has been summarized by Goetz, who argues in essence that the revised practice does not fundamentally challenge the balance between federation and *Länder*, but in fact brings it in line with the pattern of close cooperation and negotiation between levels of government and the Bonn legislative institutions typical for German federalism in other policy sectors.[17] The *Länder* have reasserted their interests on European policy by seeing to it that they have access to decision making in Brussels and that they have strong influence on German decisions with respect to the EU in areas of their jurisdiction. In addition, they have been among the strongest proponents in the EU of "subsidiarity," the principle that decision making should take place at the level most close to the citizen while still in accord with Union norms, thereby reducing the need for Community level action on matters best decided locally. Thus the outcome of the struggle between the *Länder* and the federal government concerning jurisdiction over European matters has set aright a relationship that had over the years become unbalanced. Such an adjustment is all the more appropriate in an era when member state relations with the EU, because of the increase in EU decision making, are seen as less and less in the realm of foreign policy and increasingly as part of domestic affairs.

The Impact of Community Policies

The move toward higher levels of European integration over the years has involved the shifting of powers over a number of significant public policy sectors from member state governments to the European institutions. Progress toward higher levels of policy integration has been arduous and slow in some areas. In others it developed more rapidly and completely because of the nature of agreements struck when the Communities were forged and because of the interests of powerful member states. The establishment of the ECSC and the successful policy integration in these industrial sectors so vital for the economies of the 1950s resulted from a coincidence of member state interests and skilful institution building.

The establishment of the Euratom and the EEC in 1958 led to further projects for common decision making.[18] Central to the goal of forging an ever closer union among the people of Europe was the idea of an enmeshing of member state economies, in large part through the instrumentality of trade. Thus came about the establishment of a customs union for intra-EEC trade in all industrial goods. This feature of the nascent Community was clearly of advantage to West Germany. With respect to intra-Community trade, it has often been said that the crucial bargain underlying the establishment of the EEC was one between the two most powerful founding member states, France and West Germany, whereby France, because of her large and, in the European context, relatively efficient agricultural sector, was accorded a common agricultural policy in return for the creation of a customs union for trade in all goods that was in the interest of the FRG, the nascent Community's most efficient industrial economy. Indeed, it became customary to refer to the European enterprise as a customs union with an agricultural policy.

The Common Agricultural Policy

The Common Agricultural Policy (CAP) replaced member states' farm policies. Implemented to increase efficiency and productivity in the agricultural sector, to help bring about stable food prices, and to provide a secure supply of high quality foodstuff for the Community citizens, another objective, the maintenance of a fair standard of living for those gaining their livelihood in the industry, became preeminent. Agricultural goods are traded freely within the Community and policy decisions, including those on agricultural prices, are made in

Brussels. The CAP includes a structural fund that is meant to subsidize modernization of agriculture. To realize the CAP's main objective and thus to maintain prices at levels that result in acceptable incomes for member state farmers, a levy is placed on agricultural imports from third countries. Domestically, agricultural commodities are "bought into intervention" once their price falls below a certain level. Because of the tendency for protectionist practices to lead to increased production, the CAP has often in the past led to huge oversupplies of such commodities as grains, meat, milk products, and wine, which have been bought up and stored at great cost so as not to depress prices. Exports of these high priced commodities are subsidized, again at great expense. These export subsidies have led EU's trading partners to accuse Europe of dumping these commodities and have been the cause of major trade disputes with them over the years. The cost of the CAP reached 70 percent of the Community's budget at times in the past. In recent years, measures have been implemented to reduce production of commodities in surplus supply, with the result that farm expenditures will gradually decline, and the EU's trade officials have been able to convince her trade partners that decreased production will gradually lead to a less prominent role for EU farm products on international markets.

Germany's interests, on the whole, have not been well served by the CAP. Internationally, she is interested in peaceful economic relations in her role as one of the great trading nations of the world and the disruptions caused by disputes between the EC/EU and its trading partners over agricultural trade have not served her well. As a highly industrialized country with a small agricultural sector and as a large net importer of foodstuffs, the high price European food policy is not in her national interest. Germany's contributions to the CAP amounted in 1993 to about 30 percent of total expenditures while receipts flowing to Germany amounted to only half that amount.[19] And yet her agriculture ministers have often supported high prices in Brussels. This anomaly can be explained not so much by German governments' generally pro-integration attitude (although German governments know that a price has to be paid for European cooperation) as it can by domestic politics. Despite the small number of farmers, the agricultural sector is highly organized and influential politically. Moreover, public opinion tends to be supportive of safeguarding the economic and social viability of rural areas and maintaining agricultural land in production. The CAP's increased emphasis on environmental concerns has helped to make it more palatable to the ecologically conscious German public.

Unification has led to a somewhat increased importance of the CAP for Germany. Eastern Germany has historically had a disproportionately large agricultural sector, and the GDR had a large agricultural workforce of 800,000, as well as twice as much farm land per capita as West Germany.[20] Because of its low productivity, GDR agriculture was highly subsidized. It was severely challenged by the transition to the market economy after unification, and by 1994 the agricultural workforce in the five new *Länder* had been reduced to 224,000.[21] CAP funds contributed importantly in the adjustment to more efficient production and the laying fallow of some 17 percent of farmland there.[22] But even with the additional CAP funds flowing to her as a result of the disproportionately large agricultural sector in the new *Länder*, Germany still contributes in a major way to the Community's agricultural coffers.

With continuing rationalization in a sector that has lost 3.2 million jobs in the years from 1960 to 1992 and in which a farmer who could produce sufficient foodstuffs for ten people in 1950 can now feed 80,[23] the political clout of farmers is in continuous decline. Such rationalization is proceeding apace at the European level, and the forces of free trade and globalization at the broader international level will ensure that one of the most prominent EU policies will diminish in importance as the Union is forced to adjust its very expensive and relatively inefficient subsidization policies. With its decline in importance, the CAP will be less of a drain on German finances, but it will become controversial again if the Union chooses to allow the accession of Central and East European states such as Poland, Hungary, the Czech Republic, and Slovakia, all countries in which inefficient agriculture employs a much higher percentage of the workforce than the EU average, and where implementation of the CAP would be hugely expensive. Germany, favourable toward eastward expansion of the EU, would then pay a high percentage of the resulting costs. Hence, Germany's attitude toward the CAP is likely to be crucial in this important decision also.

Trade and Commerce

Germany has always been better served by the customs union which, since its initiation in the first decade of the EEC has gradually developed into a full-fledged common market, and the attendant liberalization of intra-Community trade and commerce. The creation of the customs union led intra-Community trade to increase much more rapidly than trade with the rest of the world, and soon the member states were each other's major trading partners. The customs union led over the course of a transition period of some eleven years to the abolition among member states of such barriers to trade as tariffs and quotas. There was also set up a common trade policy, including the establishment through Community institutions of a (very liberal) regime of common external tariffs for imports from nonmember countries and the negotiation of international trade agreements by Commission officials on behalf of all member states, who collectively constitute the world's largest trading bloc. The added weight that the common negotiation of trading rules with the Community's partners has given to the representation of German interests is of great benefit for a country as dependent on foreign trade as Germany. Because of Germany's strong free trade instincts, the common position of the Community has been more liberal than it would have been without Germany's membership.

The dynamism of the European Community economies and the relative stagnation of the economies of member states in the rival European Free Trade Association (EFTA) helped, in the early 1970s, to persuade the UK, Denmark, and Ireland, and subsequently other EFTA members, to join the EC/EU, thereby strengthening it even further as a trade bloc. In the early days of the EEC, the customs union and the common agricultural policy were its most prominent policy sectors. They were complemented by the establishment of a competition policy regime necessary to ensure that the customs union would not be undermined by collusion among private firms to restrict trade and by member state governments' trade distorting practices such as unwarranted subsidization of their own firms. Because of the postwar establishment of strong antitrust legislation in West Germany, this feature of Community policy making was less controversial there than it was elsewhere.

There was only slow progress beyond the freeing of trade in goods toward the development of a true common market, a Community in which there would be free exchange of services and capital as well. Gradually, to help realize the freedom to establish services Community wide, measures were devised, for example, to allow members of the professions to establish practice in other member states without the previously existing legal impediments and thus to give them rights that nonprofessional workers had attained much earlier.[24] But while there had been quite a substantial flow of skilled and unskilled workers among member states, with West Germany as a major host country, the migration of professionally qualified persons across member state boundaries has, despite fears by some professional organizations wishing to protect their turf, been quite limited.

On the social policy front, the Community was also successful in establishing rights for migrant workers such as access to host country social programs and the portability of pensions to their homelands (including those outside the Community) once they returned. These measures were of some importance to Germany because of the large number of such workers employed in her economy. Other social policies established by the Community abolished gender discrimination in employment practices and affected other conditions of work. But beyond such quite limited measures, there has been little movement toward regulating social policies at the Community level, in large part because such member states as the UK were and continue to be reluctant to cede jurisdiction in the social policy sector to the common institutions. Similarly, there was only gradual progress in transport policy although ultimately agreement was reached to rationalize road and even air transport (to which there is no reference in the Treaty of Rome). There was little progress toward joint decision making on policies that would have threatened member state sovereignty in significant ways, particularly in the realm of cultural and education policies, let alone the sensitive areas of foreign and defence policies or domestic security.

Overall, then, there was the consolidation of a minimal set of core policies, accompanied by the gradual but steady creation of a set of Community laws in those policy sectors that became increasingly subject to Community decision making. These legal norms over the years became a powerful integrative force, interpreted by the Community's Court of Justice and accepted by member state government to be the supreme law in their field, applicable directly to persons and firms in member states. The direct applicability of European Union laws in member states is one of the features of European integration that most strikingly distinguishes the EU from other regional or international organizations, and one that has the potential to knit together its member states ever more closely. Decisions of the European Court of Justice have sometimes gone against the German government. An especially visible one, for example, struck down the centuries old *Reinheitsgebot*, a German legal measure justified for health reasons, that prevented the sale of beer containing preservatives and thus effectively prevented the sale in Germany of imported beer, most of which contained such preservatives. The Court of Justice took the view that the *Reinheitsgebot* created an unjustifiable nontariff barrier to imports. While the importance of this particular legal decision should not be overemphasized (there is, for example, no evidence of increased ill health in Germany resulting from the sale of imported beer), it does demonstrate the impact on domestic sovereignty of Community legal norms. It is now clear that in Germany and elsewhere in the EU that national courts of final jurisdiction do not have the last word on matters falling under the legal ambit of the EU.

The 1970s were an era of limited further policy integration. During that period, the Community adjusted to its first enlargement in 1973 through the accession to membership of the UK, Ireland, and Denmark, and to the economic difficulties visited on the industrialized countries by the rapid increase in energy prices brought about the actions of the Organization of Petroleum Exporting Countries (OPEC) oil cartel after the 1973 Yom Kippur War. The accession of Greece in 1981 established a Europe of Ten and marked the beginning of the expansion of the Community southward to include, by 1986, the new Iberian democracies of Spain and Portugal. The membership of three less developed countries brought with it demands by them of a redistribution of wealth among the member states in their favour including, notably, an expansion of the Community's regional policies, through which there are direct transfers of financial resources to the Community's poorer regions. An inevitable result was a greater financial burden on the more prosperous countries, West Germany foremost among them.

The early 1980s also saw a continuation of the period of stagnation in movement toward greater policy integration. Indeed, there was growing evidence of an undermining of the customs union among member states as increasingly nontariff barriers such a health standards and product safety measures were used by governments to protect their industries from the importation of competing products originating elsewhere in the Community. These developments threatened to weaken the beneficial effects of free trade for Community consumers and make the Community less competitive toward trading rivals such as the US and Japan. In reaction to these challenges and to bring about a major revitalization of the thrust toward integration, the European Commission initiated a series of measures that was accepted by the member states and helped lead to the completion of the EC's internal market by removing the impediments to the free flow of goods, services, and capital in the Community. The project became known as "Europe 1992" after the year in which the project was to be completed, and was made possible by the strengthening of decision making rules of the Community institutions through the Single European Act. These strengthened decision rules allowed the implementation of measures that led to the final transformation of the customs union into the completed internal market, or true common market of economic theory. For example, impediments to the free flow of capital among member states and the Community-wide provision of such services as insurance, which had long remained in effect, were removed by national governments. With the completion of the internal market came a new spirit of dynamism in the Community.

At present, the EU is Germany's foremost export market. One-third of jobs in Germany depend on trade with other member states.[25] Over the years, Germany's growing exports and trade surpluses have been mainly the result of intra-Community trade. In 1993, Germany imported goods worth DM 252 billion from EU countries and exported goods worth DM 289 billion. The resulting DM 37 billion trade surplus was fully 62.6 percent of Germany's total trade surplus for that year.[26] In the early 1990s, typically about 52 percent of German imports came from Community member states and about 54 percent of German exports went to EC countries.[27] With the accession of former EFTA countries in 1995, the intra-EU trade proportions will now be considerably higher. The EC/EU has over the years provided and continues now to provide Germany with secure access to the markets of other member states without fear of trade disruption through protectionist measures. Germany's economy is and continues to be closely integrated with the EU.

Another set of figures provides an indication of the costs of Germany's membership in the EU (which we have already referred to in our discussion of the CAP). Germany is, by far, the largest financial contributor to the EU, accounting for 30 percent of its budget.[28] Her gross payments in 1995 were 44 billion DM and it is expected that these payments will increase to 58 billion DM by 1999. Net payments were 21.2 billion DM in 1994, compared to the UK's 4.3 and France's 2.6 billion.[29] Given these heavy contributions to the European enterprise it is not surprising that Germany has been called Europe's paymaster, and that German officials, especially her finance minister, have in recent years continually urged fiscal restraint in EU deliberations.

In the midst of the progress toward the completion of the internal market came the fall of the Berlin Wall, and hard on its heels the uniting of Germany. That event, in turn, helped to revive and then accelerate the discussion of plans to bring about even further integration. Chancellor Kohl wished to "Europeanize" Germany in a more closely integrated Europe, both because of his strong belief in that goal and to transfer sovereignty to the common institutions to assuage any lingering fears in Europe that the new, more powerful Germany might pose a threat to economic and military security. The goal of a more integrated Europe was shared by enough European leaders (in particular France's François Mitterrand) to allow negotiations to culminate in the signing of the Maastricht Treaty in December 1991. Though the subsequent ratification by member states faced some hurdles (not least in Germany, where ratification was delayed by an unsuccessful challenge of the Treaty in the Constitutional Court), the Treaty, and with it the European Union, came into effect in late 1993. Its provisions for closer economic and especially monetary integration, and more cooperation in foreign and security policy as well as domestic security matters, have become controversial among the citizens of Germany and other member states and progress toward implementation is slow and tentative in the middle of the century's last decade. Still, by that time EU policy making had reached impressive dimensions and had a strong impact on every member state, including Germany.

The Economic and Monetary Union

The best known feature of the Maastricht Treaty, because it has dominated discussions on the Community in recent years, are the provisions on economic and monetary union (EMU). These have also been of primary concern to Germany, which has been at the centre of most schemes to further EMU. Oddly, despite the designation "European Economic Community," the European institutions have had very little direct impact on the economic and monetary policies of member states. Member states gave only limited responsibilities to Community institutions over economic matters in the founding treaties, and the political stalemate that resulted from the long period of essentially unanimity-based Council decision making meant that further transfers of sovereignty to the Community in these important and sensitive areas did not take place. Monetary policy, in the final analysis, remained a member state prerogative. Action on economic matters was limited to consultation with the view to coordination of member state policies. The Commission's role was limited largely to issuing studies and advisory opinions on matters of common concern.

In the meantime, however, the degree of economic interaction among member states increased, as intra-Community trade, which considerably outpaced the growth of trade with the rest of the world, tied their economies more closely together and made them increasingly interdependent. Because of the need to manage this interdependence and given the broader goals of European integration, there was much pressure from the Commission, the European Parliament, and some member states to go further along the road to collective action by enhancing the Community's role in fiscal and monetary policy. There are a number of practical considerations driving these proposals. One is the desirability of removing the very significant transaction costs for individuals and firms engaged in transboundary activities in a Community with multiple currencies; another is eradicating exchange rate uncertainty that dampens investment and trade, in part by its tendency to increase interest rates.[30] Moreover, were the Community able to succeed in creating a common currency, member states would benefit from advantages that can accrue from what would almost certainly become a reserve currency, from the economic advantages of pooling international reserves, and from the powerful influence the Community would exercise in international monetary negotiations and institutions.[31] Further, there is the argument that a common currency would "spread German-style price stability to other countries."[32]

Of course, measures to fix exchange rates at the EU level or to narrowly limit their fluctuations, let alone to create a common currency, have negative implications for national sovereignty, because they reduce the policy options available to governments to adjust to economic shocks of countries when, for example, a decline in demand for their products leads to a negative trade balance. It is these implications for national sovereignty that made controversial the various schemes devised over the years to increase exchange rate stability in the Community. Further complicating agreement on action toward economic and monetary integration was the fact that there existed two major schools of thought within the EC regarding the best way to bring about closer cooperation in economic and monetary matters. One group, who collectively became known as the "monetarists," included France, Belgium, and Luxembourg (as well as the EEC Commission). The monetarists argued that it was best to move quickly toward a common currency and that such moves would force more joint action on economic policies. Members of the second "economist" school, among whom West Germany was pre-eminent, considered such action dangerous, and argued that it was necessary to create the economic preconditions for a Community monetary policy. The German government, and that of the Netherlands, feared that fiscally responsible states would carry a large part of the costs incurred by the actions of less disciplined states should a common currency be created in the absence of agreements on fiscal safeguards.[33] The "economists" also argued the need for strong central institutions with the power to discipline those states not living up to their commitments in an economically more integrated Community.

In 1972, in a first attempt at EMU, the Community established a mechanism of exchange controls, referred to as the "snake in the tunnel," to stabilize currency fluctuations. This involved a 4.5 percent band width (tunnel) within which Community currencies collectively would fluctuate against the US dollar (2.25 percent on either side of a central rate), while a narrower rate band (snake) of 2.25 percent applied to fluctuations of member state currencies against each other. A system of temporary credits for weak currency countries to be repaid within a month allowed for the short-term intervention in currency markets to manage fluctuations that threatened to breach the exchange rate bands. But before long, the scheme was fatally challenged as the UK, Italy, France, and Ireland faced economic problems that caused their currencies to drop out of the snake. Only five member states, with West Germany the most prominent, stayed the course. The EMU experiment had not been a success, in large part because insufficient coordination among member states' economic policies led to continued divergence among their currencies.

The next attempt at providing monetary stability in the Community was less ambitious than the snake in the tunnel system approach to economic and monetary union. Referred to as the European Monetary System (EMS), it had its genesis in a 1977 Commission initiative, which Chancellor Helmut Schmidt pursued successfully at Copenhagen and Bremen meetings of Community heads of state and governments in 1978.[34] A prime German motivation for the EMS was to create a fixed exchange rate mechanism to take pressure off the Deutschmark, which had continually been driven up by speculators when they left the US dollar, in turn creating difficulties for West German exports and weakening other Community currencies in relation to the DM.

At the heart of the EMS was a composite currency, the European Currency Unit (ECU), composed of different amounts of member states' currencies depending on their relative economic weight and share of Community trade. The DM, reflecting Germany's economic clout had, at over 30 percent, by far the largest weighting in the ECU. The values of member states' currencies were fixed at any particular time relative to the ECU, and once thus established, were to remain fixed until a reweighting was undertaken. Participating states undertook to maintain their currencies' values within varying specified limits relative to the central rate. Most member states, West Germany among them, committed themselves to limits of 2.25 percent above and below the central rate, with a number of others, some temporarily, choosing broader limits. If two currencies became misaligned, intervention buying and selling by the respective central banks were to bring the currencies back into alignment, although devaluations and revaluations, as well as a mix of these involving several or all currencies, also became a feature of the EMS. Another feature of the system was the availability of a limited loan facility with partly subsidized interest rates for the weaker economies. The ECU was backed by a partial pooling of member state reserves, and thus became an asset which could be used to settle member state debts. By 1991, all member states except Greece and Portugal were participants of what was now being referred to as the exchange rate mechanism (ERM).

The system, however, did not lead to stability of exchange rates within the Community. In a 12-year period following its inception in 1979, there were 12 realignments of exchange rates involving one or more currencies.[35] A greater degree of stability proved elusive because of the continuing lack of convergence among member states' economic policies. As before, the tendency of speculative capital to flow into the German mark when the US dollar weakened continued to lead to its strengthening and attendant pressure on exchange rate stability among Community currencies. By the late 1980s, the number of realignments of currencies had decreased considerably, not because member states had ceded policy competence to Community institutions but because of the dominance of the West German economy. The West German *Bundesbank*'s tight monetary policy led to low West German inflation; to avoid realignments and to remain competitive, other member states had to adjust their policies accordingly. The West German *Bundesbank* had become the de facto monetary authority in the Community. Other member states were unable to influence policy directly, and indeed West German government influence was limited, given its hands-off relationship with the central bank. Of course, the primary responsibility of the *Bundesbank* is German financial stability, not the general welfare of the Community.

Such a state of affairs could clearly not continue because it engendered resentment of Germany. This became most evident in the Community currency crises of 1992 and 1993 precipitated in good part by the high interest rate policy of the *Bundesbank* when it sought to dampen the strong inflationary effects of German unification. This action affected Germany's Community partners. The French government, for example, facing a recession and thus disposed to easing monetary policy, was forced to raise interest rates and thus to reign in its economy even more to keep the franc aligned with the mark when its entreaties to the German government to ease interest rates fell on deaf ears. To the embarrassment of the British Major government, the UK pound was forced out of the ERM, as was the Italian lira. A number of member states imposed exchange controls, and a series of rounds of devaluations ensued. By August 1993, the fluctuation bands around all but the German and Dutch currencies were widened to 15 percent. Even with these wider bands, subsequent devaluations took place. It was clear that the existing mechanisms would not lead to the desired monetary stability.

The groundwork for fundamental changes in the provisions regarding economic and monetary union had previously been laid by the Maastricht Treaty. In it were established the bases of a common currency and attendant institutions and policies that are meant, once implemented, to ensure that the Euro, as the new currency is to be named, will be managed in a manner that corresponds closely to the present management of the German mark. There is to be a central bank, patterned on the *Bundesbank*, with representation from participating member states, but independent of member state government influence. A set of very stringent conditions applies for entry: participating member states' national debts are not to exceed 60 percent and deficits are not to exceed three percent of GNP, and there are provisions meant to ensure that inflation rates of qualifying member states remain low and within a very narrow range of each other. A time frame for implementing EMU is provided for the Maastricht Treaty, and it is quite clear that only those member states meeting the conditions of entry are to be allowed to participate. Those unable to meet the conditions are to be excluded until the conditions are met. The Council of Ministers is to be empowered to manage fiscal policies to ensure monetary stability with powers to discipline member states whose practices militate against that goal. A time frame for implementing the EMU among the qualifying member states is laid out. Implementation of EMU involves a shift of powers to the EU institutions that represents a major step toward a higher level of European integration and an attendant loss of member state sovereignty. It is for that reason that the plan has engendered great controversy in such member states as the UK, France, and Denmark.

In Germany, controversy over the economic and monetary union provisions of the Maastricht Treaty has been less over a loss of sovereign powers than over the potential loss of the mark, perhaps the single most important national symbol because it signifies the elements of their collective lives, economic welfare, and stability, that Germans could allow themselves to be proud of. Many Germans, in some 1996 and 1997 opinion polls a substantial majority, have expressed strong reservations about the Euro because they are afraid that an EU monetary policy will lead to financial and economic instability. To counteract these fears, Germany's finance minister, Theo Waigel, has repeatedly promised that there will be no watering down of the entry criteria, and has even advocated that they be made more restrictive. In early 1996, to profit politically from the anti-EMU mood and discredit Chancellor Kohl and the pro-EMU Christian Democratic Union (CDU) as well as its Free Democratic party partner in government, SPD leader Oskar Lafontaine unsuccessfully attacked the move toward a common European currency in a series of Land elections. At the same time, Mr. Kohl was facing a major political crisis as the vaunted consensus among government, industry, and labour threatened to break down over the Kohl government's moves to pare back the German welfare state, actions taken in part to ensure that Germany remained competitive in international trade, but also to ensure that German social spending would not lead to a budget deficit greater than that allowed prospective entrants into the EMU. It has become increasingly clear that, much as has occurred in its fellow member states, the road to EMU in Germany is getting rocky and politically risky. In 1997 it appears possible, though still not overly likely, that the question of German participation in

EMU could become an issue in the 1998 federal election, pitting a fiercely proparticipation CDU/CSU against a skeptical if not hostile SPD that is willing to gamble riding the crest of a wave of popular opposition to German participation in EMU to electoral victory.[36] Such a development would mark a severe setback to Mr. Kohl's vision of a Germany ever more strongly ensconsed in a united Europe.

The Maastricht Treaty was and is about more than EMU. Its most ardent supporters saw it as a major milestone toward a more closely integrated Europe whose political institutions were still too much cast in an intergovernmental, as opposed to supranational, mold. These supporters could point out that though the EU boasts a Parliament directly elected by member state citizens, this Parliament still has limited powers and that during European elections, national and not European issues are usually at centre stage because citizens do not find European issues, and therefore the work of Parliament, sufficiently important to make it the focus of much attention. Hence, in Germany (as in other member states) elections to the European Parliament have effectively become plebiscites in which parts of the electorate can safely register a protest vote or send national politicians signals, for example by voting heavily for radical parties such as the Republicans, without directly affecting the fate of governments or even the fate of European policies and institutions. This state of affairs provides evidence for the fact that the EU and its institutions have had only limited impact on political life in its member states.

The "nationalization" of European elections also demonstrates the "democratic deficit" of the EU institutions because it is a reflection of the fact that the institutions are not directly accountable to the people. The Council of Ministers, the European Commission, and the European Court of Justice, and not the European Parliament, are still the primary actors in the EU. They are likely to remain so, and a European consciousness is likely to make little headway, until the citizens of member states find reason to take greater interest in EU affairs and direct their national politicians to enhance the powers of its institutions.

More interest in European affairs among citizens of member states would be engendered should these politicians agree to transfer a greater degree of jurisdiction over policies to European institutions, as indeed will occur once the EMU provisions of the Maastricht Treaty are implemented. It will also be raised once the home and justice affairs provisions of the Treaty on European Union (the formal name of the Maastricht

Treaty) are fully in effect, that is, if the removal of frontier controls between member states is totally implemented and once the provisions for cooperation in dealing with international crime, terrorism, and drug trafficking are implemented and EU wide norms on immigration and asylum are established.[37] These matters are of major concern to Germans given their country's position at the crossroads of Europe and its attractiveness to those from third countries wishing to escape violence and poverty, such as the over 400,000 refugees from the former Yugoslavia harboured by Germany. Greater integration on these matters would benefit Germany since these problems are more effectively dealt with at the EU rather than the national level and because they would lead to a sharing of the burden of the refugees and asylum seekers that Germany, among EU member states, has had disproportionately to bear.

Foreign Policy and Security

A final major European policy area touched on by the Maastricht Treaty, foreign and security affairs have always been controversial in the Community context. For years some member states, France foremost among them, were unwilling to allow discussion of these in the Community context. Over the years, attitudes softened somewhat, and a system of consultation among member states on foreign and security matters was instituted, though outside the purview of the Community institutions and therefore in an intergovernmental context and mode. For example, the chief political officials of foreign offices meet periodically to discuss matters of common concern, and member state diplomatic personnel cooperate in third country capitals and in international organizations. Over time, the Commission has won the right to participate in meetings of heads of state and governments called to discuss such political matters, but these forums remain explicitly outside the common framework of EU decision making. Member states have been notoriously unable to come to common decisions on major foreign policy crises such as the breakup of the Yugoslav federation or the Gulf War.

The Maastricht Treaty does little to remedy this state of affairs. There were some new accents. In the case of foreign policy, the Council of Ministers, having agreed unanimously on a common policy, may also decide, again unanimously, that certain measures required to implement the policy should be taken by majority vote. But the UK insisted that, even if there is a common policy, member states can go their own way "in case of imperative need."

The Treaty makes reference to the eventual framing of a common policy which might in time lead to a common defence. The Western European Union (WEU), a defence-oriented organization grouping ten of the member states,[38] is identified as an integral part of the development of the EU, which may request the WEU to elaborate and implement decisions and actions of the EU that have defence implications. All member states are entitled to join the WEU; what is still in dispute is whether WEU is subordinate to the EU or not. A review of the defence arrangements continues in the course of the 1996–97 series of Intergovernmental Conferences (IGC) during which are being negotiated revisions of the Treaty on European Union, as well as such issues as enlargement of the EU and the concrete steps toward the implementation of EMU.

Germany has pressed for additional common decision making in these meetings. The Kohl government is eager to move toward more integration in the areas of foreign affairs and defence. It wishes to have qualified majority voting extended to all areas, a position still opposed by a number other member states.[39] A French-German compromise agreement reached in February 1996 would allow for "constructive abstention" in matters of foreign and security policy, allowing members of the WEU to abstain from common action desired by other members rather than block such an undertaking as is presently the case.[40] Thus those member states wishing to undertake common action would be able to press ahead, even if this were to lead to a multi-level or multi-speed Europe in which the most pro-integration member states form a solid central core of increasingly highly integrated decision making and leave behind those that are not willing to commit themselves to common decisions on foreign policy and defence. A similar prospect faces the EU on EMU, because as it now appears, only a fraction of the member states will meet the criteria for participation at the first instance that the scheme is initiated.

What will result from the Intergovernmental Conferences is still unclear at this writing. In part the IGC is hostage to outcomes of national elections, in the foreseeable future. What seems more safe to predict is that Germany is almost certain to be at the forefront of any moves to carry European integration forward. That has been the history of Germany in the integration process so far, and is likely to continue to be so for some time to come.

ACKNOWLEDGEMENT

I am grateful to Martin Hering for research assistance in the preparation of this chapter.

NOTES

1. These processes have resulted in the creation of a number of different European communities. The first, established in 1952, was the European Coal and Steel Community (ECSC). In 1958 were inaugurated the European Economic Community (EEC) and the European Atomic Energy Community (Euratom). The institutions of these three communities were amalgamated in 1967, and it became customary to refer to the resulting organization, both as a set of institutions and as a collectivity of member states, as the European Community (EC). In 1994, after the ratification of the Maastricht Treaty and thereby the acceptance by member states of additional measures to unify Europe, the Community became known as the European Union (EU).

2. The title "paymaster of Europe" is often used, but not favoured by German governments.

3. British, Irish, and Danish accession to the EEC in 1973 led to a Community of Nine, Greece's accession in 1981 resulted in the Ten, soon to become the Twelve with Spanish and Portuguese accession in 1986, and Fifteen when Austria, Finland, and Sweden joined the EU in 1995.

4. George Ross, *Jacques Delors and European Integration* (New York: Oxford University Press, 1995), p. 49.

5. Also known as the Treaty on European Union.

6. "The Urge to Shove," *The Economist*, 6 January 1996, p. 39.

7. "Germany, Israel Celebrate New Harmony," *Globe and Mail*, Saturday, 27 January 1996, p. A9.

8. "The Urge to Shove," p. 39.

9. Renata Fritsch-Bournazel, *Europe and German Unification* (New York and Oxford: Berg Publishers Inc., 1992), pp. 157–58.

10. Fritsch-Bournazel, *Europe and German Unification*, p. 162.

11. Cited in Fritsch-Bournazel, *Europe and German Unification*, p. 155.

12. For a comprehensive treatment of this subject see Hans J. Michelmann and Panayotis Soldatos, eds., *Federalism and International Relations* (Oxford: Clarendon Press, 1990).

13. Klaus H. Goetz, "National Governance and European Integration: Intergovernmental Relations in Germany," *Journal of Common Market Studies* 33, no. 1 (1995): 92.

14. The discussion here is based in part on Hans J. Michelmann, "The Federal Republic of Germany," in *Federalism and International Relations*, ed. Michelmann and Soldatos, pp. 222–27.

15. Michelmann, "The Federal Republic of Germany," pp. 227–28.

16. Goetz, "National Governance and European Integration," p. 106.

17. Goetz, "National Governance and European Integration," p. 111.

18. Contrary to expectation in the late 1950s, Euratom proved a less than successful integration scheme among other reasons because of the much higher than expected development costs of nuclear technology, cheap supplies of competing hydrocarbon

fuels, and France's development of its nuclear striking force and consequent less than enthusiastic participation in European-level nuclear cooperation.

19. Elmar Brok, "Der Zahlmeister ist tot—es lebe der Nutzniesser!" in Jochen Borchert et al., *Europäische Integration und deutsches Interesse* (Sankt Augustin: Konrad-Adenauer-Stiftung, 1994), p. 25.

20. Horst Schilling, "Probleme bei der Anpassung der ostdeutschen Landwirtschaft und den EG-Agrarmarkt," in *Die Vereinigung Deutschlands in europäischer Perspektive,* ed. Wolfgang Heisenberg (Baden-Baden: Nomos, 1992), p. 229.

21. Bundesministerium für Arbeit und Sozialordnung, *Statistisches Taschenbuch 1995* (Bonn, 1995), Table 2.4.

22. Hans Mittelbach, "Zur Lage der Landwirtschaft in den neuen Bundesländern," *Aus Politik und Zeitgeschichte* B33/34 (1995): 18.

23. Borchert et al., *Europäische Integration und deutsches Interesse*, p. 7.

24. The difficulties in attaining agreement on the migration of physicians, the first profession to enjoy the freedom to establish practice in a member states beyond the physician's home state, are documented in Hans J. Michelmann, "Credentials, Jurisdiction and Mobility: Physicians in the European Community," *Revue d'intégration européenne/Journal of European Integration* 2, no. 3 (1979): 203–29.

25. Brok, "Der Zahlmeister ist tot—es lebe der Nutzniesser!" p. 20.

26. Brok, "Der Zahlmeister ist tot—es lebe der Nutzniesser!" p. 22.

27. Statistisches Bundesamt, *Statistisches Jahrbuch 1994 für das Ausland* (Wiesbaden, 1994), pp. 105–6.

28. Brok, "Der Zahlmeister ist tot—es lebe der Nutzniesser!" p. 22.

29. Gerd Langguth, "Ein starkes Europa mit schwachen Institutionen?" *Aus Politik und Zeitgeschichte* B1/2 (1996): 43.

30. Dennis Swann, *The Economics of the Common Market*, 8th ed. (London: Penguin Books, 1995), pp. 204–5.

31. Swann, *The Economics of the Common Market*.

32. "The Etiquette of Merging Currencies," *The Economist*, 9 December 1995, p. 80.

33. Swann, *The Economics of the Common Market*, pp. 210-11.

34. Swann, *The Economics of the Common Market*, p. 220.

35. Swann, *The Economics of the Common Market*, p. 229.

36. "Sweaty Palms," *The Economist*, 3 May 1997, p. 44.

37. On these issues, see Kurt Schelter, "Innenpolitische Zusammenarbeit in Europa zwischen Maastricht und Regierungskonferenz 1996," *Aus Politik und Zeitgeschichte* B1/2 (1996): 23.

38. Finland, Sweden, Austria, Denmark, and Ireland are observers only.

39. "The Cavillers Aren't Just British," *The Economist*, 10 May 1997, p. 48.

40. "Chirac Astride the World," *The Economist*, 11 May 1996, p. 46.

2

Phoenix From the Ashes

Contending Theoretical Perspectives on German Foreign Policy

CHRISTIAN TUSCHHOFF

German foreign policy after the end of World War II is reminiscent of the Egyptian myth that served as a symbol of immortality. Ancient Egyptians worshipped a fabulous bird called the phoenix. The phoenix was very large with a shining scarlet and gold plumage and a melodious cry. Only one phoenix existed at any given time in history and lived for 500 years. When it was time to die, the phoenix flew graciously to the Sun Heliopolis in Egypt, where it immolated itself on the altar of fire. Then, a new phoenix miraculously rose from the ashes of its predecessor.

In 1945, Germany suffered a military defeat, political surrender, and enormous destruction and felt morally guilty. The four occupying powers, the United States, Great Britain, France, and the Soviet Union, divided the country into four zones in an effort to eliminate or, at least, to control the country that had caused two major world wars in the first half of the twentieth century. Yet 50 years later a united Germany emerged as a sovereign and powerful state in the center of Europe. The Federal Republic of Germany (FRG) essentially achieved all foreign policy goals it had set during the Cold War. These goals were:

- full sovereignty over domestic and foreign affairs;
- unification with those parts of Germany in the East that came under communist rule;
- building a strong democracy based on a market economy that facilitated prosperity for its citizens;
- establishing armed forces for national and collective defense purposes;
- rejecting neutralism and aligning itself with Western democracies;

- creating a friendly European environment and maintaining peaceful and friendly relations with its neighbours;
- developing good relations with Israel and the Jewish community.

If the four powers that took charge of the special rights and responsibilities for Germany had intended to keep it divided and under close control in order to maintain stability in central Europe, they had failed.[1] With a population of 81 million people, a territory of 138 thousand square miles, a gross domestic product of almost $3 trillion, and armed forces of 340,000 troops, the FRG is mighty again and outnumbers all potential competitors in Europe with the exception of Russia. These remarkable achievements need to be explained. Why did Germany succeed in achieving her most fundamental goals while its allies and opponents failed to contain it? How did the Federal Republic manage to rise to its current status while its immediate competitors—France and Great Britain—lost their colonial empires and struggled to keep their position as European powers during the same time span?

Rather than offering a historical account of German foreign and defense policy,[2] this article examines the situation from the two different theoretical perspectives of realism and institutionalism.[3] Such an approach has several advantages where political science is concerned: (1) it offers causal explanations for foreign policy rather than a pure description; (2) it highlights various key aspects of German foreign policy while avoiding details irrelevant to the causal explanation; (3) it helps readers to use common theories of international relations and foreign policy analysis to understand different countries' foreign policies; and (4) it offers theory-based parameters that both help to predict the future direction of German foreign policy and enables the reader to discern whether or not policies improve or impair stability.

Realism: The Security Dilemma
and Relative Gains

In the realist world view, states are the single most important actors in international relations.[4] They essentially perform similar functions. There is no world government. Because there is no authority above and beyond states, they must act as equals rather than specialize in certain functions. The structure of an international system that lacks a common government, and in which states, as the constituent units, act as formal equals, is called anarchy. Since states cannot resort to a higher authority for protection, they must rely on self-help for their own national security, which, in turn, guarantees their very existence. When states attempt to establish national security, they pose a threat to other states that then respond in kind, because states cannot trust each other in an anarchical environment. The action-reaction sequence performed by states trying to achieve security with regard to one another is called the "security dilemma." One state poses a threat to the other states that respond by trying to protect themselves and, as a consequence, undermine the security of all others. When a state attempts to improve its security, others, in all likelihood, take countermeasures that imperil the state's security again. In such an environment, states seek to behave as "defense positionalists," that is they constantly seek to maintain or improve their position relative to others. This pattern of behaviour is called "relative gains seeking," that is states constantly guard against the decline of their capabilities relative to other states.[5]

However, while states are equals—in the sense that they all perform similar functions—they differ in their capability to achieve security. A state's security is determined by its own capability in comparison to capabilities of other states. Not every state can afford to achieve security all by itself. Given the limits of resources, states must cooperate to defend against a threat. To this end, states form alliances based on common interests and in response to specific threats. Realists maintain that there are two ways of forming an alliance. Should there be a growing threat from a powerful state, a number of less powerful states form an alliance to keep collectively the balance that each would not be able to maintain on an individual basis. Alliances form out of creating a balance. Should a small state seek protection from a larger one against threats from other small states, an alliance is formed by "bandwagoning." Yet even when allied, states seek to retain some independence and avoid division of labour within the alliance.

They also seek to exclude their own capabilities from multilateral control measures.

German Foreign Policy: A Realist Explanation

German foreign policy has been determined by the "international stage."[6] The international system constrains and shapes foreign policy. The theory of realism would maintain that the FRG was forced to achieve security without having the essential military capabilities because it had been disarmed after World War II. In the early years—between 1949 and 1955—its security depended on the protection provided by other countries. Deprived of the resources of national defense, the FRG could pursue an independent course in between East and West, but was forced into an alliance. Two basic options remained for the FRG: it could either ally itself with the militarily weak North Atlantic Treaty Organization (NATO) to balance the threat from the Soviet Union or bandwagon with the Soviet Union. The FRG decided to join the Western alliance for two reasons. First, the occupying powers—the United States, France, and the United Kingdom—had forced both a constitution and a particular form of government upon West Germany that entailed basic principles such as democracy, the market economy, federalism, social responsibility, and the observation of human rights. Self-preservation, that is, the protection of these constitutive principles, required to align the country with the West because the other option—bandwagoning with the Soviet Union—was synonymous with the abandonment of just these principles that have come to constitute FRG.[7] Second, the package-deal of the so-called Paris Treaties of 1954 that the FRG negotiated with the West offered opportunities to seek relative gains. Such gains included equality with other Western countries, equal treatment within the North Atlantic Alliance and—most important of all—the opportunity to rearm and, ultimately, to provide for national security by itself. From a realist perspective it is important to understand that West Germany's fundamental decision to join NATO was not a matter of choice but the logical consequence of constraints imposed by the international system.

In the period between 1955 and 1968, the FRG made use of opportunities to amend its security by making relative gains. It built solid armed forces to improve its capability of national defense. However, given the threat from Soviet and other Warsaw Pact forces, it still depended on allied protection for both nuclear deterrence and conventional defense purposes. As part of the 1954 Paris Treaties, Germany was prevented from producing nuclear, biological, and chemical weapons on its own soil and had to accept severe restrictions on the production of heavy weapon systems, such as missiles or battleships. Moreover, West German armed forces were put under the exclusive operational command of NATO headquarters. The FRG could not convert its improved military capability into more political independence from the alliance. While the FRG had gained significant military capability, the other allies maintained command and control over these assets. Within NATO, both West Germany and its allies made relative gains. According to the realist approach, France must have perceived West Germany's relative gains as perilous to its own security and, for this reason, terminated defense cooperation among allies. It chose to leave NATO's military integration in 1966 to pursue a more independent defense policy, but remained a member of the alliance. Thus, France hedged against disproportionate German gains. The Soviet Union and the other Warsaw Pact countries had their own armament programs in place to balance against the improvement of NATO's collective defense. Realists point to the fact that neither side gained sufficient capability to upset the existing bipolar balance of power in the international system. Most prominently, French attempts to change the bipolar into a tripolar system failed, partly because France did not possess sufficient capability to offset the existing distribution of power and, partly, because West Germany preferred to depend on the familiar American rather than French protection.

The FRG was forced to remain in NATO and did not gain the option of either national defense or shifting alliances. But when the federal government started negotiations with the Soviet Union, the East European countries, and the German Democratic Republic (GDR), the question arose whether the new *Ostpolitik* would amount to such an option. Though *Ostpolitik* created some headaches in Washington, Paris, and London, realists argue that it represented Germany's attempt to join the Western bend towards a policy of détente with the Soviet Union. They reasoned that *Ostpolitik* was forced upon West Germany, which was increasingly concerned that it might become isolated within the Western alliance if they did not settle their special conflicts with Moscow, East Berlin, Warsaw, and Prague. Rather than using the opportunity to improve national independence, *Ostpolitik* sought to maintain the existing bipolar balance of power and to reconcile special West German interests—such as unification and human rights for German minorities in East European countries—with Western détente policies. Equally important from a realist perspective, *Ostpolitik* neither changed the bipolar balance of power in the international system nor did it make West Germany less dependent on its Western allies. Instead, it confirmed the continuing dependence of FRG upon the Western security guarantees and policy support. The distribution of gains remained even because *Ostpolitik,* as an integrated part of détente, made East-West confrontation less risky and more predictable. It freed the West from supporting German unification beyond symbolic declarations and reduced the risks of defending the FRG and GDR. It helped Washington, London, and Paris to improve their relations with East Berlin, other Eastern European capitals, and, most important of all, Moscow. The Eastern bloc profited from *Ostpolitik* just as much because it reduced their risk of war in Europe and opened up new opportunities of diplomatic relations with the West and Third World countries.

While détente reduced international tension and diminished the risk of a European or global war, realists state that it did not loosen the tight international grip that constrained West German foreign policy. Helmut Schmidt, the German chancellor from 1974 to 1982, attempted to base his more assertive policies on the assumptions that (1) *Ostpolitik* had reduced the FRG's dependence on the West; (2) détente had profoundly changed the nature of East-West relations from confrontation to partnership; and, (3), that military force had lost some of its significance in matters of power and was increasingly complemented by economic factors. Schmidt concluded that West Germany had a vested interest in détente and was determined to mediate between the United States and the Soviet Union once Soviet military programs began to accelerate during the second half of the 1970s and the invasion of Afghanistan in 1979 caused superpower cooperation to terminate. However, mediation overtaxed West German leverage and demonstrated that the FRG could not pursue national interests independent of its Western allies. Rather, Schmidt ran the risk of becoming isolated in the Western camp as soon as France, under the leadership of President François Mitterrand, followed the American lead in opposing the Soviet Union's global aspirations. Unable to overcome bipolarity, Germany was forced to go along with its NATO partners again. Symbolically, it had to support the boycott of the 1980 Summer Olympics in Moscow. More substantially, it had to abide by and implement NATO's so-called double track decision that called for the deployment of Pershing II and cruise missiles should the Soviet Union fail to reduce its intermedium range nuclear forces as a result of arms control negotiations. Wide public protests in West Germany, based on the perception that the American Reagan administration was not seriously negotiating with Moscow but was using arms control as a cover for a new arms race, fell short of preventing NATO missile deployments on West German soil. Moreover, the FRG was forced to go along with its Western allies and put economic relations with the East on hold. The United States prevailed in its effort to expand the Coordinating Committee for East-West Trade Policy (COCOM) list of strategically important goods that were excluded from trade. Schmidt was proven wrong on all of his three aforementioned assumptions. While reducing some of the West German defense burdens, détente did not end the FRG's dependence on its allies. The nature of East-West relations did not change but remained confrontational. Finally, not economic, but military factors prevailed as the greatest signifier of power in international affairs. A change of government from a center-left to a center-right coalition forced Helmut Schmidt out of the Chancellery. He was replaced by Helmut Kohl who strongly supported allied policy toward the Soviet Union and Eastern Europe. Some realists cite the change in government as further evidence proving their case that external factors determine West German politics. From Adenauer to Schmidt, four out of five chancellors lost power, not at the ballot, but in the midst of their regular terms. All four stumbled over external affairs.[8]

The end of the Cold War fundamentally changed the global distribution of power.[9] The demise of the Soviet Union and the dissolution of the Warsaw Treaty organization not only altered the balance from bipolarity to unipolarity but also helped the FRG to make extraordinary gains. It brought an end to the division of the country and left it to Germany to determine its international alignments in the future. The residual rights and responsibilities of the four powers that formerly occupied Germany ceased to exist; the Federal Republic of Germany thus gained full sovereignty over its internal and external affairs and received permission to assume national command over its armed forces. Moreover, the FRG gained power to choose from a broader menu of options which security organization it considered appropriate to use in a particular crisis situation.

The constant tension between Anglo-Saxon and French concepts of the shape of a new European security architecture assigned Germany the pivotal role as a potential mediator.

In turn, Germany accepted arms control limitations such as the renunciation of the production and possession of, and control over, weapons of mass destruction as well as a ceiling of 370,000 troops in its armed forces. The FRG recognized existing borders in Europe as permanently inviolable and changed its constitution and laws accordingly. Since then, the FRG has moved steadily to expand its foreign manoeuverability. Step by step the government undermined domestic restrictions against the use of armed forces for missions beyond national and allied defense. The German military started participating in non-European operations. New plans suggest that armed forces will assume greater mobility and develop a long range transportation capability. Furthermore, the FRG demanded permanent membership in the Security Council of the United Nations, including veto power. These changes signal a shift away from checkbook diplomacy. No longer will Germany be accused of being an "economic giant but a political dwarf." Whereas other European countries have also improved their security, because they, too, are no longer vulnerable to a Soviet attack, their post-Cold War gains are far less significant than Germany's. They did not increase in size of territory, population, or economic potential. The post-cold war distribution of power unevenly favoured the FRG. According to realist theory, such an uneven redistribution of power should be of concern to Germany's neighbours. The new balance, realists predict, will be as unstable as it used to be in the nineteenth century because Germany is too large to be equal and too small to become an irresistible hegemon. They expect that Europeans will find a more stable balance possibly by forming an anti-German alliance. Other theorists do not share such a pessimistic outlook because they explain foreign policy by referring to other causes than the distribution of power.

Institutionalism: Integration and Absolute Gains

One theory that contradicts realist explanations and predictions is called institutionalism.[10] Its proponents agree with realists that states determine their national interests on the basis of the anarchical self-help system and the distribution of power. However, international institutions, such as organizations, principles, rules, and procedures, can also affect the interest and actions of states. They constrain the options a government may consider. Because institutions affect all states in a similar way they help governments to predict the behaviour of other states. Institutions may thus lead a way out of the security dilemma and offer opportunities for peaceful change.

Institutions facilitate mutual trust among states to an extent that states do not only behave as defensive positionalists, but agree to settlements that do not always distribute costs and benefits evenly among the participating parties. States seek settlements that provide them some *absolute* gains. They expect that they will benefit from institutional cooperation in the long run, so not every agreement must be reciprocal. Rather than seeking such specific reciprocity in every agreement, states expect to benefit equally from enduring cooperation. Thus, institutions prolong the duration of the expectation of states from a one-time agreement to a series of consecutive settlements. They also change the outlook from seeking specific to general reciprocity.[11]

What is of equal importance is that states do not always insist on maintaining a minimum of independence such as an "exit option" from international organizations and avoiding outside control of their power resources but often choose to trade their autonomy for mutually beneficial cooperation by constructing international regimes. Governments sometimes agree to future constraints on their foreign policy because they seek to limit the options available to their successors.

Institutions alleviate problems resulting from any uncertainty about the intentions of the other actors because they reduce the range of expected behaviour. They, therefore, alter the conception of national interests and generate mutual confidence. Institutions facilitate international cooperation because they generate converging expectations and provide critical information that makes the behaviour of other states more predictable. Thus, organizations reduce the risk and the cost of cooperation and support states in their efforts to maximize their gains both individually and collectively. They also catalyze further agreements.

German Foreign Policy: An Institutionalist Explanation

German foreign policy looks different from an institutionalist perspective than it does from a realist one. The FRG not only sought to achieve sovereignty and security, but also strove for economic prosperity. It also understood the tension among these goals and often chose deliberately to trade away sovereign rights for security and prosperity. It relinquished control over its coal and steel industry in 1951, when it agreed to join the European Coal and Steel Community (ECSC). These industries fell under the control of a supranational authority. The institutional framework of the ECSC served as a model for further European organizations such as the European Economic Community (EEC) founded in 1957, the European Community (EC) founded in 1967, and the European Union (EU) founded in 1991. The organizational framework of the EEC represented a combination of relinquished, pooled, and retained sovereignty. It consisted of a High Authority (later the European Commission), a Council of Ministers, an Assembly, and a Court. The High Authority was a sovereign subject of international law and operated independently from member states. It initiated legislation and oversaw its implementation. However, legislation was the domain of the Council of Ministers, composed of national representatives whose vote depended on the instructions of each national government. Members retained sovereignty to implement policies as agreed upon by the Council of Ministers. Members relinquished their authority to initiate and oversee national coal and steel policies, but they pooled their sovereignty in the Council of Ministers because legislation on these policies were codetermined by national governments. Members also retained their sovereignty to implement common European policy.

The FRG agreed to such partial relinquishment and pooling of sovereignty because it received equal treatment with other European states and expected to maximize gains such as access to international markets, a steady flow of energy, and inexpensive steel and energy. Once these expectations were met, the FRG agreed to broaden the realm of European integration operating under similar international arrangements to include agriculture, foreign trade, and social and domestic security policies. The FRG complied with European policies even in cases in which they were detrimental to national interests.

Whenever the European Court of Justice ruled against FRG, it enacted the verdict.[12] Moreover, German courts have been actively seeking to invoke the "direct effect doctrine" according to which European law takes precedence over national law.[13] Also, the FRG did not withdraw its membership in the EC even when it became evident that the Community was producing enormous inefficiencies, particularly in the realm of agriculture.[14] Rather than using the exit option, that is to leaving the EC, Germany used its "voice option"[15] and initiated reforms, including changing the rules from unanimous to qualified majority voting in the Council of Ministers as instituted by the Single European Act of 1987. Qualified majority voting represents yet another partial relinquishment of national sovereignty because the process of codetermination no longer depends on unanimous consensus. Instead, it depends on coalition building. Such evidence supports institutionalist claims that institutions alter the very definition of a state's national interests by altering the incentives and constraining the options under government consideration. Even when an outcome is perceived detrimental to or contradicts national interest—such as European agricultural policy or lowering quality standards for certain products—the FRG consistently accepted European decisions. Institutionalists hypothesize that the FRG did not insist on making relative gains but accepted absolute ones. It also based its behaviour on the principle of general, rather than special, reciprocity. More evidence from Germany's European policy underscores this finding. While West Germany had to accept painful European intrusions into its economy and domestic affairs, it benefited enormously from a broad access to European markets, high-tech cooperation, and European subsidies for economic development and restructuring. As international economists observe, the mutually beneficial relationship with Europe will most likely continue even in the post-Cold War era because the four tasks ahead—(1) modernization of East European economies and societies; (2) the deepening of West European integration; (3) success in a fiercer international competition; and (4) the peaceful engagement of a united Germany in Europe—must all be based on general reciprocity. No single European country can afford to go it alone. Mutual interdependence among European states has reached a level that makes the exit option simply too expensive. Europe needs Germany as much as Germany needs Europe.[16] However, deepening integration in an effort to improve Europe's abilities to shoulder the burden of the future requires the enforcement of more and deeper internal adjustments against steadily growing domestic opposition. One such adjustment would be a common European currency.

When the FRG joined NATO in 1955 critics argued that the West German government had sacrificed the national goal of unification and, thus, accepted the permanent division of country and the German nation. Opponents also believed that the Western alliance had unduly constrained

West German national defense, and that the FRG had agreed to detrimental arms control arrangements that permanently limited its ability to defend itself. Moreover, Western allies had not committed themselves to a forward defense of West Germany, but were more likely to use West German territory as a buffer zone or, even, the likely battlefield for their own individual national defense purposes. Furthermore, critics claimed, West German rearmament, under the rubric of NATO would have been an invitation to the Soviet Union to start a preventive war. As a better way to pursue national interests, these critics proposed a system of national defense outside NATO and without an offensive force posture that neither threatened the West nor provoked the East. A strictly neutral FRG would also have a better chance of achieving unification.[17] These liabilities notwithstanding, the FRG gambled and joined NATO because it hoped to reduce the risks involved, turn its allies soft political promises to defend the FRG into hard military commitments, and, ultimately, frustrate the Soviets into giving up East Germany. When making its decision to either become a NATO member or to remain neutral, the FRG based its choice not only on the specific reciprocity of trading alliance membership and arms control for sovereignty and rearmament, but also on the expectation that its new allies would substantiate their political promises militarily, agree to a more equal share of security and defense responsibilities, and support the German goal of national unification. Bonn calculated that NATO membership would empower West Germany to block any quadrilateral deal detrimental to its national interests and that it could steadily improve its ability to shape policies of the alliance as a whole. In other words, the FRG based its decision in part on the expectation that the behaviour of its allies was predictable, that they would comply with the 1954 agreements, which NATO helped to monitor, verify, and enforce, and on the fact that West Germany felt it could, therefore, trust the West as much as the West could trust the West Germans. Bonn's choice was based on absolute gains as outlined in the Paris Treaties as well as on the expectation that more absolute gains would follow.

These West German expectations became reality on a number of occasions when NATO allies renegotiated the sharing of security risks and defense burdens. Most importantly, Bonn's opposition to attempts of the American Kennedy and Johnson administrations to base European deterrence and defense almost entirely on conventional weapons prevailed when NATO finally agreed on the new military strategy of "flexible response."[18] It also prevented Washington and London from making concessions to Moscow and East Berlin on issues of German unification and the status of Berlin. The FRG further succeeded to harden its allies soft political promises to defend West Germany. NATO moved its defense line from the Rhine eastward to the Elbe and installed a "forward defense." With growing military force contributions to NATO's collective defense, West Germany demanded and received a bigger share of command positions in NATO's military headquarters and German civil servants hurried to NATO's political headquarters to fill in the growing share of German personnel slots. Moreover, the allies established and improved procedures to coordinate national and multilateral defense planning as well as nuclear consultation.[19] These silent institutional revolutions proved to be critical not only in building a dense communication network between Bonn and NATO headquarters, but also in forcing West German national security interests onto NATO's agenda. Undoubtedly, the FRG's relative influence over NATO's policies grew, particularly during the 1960s and early 1970s. As a result Germany improved its national security by reducing risks, redistributing residual risks among allies, and expanding political influence in NATO. In short, NATO, as an organization, helped member states to maximize gains. FRG benefited unequally from these gains. This finding supports institutionalist propositions and suggests the addendum that institutions even facilitate peaceful change by permitting the redistribution of power.[20] According to institutionalism, France's decision to leave NATO's military integration was motivated by the desire to unblock further cooperation among the other allies rather than to hinder disproportionate West German gains. It helped NATO to maintain cohesiveness rather than intensifying centrifugal forces after France had left the military integration.

However, West Germany failed to persuade its allies to agree on the Multilateral Force (MLF).[21] This nuclear force would have largely undermined the FRG's renunciation of a nuclear capability in 1954 and dramatically improved its influence on NATO's nuclear decision making. But London and other capitals correctly perceived such relative gains for Bonn as their relative loss and obstructed the agreement. West Germany had to settle for the second best solution: the creation of a NATO Nuclear Planning Group (NPG) that offered absolute gains to all relevant partners.

Also, the deployment of Pershing II and cruise missiles in 1983 as a result of NATO's double-track decision in 1979 redistributed risks among allies because these missiles targeted the Soviet Union while most other European Intermediate Range Nuclear Forces (INF) were aimed at East European targets. Pershing II and cruise missiles increased the chances that a European war would spread to America. American deployments met a long-standing West German demand "to couple" European and American security.[22] It was a final military measure to reinforce the principle of indivisibility of threats to the collectivity upon which NATO was founded originally. American missile deployments again served as an instrument to harden Washington's nuclear deterrence and defense commitments to Europe. The resulting reinforced principle of indivisibility of threats proved to be stronger than any neutralist demands of the German peace movement. In short, West Germany successfully maximized both national and collective security gains within NATO.

During the Cold War, it proved to be much more difficult to establish new organizations that could rival NATO's predominance in European defense issues. Even in the post-Cold War era, serious attempts to expand the European Union's authority into foreign and security policy and develop the Western European Union (WEU) into its defense arm has produced no militarily effective result.[23] Furthermore, while German-French relations proved to be crucial in determining economic policies and moving European integration forward, cooperation in the area of defense and security remained too weak to provide an alternative to NATO. Both sides considered regular biannual consultations as agreed in the Elysee Treaty of 1963 to be most valuable procedures in coordinating both economic and other policies in the realm of "low" politics. France became the single most important trading partner of the FRG and both countries have derived some important absolute gains from the continuing relationship.[24]

While it is agreed that improvements in German-French relations supplemented rather than replaced transatlantic cooperation, the same can also be said about *Ostpolitik*. The principles of mutual recognition of territorial integrity, refraining from violence, and noninterference in domestic affairs were mere political promises without military substance that would have significantly improved the FRG's national security. These soft declarations, while important to develop political and economic relations, could not replace the hard military security guarantees of NATO.

Nor could agreed consultation procedures outweigh Germany's cooperation with the West. Institutions created by treaties with the Soviet Union, Poland, Czechoslovakia, the GDR, and, finally, the Helsinki Final Act of the Conference on Security and Cooperation in Europe (CSCE) remained too weak to offer a viable alternative to NATO. Also, economic cooperation with East European countries remained insignificant compared to growing relations with Western Europe and the United States. *Ostpolitik* could not change West Germany's foreign policy preferences.

When the prospect of unification reopened the option of a neutral and nonaligned Germany, the FRG moved quickly to reassure its allies of its continuing allegiance to the West symbolized by its membership in NATO and the European Union. Implementation of the Single European Act, agreement and ratification of the Maastricht Treaty, as well as the Schengen agreement, all linked Germany closer to its West European neighbours more than ever before. The Maastricht Treaty envisions a common European currency by the end of the twentieth century.[25] The FRG reaffirmed its previous renunciations of the production of weapons of mass destruction and expanded it to include possession and control. NATO developed a new force structure that now encompasses multinational corps and even some multinational divisions. Such deepening of military integration not only contains German armed forces by firmly linking them to allied forces, but also compensates for the dwindling of alliance cohesion as a result of a rapidly declining external threat.[26] To reassure France, that still does not participate in NATO's military integration, Germany agreed to form a Euro-Corps that accommodates French forces in Germany and broadens German-French cooperation into the area of military defense. All indicators point in the direction that is Germany reinforcing self-integration rather than renationalizing foreign and defense policies.[27] No evidence shows that the FRG has considered bringing to an end its membership in international institutions or has pursued policies contrary to agreed principles or consultation procedures. On the contrary, all evidence strongly supports the institutionalist propositions that German preferences and polices have been both constrained and shaped by international institutions.[28] Even the most controversial example, Germany's self-assertive policy toward the former Yugoslavia, was based upon principles agreed by the European Union even though the Federal Republic threatened to implement these principles unilaterally if other countries refused to cooperate.[29]

Conclusion

While using almost the same evidence from history, realism and institutionalism paint quite different pictures and provide contradictory answers to the questions asked at the beginning of this chapter. Realism maintains that states succeeded in maintaining a stable balance during the Cold War. The history of the FRG's foreign policy is a history of keeping a delicate balance among Europeans. East and West countered every West German attempt to gain more foreign policy options to achieve national security in an effort to maintain stability before 1989. The collapse of the Soviet Union and the Warsaw Treaty Organization radically altered the stable distribution of power among European states. Europeans can no longer contain German foreign policy by themselves. Institutionalism sees a more incremental rise of West German power since 1955. During the Cold War, West German foreign policy was a history of confidence-building among neighbours. European states created international institutions to contain, accommodate, and, most importantly, modernize, as well as pacify West Germany so that it could no longer poses a menacing threat to their security. Unification emerged as an end result of a long process of steadily growing German power. It occurred with the consent of other countries and does not upset the stability in Europe as long as the FRG remains firmly embedded in international organizations.

Realism and institutionalism also differ in their explanation of when and why the German phoenix rose from the ashes. Realists believe that Germany's essential gain of power occurred after 1989 as a result of the demise of the Soviet empire and the subsequent German unification. These basic alterations in the distribution of power in the international system account for German gains in the post cold war world. Both the global and the European systems are less stable today than they have been during the last 50 years. The bipolar system of the Cold War era has given way to a unipolar system with the United States as the sole remaining superpower. The European system is unbalanced because Germany is bigger and more powerful than any of the other European countries except Russia. According to realism, today's German phoenix is similar to that of the nineteenth century's.

Two possible future scenarios derive from the realist vision contingent upon either the global or the regional picture. The first scenario is global. It maintains that over time Europe might feel threatened by the United

States as the sole remaining superpower. European states will be compelled to balance by forming an anti-American alliance around a German core in order to restore global stability. If Europeans ever overcome their parochial national interests it will be because of a unifying threat from the other side of the Atlantic. The second scenario is regional. Neighbours perceive the newly unleashed Germany as an imminent danger against which they must balance by forming an anti-German alliance in order to restore regional stability. Both scenarios are based on the assumption that the post-Cold war era will be less stable than the Cold War itself. Realists anticipate more great power conflicts and that war is not totally unlikely. States need to find a new stable balance of power and minimize conflicts during the transition from an unstable unipolar to a new and stable bipolar distribution of power. Germany's role is pivotal in both scenarios.

Institutionalists believe that Germany's growth was more steady than abrupt and thus occurred gradually over the last 50 years. The German phoenix of the second half of this century is completely new and has nothing in common with its predecessor. International institutions have underscored the growth of German power. They may support aspirations of others as well. These institutions will persist. Furthermore, not only will Germany remain firmly embedded in international institutions, but these arrangements have also changed the character of the German state and society. The FRG will continue to pursue policies within the limits of existing international institutions. Neighbours, allies, and opponents have nothing to fear from the tamed republic. Conflict may occur, but it will be channeled and resolved within institutional arrangements. It is in Germany's best interest to maintain and develop these institutions as a way to stabilize international relations. The FRG may even be able to play a mediating role between its American, West European, and East European partners by avoiding the disruption of existing partnerships. Germany will play a pivotal role in linking allies together and deepening institutional integration. Strong international institutions will also support the transition process of Central and East European countries toward democracy and market economy. Germany's prosperity not only sets the standard for these countries, but the history of the Federal Republic of Germany over the last 50 years serves as a model of a country which has transformed itself successfully.

NOTES

1. For a final attempt to stop German unification because Germany was perceived to be "by its very nature a destabilizing rather than a stabilizing force in Europe," see Margaret Thatcher, *The Downing Street Years, 1979/1990* (New York: Harper Perennial, 1993). Quote ibid., p. 791.

2. Wolfram Hanrieder, *Germany, America, Europe: Forty Years of German Foreign Policy* (New Haven: Yale University Press, 1989); Christian Tuschhoff: "Wiederbewaffnung, Westbindung und Wiedervereinigung. Konstitution, nachholende Entwicklung und Rekonstitution deutscher Sicherheitspolitik nach 1949," in *Deutschland und der Westen im 19. und 20. Jahrhundert. Teil 1: Transatlantische Beziehungen*, ed. Jürgen Elvert and Michael Salewski (Stuttgart: Franz Steiner Verlag, 1993), pp. 165–214; Gregor Schöllgen, *Die Macht in der Mitte Europas. Stationen deutscher Außenpolitik von Friedrich dem Großen bis zur Gegenwart* (Munich: Verlag C.H. Beck, 1992); Helga Haftendorn, *Sicherheit und Entspannung. Zur Außenpolitik der Bundesrepublik Deutschland 1955–1982* (Baden-Baden: Nomos Verlagsgesellschaft, 1983); Helga Haftendorn, *Sicherheit und Stabilität. Außenbeziehungen der Bundesrepublik zwischen Ölkrise und NATO-Doppelbeschluß* (Munich: Deutscher Taschenbuch Verlag, 1986); Christian Hacke, *Die Außenpolitik der Bundesrepublik Deutschland. Weltmacht wider Willen?* (Frankfurt and Berlin: Ullstein Verlag, 1997); Frank R. Pfetsch, *Die Außenpolitik der Bundesrepublik 1949–1992*, 2nd ed. (Munich: Wilhelm Fink Verlag, 1993); Timothy Garton Ash, *In Europe's Name: Germany and the Divided Continent* (New York: Random House, 1993). A detailed documentation can be found in Auswärtiges Amt, ed., *Außenpolitik der Bundesrepublik Deutschland. Dokumenten von 1949–1994* (Cologne: Wissenschaft und Politik, 1995).

3. For an assessment of realism and institutionalism see Joseph M. Grieco, *Cooperation among Nations: Europe, America, and Non-Tariff Barriers to Trade* (Ithaca, NY: Cornell University Press, 1990); Arthur A. Stein, *Why Nations Cooperate: Circumstance and Choice in International Relations* (Ithaca, NY: Cornell University Press, 1990); Gunther Hellmann and Reinhard Wolf, "Neorealism, Neoliberal Institutionalism, and the Future of NATO," *Security Studies* 3, no. 1 (Autumn 1993): 3–43.

4. Kenneth N. Waltz, *Man, the State, and War: A Theoretical Analysis* (New York: Columbia University Press, 1954); Robert Gilpin, *War and Change in World Politics* (New York: Cambridge University Press, 1981); Barry Buzan, Charles Jones, and Richard Little, *The Logic of Anarchy: Neorealism to Structural Realism* (New York: Columbia University Press, 1993); Stephen M. Walt, *The Origins of Alliances* (Ithaca, NY: Cornell University Press, 1987). For a critique of realism see Paul Schroeder, "Historical Reality vs. Neo-realist Theory," *International Security* 19, no. 1 (Summer 1994): 108–48 and the following debate "Correspondence: History vs. Neo-Realism: A Second Look," *International Security* 20, no. 1 (Summer 1995): 182–95.

5. For a distinction between relative and absolute gains see *Neorealism and Neoliberalism: The Contemporary Debate*, ed. David A. Baldwin (New York: Columbia University Press, 1993).

6. Josef Joffe, "The Foreign Policy of the Federal Republic of Germany. Tradition and Change," in *Foreign Policy in World Politics*, ed. Roy C. Macridis, 8th ed. (Englewood Cliffs, NJ: Prentice Hall, 1992), pp. 68–107.

7. Werner Link, "Die außenpolitische Staatsräson der Bundesrepublik Deutschland. Überlegungen zur innerstaatlichen Struktur und Perzeption des internationalen

Bedingungsfeldes," in *Demokratie und Diktatur. Geist und Gestalt politischer Herrschaft in Deutschland und Europa*, ed. Manfred Funke et al. (Bonn: Bundeszentrale für politische Bildung, 1987), pp. 400–16.

8.   Joffe, "The Foreign Policy of the Federal Republic of Germany," pp. 93–94.

9.   John J. Mearsheimer, "Back to the Future: Instability in Europe after the Cold War," *International Security* 15, no. 1 (Summer 1990): 5–56; Kenneth N. Waltz, "The Emerging Structure of International Politics," *International Security* 18, no. 2 (Fall 1993): 44–79; "Correspondence," *International Security* 19, no. 1 (Summer 1994): 195–99.

10. Robert O. Keohane, *After Hegemony: Cooperation and Discord in the World Political Economy* (Princeton: Princeton University Press, 1984); Robert O. Keohane, *International Institutions and State Power: Essays in International Relations Theory* (Boulder, CO: Westview Press, 1989); Oran R. Young, *International Cooperation: Building Regimes for Natural Resources and the Environment* (Ithaca, NY: Cornell University Press, 1989); Stephen D. Krasner, ed., *International Regimes* (Ithaca, NY: Cornell University Press, 1983). For a realist critique of institutionalism see John J. Mearsheimer, "The False Promise of International Institutions," *International Security* 19, no. 3 (Winter 1994/95): 5–49 as well as the following debate Robert O. Keohane and Lisa L. Martin, "The Promise of Institutionalist Theory," *International Security* 20, no. 1 (Summer 1995): 39–51; John J. Mearsheimer, "A Realist Reply," *International Security* 20, no. 1 (Summer 1995): 82–93.

11. For the distinction between specific and general reciprocity see John G. Ruggie, ed., *Multilateralism Matters: The Theory and Praxis of an International Form* (New York: Columbia University Press, 1993).

12. Anne-Marie Burley and Walter Mattli, "Europe Before the Court: A Political Theory of Legal Integration," *International Organization* 47, no. 1 (Winter 1993): 41–76 and the following debate Geoffrey Garrett, "The Politics of Legal Integration in the European Union," *International Organization* 49, no. 1 (Winter 1995): 171–81; Walter Mattli and Anne-Marie Slaughter, "Law and Politics in the European Union: A reply to Garrett," *International Organization* 49, no. 1 (Winter 1995): 183–90.

13. Martin Shapiro, "The European Court of Justice," in *Europolitics: Institutions and Policymaking in the "New European Community,"* ed. Alberta M. Sbragia (Washington, DC: The Brookings Institution, 1992), pp. 126–27. It should be noted though, that the German Federal Constitutional Courts ruling on the Maastricht Treaty represents a severe setback to the direct effect doctrine.

14. Fritz Scharpf, "The Joint Decision Trap: Lessons from German Federalism and European Integration," *Public Administration* 66, no. 3 (Autumn 1988): 239–78.

15. For the distinction between "exit" and "voice" see Albert O. Hirschman, *Exit, Voice, and Loyalty: Responses to Decline in Firms, Organizations, and States* (Cambridge, MA: Harvard University Press, 1970).

16. Reinhard Rode, "Deutschland: Weltwirtschaftsmacht oder überforderter Euro-Hegemon?" *Leviathan* 19, no. 2 (1991): 229–46; Andrei S. Markovits and Simon Reich, "Should Europe Fear the Germans?" in *From Bundesrepublik to Deutschland: German Politics after Unification,* ed. Michael G. Huelshoff, Andrei S. Markovits, and Simon Reich (Ann Arbor, MI: University of Michigan Press, 1993), pp. 271–89; James Sperling, "A Unified Germany, a Single European Economic Space, and the Prospects for the Atlantic Economy," in *Germany and the European Community*, ed. Carl F. Lankowski (New York: St. Martin's Press, 1993), pp. 179–216.

17. Christian Tuschhoff, *Die Grundsteinlegung deutscher Sicherheitspolitik, 1949–1955* (Münster: Lit Verlag, 1994).

18. Christian Tuschhoff, "Strategiepoker: massive Vergeltung—flexible Antwort," in *Das Zeitalter der Atombombe,* ed. Michael Salewski (Munich: C.H. Beck Verlag, 1995), pp. 167–88.

19. Joerg F. Baldauf, "Implementing Flexible Response: The US, Germany, and NATO's Conventional Forces" (dissertation, Massachusetts Institute of Technology, Cambridge, MA, 1984); Frederic L. Kirgis, Jr., "NATO Consultations as a Component of National Decisionmaking," *American Journal of International Law* 73, no. 3 (July 1979): 372–406; Christian Tuschhoff, *Machtgewinn auf leisen Sohlen. Deutschland, Kernwaffen und die NATO* (Baden-Baden: Nomos Verlagsgesellschaft, forthcoming).

20. Manfred Efinger, Volker Rittberger, Klaus D. Wolf, and Michael Zürn, "Internationale Regime und internationale Politik," in *Theorien der Internationalen Beziehungen. Bestandsaufnahme und Forschungsperspektive (Politische Vierteljahresschrift* 31, no. 21 (1990)), ed. Volker Rittberger (Opladen: Westdeutscher Verlag, 1990), pp. 263–85.

21. Wilfried L. Kohl, "Nuclear Sharing in NATO and the Multilateral Force," *Political Science Quarterly* 80, no. 1 (March 1965): 88–109.

22. Ernst-C. Meier, *Deutsch-amerikanische Sicherheitsbeziehungen und der NATO-Doppelbeschluß* (Rheinfelden: Schäuble, 1986); Susanne Peters, *The Germans and the INF Missiles: Getting Their Way in NATO's Strategy of Flexible Response* (Baden-Baden: Nomos Verlagsgesellschaft, 1990).

23. Mathias Jopp, *The Strategic Implications of European Integration,* Adelphi Paper 290 (London: International Institute for Strategic Studies, 1994).

24. Philip H. Gordon, *France, Germany, and the Western Alliance* (Boulder, CO: Westview Press, 1995).

25. Michael J. Baun, "The Maastricht Treaty as High Politics: Germany, France, and European Integration," *Political Science Quarterly* 110, no. 4 (Winter 1995/96): 605–24. Wilhelm Schönfelder and Elke Thiel, *Ein Markt—eine Währung. Die Verhandlungen zur Europäischen Wirtschafts- und Währungsunion* (Baden-Baden: Nomos Verlagsgesellschaft, 1994).

26. Christian Tuschhoff, "Die politischen Folgen der Streitkräfte–Reform der NATO," *Aus Politik und Zeitgeschichte* B15/16 (1993): 28-39; Karl Lowe and Thomas-Durell Young, "Multinational Corps in NATO," *Survival* 33, no. 1 (January/February 1991): 66-77; Alexander Moens and Christopher Anstis, eds., *Disconcerted Europe: The Search for a New Security Architecture* (Boulder, CO: Westview Press, 1994); Catherine M. Kelleher, *The Future of European Security: An Interim Assessment,* Washington, D.C.: The Brookings Institution, 1995); David G. Haglund and Olaf Mager, *Homeward Bound? Allied Forces in the New Germany* (Boulder, CO: Westview Press, 1992).

27. Gunther Hellmann, "'Einbindungspolitik': German Foreign Policy and the Art of Declaring 'Total Peace,'" in *Die Zukunft der Außenpolitik. Deutsche Interessen in den internationalen Beziehungen,* ed. Jörg Calließ and Bernhard Moltmann (Rehburg-Loccum: Loccumer Protokolle 67, 1994), pp. 86–127. Jeffrey J. Anderson and John B. Goodman, "Mars or Minerva? A United Germany in a Post-Cold War Europe," in *After the Cold War: International Institutions and State Strategies in Europe, 1989–1991,* ed. Robert O. Keohane, Joseph S. Nye, and Stanley Hoffmann (Cambridge, MA: Harvard University Press, 1993), pp. 23–62.

28. Klaus D. Wolf, "Das neue Deutschland—eine 'Weltmacht'?" *Leviathan* 19, no. 2 (1991): 247–60; Beate Kohler-Koch, "Deutsche Einigung im Spannungsfeld internationaler Umbrüche," *Politische Vierteljahresschrift* 32, no 4 (December 1991): 605–19.

29. Volker Rittberger, "Nach der Vereinigung—Deutschlands Stellung in der Welt," *Leviathan* 20, no. 2 (1992): 207–29; Harald Müller, "German Foreign Policy after Unification," in *The New Germany and the New Europe,* Paul B. Stares, ed. (Washington, DC: The Brookings Institution, 1992), pp. 126–73.

3

Germany Divided, Germany Unified
The National Question, 1945-1990

MATTHIAS ZIMMER

I "What belongs together is growing together."

Willy Brandt's famous quotation from his speech in Berlin on 10 November 1989, the day after the Berlin Wall came down, was not only an optimistic prediction for the future, but quintessentially captured a major task in postwar German history. Germany was divided in the wake of the Cold War, a division that was cemented by the Wall when it was erected in 1961 to seal off East Germany from West Germany. The essence of the German question in the years following the division of Germany was: How could a country that was divided against its will be brought together, and how could people who were separated from each other be united again? Would the artificial division in two separate and separated states create two different identities in East and West, thus effectively dissolving the German nation? Or would the common identity of Germans in East and West prevail over the political division? The answer to this question took 40 years to work itself out. The parallel creation of two German states in 1949 marked a first peak in Germany's postwar history, the unification of Germany in 1990 ended Germany's postwar history.

Following Germany's unconditional surrender in May 1945, it was occupied by the victorious Allies and divided in four zones of occupation. Berlin, the German capital, became a microcosm of the occupational regime. The city, located in the Soviet Zone of Occupation, was divided into four occupation zones itself and treated as a separate entity. The future of Germany was in the hand of the Allies who had assumed supreme authority in Germany on 5 June 1945. With the unconditional surrender Germany became "subject to such requirements as may now or hereafter be imposed upon her."[1] Germany was divided for occupational purposes only, as the Allies were quick to emphasize. The Potsdam Agreement of August

1945 reflected this intention. It stipulated a "uniformity of treatment of the German population throughout Germany" and declared the intention of the Allies to establish central administrative departments for all of Germany, although for the time being there would be no central German government. But the declarations at Potsdam never translated into practice. Between 1945 and 1947, the United States and the Soviet Union increasingly came to perceive each other as enemies. In this formation phase of a new world order that became to be known as the East-West Conflict the division of Germany was sealed because the conflict lines ran through Germany. The subsequent mutual delimitation of spheres of influence led to the formation of the liberal-democratic Federal Republic of Germany (FRG) and the communist German Democratic Republic (GDR). Germany was torn between East and West; German unity fell victim to the East-West Conflict.[2]

The East-West Conflict was at the cradle of the division of Germany; the solemn declaration ending the Cold War at the Paris Conference on Security and Cooperation in Europe (CSCE) in September 1990 was at the cradle of German unification in 1990. Division and unity in the years after 1945 were consequences of the East-West Conflict, and German politicians had to take this fact into account. The foreign policy principles of the FRG thus were a product of necessity rather than choice. Located on the dividing line of the East-West Conflict, the security of the FRG could be safeguarded only by close cooperation with the West. The alliance with the western democracies thus became the *raison d'état* of the FRG—her guiding principle in foreign policy.[3] It has been argued that the implementation of this principle, together with the political and military integration of the FRG into the institutions of the West, would inevitably deepen the division of Germany, but this criticism did not stand the test of reality. The FRG had always claimed that the implementation of a liberal democratic order and the integration into the West were in the interest of all Germans. The preamble of the 1949 Basic Law (Constitution) of the Federal Republic of Germany explicitly stated that the Basic Law was enacted also "on behalf of those Germans to whom participation was denied." The revolution of 1989 in East Germany and the subsequent rush to unification proved that this claim was not hollow. German unification came about on the basis of the FRG Constitution adopted in 1949.

A Difficult Start: Freedom Versus Unity?

The Federal Republic of Germany was a child of the Cold War, founded on the debris of the Third Reich. Even the Western Allies were not entirely convinced that the German menace had been contained once and for all and only slowly released the FRG into sovereignty. Between 1949 and 1955, the FRG was not a sovereign state. Even after the termination of the occupation regime in 1955, the Three Powers—the United States, Great Britain and France—retained the "rights and duties, exercised or held by them with regard to Berlin and Germany as a whole, including German unification and a peace settlement."[4] In other words, although West Germany became formally sovereign in 1955, the question of German unification never was a question to be decided by the Germans only. The residual rights of the Allies ensured them a right to a say in this matter. The Allies were not in principle opposed to German unification, but attached conditions to it. In the Paris Treaties of 1954 they had formally agreed to cooperate "to achieve...their common aim of a reunified Germany enjoying a liberal-democratic constitution, like that of the Federal Republic and integrated within the European community."[5] But this became precisely the pitfall of the politics of unification: As long as the East-West Conflict would shape European political geography, the likelihood of German unification on western terms was nonexistent. Western support for any other solution to the German question but on western terms was equally unlikely.

Konrad Adenauer, the first chancellor of the FRG, had instinctively seen the danger of the impending division of Germany after the end of the war.[6] The part of Germany occupied by the Soviet Union was, according to Adenauer, lost for the time being. Consequently, the western parts of Germany had to be united and integrated into the West because this was, in Adenauer's view, the only remedy to withstand the threat of communist expansionism. At the same time, the western integration of the FRG would serve to mitigate the fears of Germany's neighbours concerning a resurgence of German power. If the FRG could be interconnected with the western democracies on a variety of levels, she would cease to be a threat to European security. Adenauer hoped that this strategy of integration would not only enhance West German security, but would also raise the FRG to the position of a sovereign and equal partner in the western alliance. If West Germany's relations with the West would be based on partnership, the West could not come to a separate agreement with the Soviet Union that might be harmful to the FRG. Adenauer's fear, which has been labeled as "Potsdam complex," was not entirely unfounded, because until 1955 the specter of a four-power conference on Germany was haunting the chancellor. In Adenauer's view, such a separate agreement not only threatened his triple aims of western integration, equality, and sovereignty; moreover, an agreement on the basis of the status quo would have cemented the division of Germany.

West Germany's integration into the West was an aim in itself for Adenauer, but at the same time the means to achieve equality and sovereignty. He frequently emphasized that his policy of integration was not only compatible with national unification, but would speed up the process of unification. He argued that the Soviet Union would only agree to a solution of the German question on western terms if the West could negotiate from a position of strength. West Germany's alliance with the western democracies enhanced in Adenauer's view not only the leverage of the western alliance, but also of Germany. The domestic dimension of the policy of strength materialized in the economic upswing of the FRG. The so-called *Wirtschaftswunder*, the economic miracle of the 1950s, had a magnetic effect on the less well-to-do Germans in East Germany. West Germany became a beacon of prosperity and democracy, thus threatening the stability of the East German regime. The constant flow of resettlers from East to West Germany and the uprising in East Germany in June 1953 proved that East German stability indeed was fragile and stood on feet of clay.

Closely related to the policy of strength was the principle of free choice. Adenauer maintained that a unification of Germany was to have two prerequisites. The first prerequisite, free elections in Germany as a whole, would marginalize the ruling communist party in East Germany and reveal its puppet character. The second prerequisite concerned the foreign policy choices for a unified Germany. Adenauer vehemently opposed a neutralization of Germany and argued that a unified Germany should be free to decide its place in Europe—and this place for Adenauer was undoubtedly within the western alliance.

The principle of free choice explains the dismissal of Stalin's note in March 1952. Stalin had offered a unified Germany with its own army under the condition that Germany was neutralized and would not enter any coalition that was directed against a country that had participated with its armed forces in the war against Germany. This would have excluded Germany's participation in the European Defense Community (EDC), which was negotiated at the time. Stalin's offer has been interpreted as a tactical manoeuver to torpedo the negotiations and the FRG's integration into the western alliance. The alternative that Stalin offered, a neutral

Germany with its own national army, was neither in the interest of Adenauer nor the western allies. Adenauer equated neutralization with the transformation of Germany to a Soviet-style regime, and although he may have been "more American than the Americans" when he immediately smothered all attempts to plumb the ramifications of Stalin's offer, he was backed up by the western allies.[7] The question remained over the next decades if a chance for unification had been missed in 1952. Even with the evidence from the Soviet archives at hand, the question can not be answered conclusively. Adenauer's immediate reaction was as much caused by his deeply rooted suspicion of the motives of Soviet foreign policy as by the insight that Germany was neither the addressee of the note nor at liberty to negotiate the terms of unification on its own. His strategy thus was to align the western allies and prevent an agreement of the four Powers over the heads of the Germans, which would have destroyed his entire political strategy.

In 1955, Adenauer achieved his main goal in the FRG's relations with the West. The optimistic mood with regard to unification had given way to a more sober and pessimistic perspective. The project of a EDC had foundered in the French National Assembly in 1954, and for a brief moment it seemed that Adenauer's strategy of integration with the West had failed. The swift integration of the Federal Republic into NATO solved the crisis. The FRG of Germany became sovereign and the occupation statute was terminated. Re-armament and the introduction of a general draft were the FRG's contributions to the western alliance. With the creation of the Warsaw Pact in the East, the formation of two opposing blocks in Europe was concluded.

The political strategies in dealing with the East-West Conflict henceforth took the status quo into account. The Soviet Union subsequently sought a contractual agreement that would legitimize the status quo in Europe, a process that culminated in the CSCE in the 1970s. The western allies tried to reduce the level of tensions on the basis of the status quo without explicitly recognizing it. Détente and disarmament became popular catchwords; the German national question, potentially endangering the status quo, was put on the back burner. Adenauer's equation that western integration and a policy of strength would almost automatically result in the unification of Germany did not work out. His attempt to tie together détente and disarmament with some progress in the German question failed because the western allies rejected the link. Until 1955 the

Federal Republic of Germany had tried to achieve unification on western terms. Ironically, the very moment that the western allies contractually agreed to support the FRG in her quest for unification on western terms in the Paris Treaties in 1954, the overall strategic environment made this particular aim politically undesirable. The FRG's policy became defensive in nature, trying to prevent a recognition of the status quo and maintaining the legal principles that justified her aim of unification. The erection of the Berlin Wall in 1961 was the hour of disillusionment for West German politicians not only because the division of Germany was physically and visibly cemented, but because the western allies apparently accepted the new situation and only resorted to verbal protest.[8] The years after 1955 had marked the limits of the FRG's quest for unification. Unwilling to draw the necessary conclusion from the fact that the attempts at solving the national question were in a stalemate, the FRG's policy ossified to a formalistic insistence on legal principles and potentially undermined the strategy of the United States to initiate a global approach to détente with the Soviet Union.[9] Only with the succession to power of the coalition between Social Democrats and Liberals in 1969 the FRG was able to break the deadlock and free herself from the self-blockade of the preceding years.

A New Approach: *Ostpolitik* and Détente

In the years after 1969, the Social-Liberal Coalition under Chancellor Willy Brandt implemented a new policy that complemented Adenauer's integration in the West with a flexible and innovative approach concerning the FRG's relations with the East.[10] At the core of Brandt's concept was the acceptance of the status quo and a new approach to the national question that took into account the interests of the Soviet Union and Eastern Europe. With regard to the German Democratic Republic, the Social-Liberal Coalition reversed the policy of isolation pursued by the former German governments. Brandt and his government tried to achieve a *modus vivendi* with East Germany on a contractual basis. The new approach had to be buttressed by an overall policy of relations with the East, especially with the Soviet Union. Brandt's first step was to conclude the Moscow Treaty with the Soviet Union, recognizing the existing territorial realities in Europe. In the treaty, the FRG declared not to have territorial claims against anybody now and in the future and particularly recognized the inviolability of the Oder-Neisse line,

Poland's western frontier.[11] This part of the treaty was highly contentious. After the war, German territory east of the Oder-Neisse line had been ceded and placed under Polish administration pending a final settlement in a peace treaty. A small portion of East Prussia was placed under Soviet administration. Did Brandt's recognition of the territorial realities "sell out" German interests, as he was accused of doing by the conservative opposition? Brandt declared that nothing had been given away that had not already been lost. The territories east of the Oder and Neisse were lost in Brandt's assessment as a result of Hitler's heinous crimes. Moreover, the allies had declared in Potsdam that the territorial arrangements would be preliminary, pending the final settlement in a peace treaty that would legally sanction the transfer of territory. The FRG could certainly not speak for a unified Germany which eventually would part in a peace treaty, and the Moscow Treaty would, therefore, not be legally binding to a unified Germany. The FRG also insisted that the right to national self-determination was not affected by the treaty and attached a letter to the treaty emphasizing that the recognition of territorial realities "does not conflict with the political objective of the Federal Republic of Germany to prepare for a state of peace in Europe in which the German nation will recover its unity in self-determination."[12] Even if Germany could not be united in the foreseeable future, Brandt was convinced that the option for unification should not be surrendered. By recognizing territorial realities in Europe, the West German government had removed an obstacle in the improvement of East-West relations. Bonn's obstinate refusal to recognize the existing borders had, in previous years, not only foiled the FRG's own cautious attempts to pursue a more conciliatory approach in her relations with the East, but had also impeded global détente. Henceforth, the policy of détente was decoupled from the intricate German question, and the strategies to solve the German question were decoupled from the mood swings in the East-West relations in general. The treaty with the Soviet Union in 1970 was the prelude to subsequent treaties with Poland (1970) and Czechoslovakia (1973), as well as for the treaty with East Germany in 1972.

Especially with regard to East Germany, the Social-Liberal coalition tried to break new ground. At the very beginning of his tenure Chancellor Brandt had for the first time officially recognized the existence of the German Democratic Republic when he spoke about two German states in his inaugural address in 1969. He stopped short of a legal recognition; relations between the two German states should have a special character. The special character was captured in the phrase of two states in Germany that are not foreign to each other. The Treaty on the Basis of Relations Between the Federal Republic of Germany and the German Democratic Republic, signed in 1972, further underlined the peculiar mixture of inter- and intrastate relations.[13] Although both German states agreed to "develop normal good-neighborly relations with each other on the basis of equal rights" (Article 1), they established permanent missions at the respective seats of governments instead of embassies, as is common in international law. The treaty ended the FRG's claim to be the sole representative of all German people by stipulating that "neither of the two states can represent the other or act on its behalf" (Article 4); moreover, the jurisdiction of each of the two states was to be confined to its own territory (Article 6). With the recognition of the GDR, the so-called Hallstein doctrine became obsolete. This doctrine had served Bonn well since the mid 1950s to isolate internationally the GDR by preventing diplomatic recognition by third nations. Henceforth, third nations could establish diplomatic relations with East Germany without risking breaking off diplomatic relations with West Germany. The GDR had achieved its goal of equality and international recognition, although relations with West Germany were short of full international recognition.[14] Both German states became members of the United Nations in 1973.

What did the FRG gain from the contractual relaxation of tensions? Did not the *Ostpolitik*, the policy of détente with the East, give away legal positions and sacrifice the quest for national unity? Critics of Brandt's policy indeed argued that the *Ostpolitik* went too far. But beyond the political quarrel there was a consensus in the West German Parliament to the effect that "the treaties did not anticipate a peace settlement for Germany by treaty and do not create any legal foundation for the frontier existing today," that merely a *modus vivendi* was established that did not affect the "inalienable right to self-determination."[15] The treaties might be binding for West Germany, but would certainly not be legally binding for a united Germany.

Brandt's policy may seem static, merely recognizing the obvious and adapting Bonn's *Ostpolitik* to an international environment strongly in favour of détente. But Brandt's conception of *Ostpolitik* aimed beyond the status quo. It rested on the idea that the status quo could only be overcome and transcended by recognizing it. The refusal to recognize the realities of the postwar world had not advanced the cause of German unity, because it was exactly this refusal that had preserved the division. Brandt perceived unification to be a long-term process in which the two German states had to come closer in a series of small steps. This basic idea had first been sketched out by his aide Egon Bahr, who in 1963 had proposed a "change through rapprochement" to gradually transform the German question. More important than the insistence on national unity and unification was the idea to cooperate with the regime in East Germany and to soften it up in the process. A democratization in East Germany would eventually redefine the German question. The underlying assumption of this policy was that capitalism and socialism would converge due to the constraints of the industrial society. The converging point would be some variant of democratic socialism; the East German regime would be democratized, and in West Germany the principle of social justice and equality would be firmly established in state and society, a move which the Social-Liberal Coalition undertook in a series of reform bills.

Overcoming the division of Germany thus was a long-term process in Brandt's view. For the time being, conditions had to be created that would keep the national consciousness alive and the German question open. The rights and responsibilities of the allied powers provided the legal context for Germany as a whole since those rights and responsibilities could be terminated in a peace settlement with a united Germany only. Brandt also emphasized the maintenance of the unity of the nation. Maintaining national unity required the free flow of ideas, communication between people in East and West Germany, required a permeation of the Wall that sealed off Germans in the East from Germans in the West to keep alive the sense of unity. Brandt's approach was subversive, inherently threatening the stability of the East German regime that rested on the deliberate separation from the West. Thus, the treaty between the FRG and the GDR reflected two differing realities. For the communist regime in East Germany, it was a treaty that acknowledged the division of Germany and the equality of the GDR in international relations. For the West German government it was a treaty that was primarily intended to alleviate the situation of the people under East German rule and, on second thought, a treaty that initiated a policy of national unification rather than concluding it.

National unity was not to be achieved by the Germans on their own, but had to be embedded in a pan-European context. The German question was Europeanized; its resolution required overcoming the division of Europe. Brandt's *Ostpolitik* aimed at a European peace order by means of détente. Adenauer's priorities thus had been reversed: further progress in the German question was not seen as prerequisite to, but a consequence of détente. Moreover, détente was to prevent the further deepening of the division and mutual estrangement of the divided parts of Germany and Europe.

Ostpolitik did not end with the bilateral agreements of the early 1970s. The bilateral policy of détente was complemented by the CSCE. Such a conference had been on the political agenda of the Soviet Union for almost two decades, primarily to reach a multilateral agreement buttressing and recognizing the status quo in Europe. The western countries had their own agenda for the CSCE; they emphasized the human rights component in the relationship among states in Europe. Thus, the Final Act of the Conference reflected, in four "baskets," a minimum consensus that was reached by a process of give-and-take.[16] The first basket consisted of a declaration on principles guiding the relations between the participating states. The principles contained the rights of sovereign equality, renunciation of force, inviolability of frontiers, territorial integrity, peaceful settlement of disputes, nonintervention in internal affairs, respect for human rights and fundamental freedoms, equal rights and self-determination of peoples, cooperation among states, and fulfillment in good faith of the obligations under international law. The third basket contained those principles that reflected the interests of the West—cooperation in humanitarian affairs, the exchange of information and working conditions for journalists, cultural cooperation, reunion of families, freedom of travel, and free movement.

Over time, the West came to regard the principles contained in the third basket as a lever to influence the regimes in the Communist bloc; although the Communist countries emphasized nonintervention in domestic affairs. The CSCE agreement was not legally binding, but a declaration of intent. But by signing the agreement, the West (and increasingly opposition movements in Eastern Europe) could argue that the eastern signatories did not live up to the expectations. The continuation of the CSCE process in a series of follow-up conferences were sometimes turned into a tribunal on the human rights record of the communist bloc countries and reflected the deterioration of East-West relations in the late 1970s and early 1980s. Static and dynamic elements of the *Ostpolitik* seemed to balance one another.[17] Only in hindsight does it become clear that the CSCE accord had implanted an explosive charge in the socialist countries that, slowly and with time delay, had its effect in 1989.

But in the 1970s, these events could not have been foreseen. *Ostpolitik* was an issue fiercely debated in the public domain. The conservative opposition, which had lost the elections in 1969 by a small margin, vehemently opposed Brandt's new approach.[18] They argued that Brandt would give away rights in return for declarations of intent, that *Ostpolitik* meant the renunciation of the goal of unification, that the establishment of official relations with the GDR would lend legitimacy to a regime that had none whatsoever. The Bavarian state government, ruled by the conservative Christian Social Union (CSU), took the treaty with East Germany to the Federal Constitutional Court, arguing that the recognition of the GDR violated the Basic Law. The Court, by a majority vote, rejected the arguments brought forward by the Bavarian government, but drew a fine line for West German politicians. It declared that no constitutional body "may abandon the restoration of national unity as a political goal" and required the constitutional bodies "to work toward the attainment of this goal in their policies and to refrain from doing anything that would thwart the aim of reunification."[19] The Federal Constitutional Court reaffirmed the conservative position on national unification, but gave politicians some leeway; political strategies that were not explicitly aimed at the unification of Germany were permitted as long as the case could be made that this particular strategy actually furthered the aim of unification. And indeed, the rationale of *Ostpolitik* seemed peculiar: To stabilize a regime in order to liberalize it and to approve of a status quo in order to transcend it—those were exercises in political dialectics that required some sophistication.[20] But the core of Brandt's *Ostpolitik* remained intact, even after the Social-Liberal Coalition was succeeded by the conservative Christian-Liberal Coalition in 1982. The major elements of this consensus were:

1. The emphasis on the special character of the relations between the two German states. The Federal Constitutional Court had summarized this special relationship with regard to the Treaty between the FRG and the GDR by pointing to its dual character: it was "in essence" a treaty under international law, "in substance" a treaty that regulated intra-German relations. The FRG would not consider the GDR a foreign country; the frontier between the two states would not have the character of a frontier dividing sovereign states. East

Germany profited from this interpretation because the trade between both German states was not considered foreign trade under the regulations of the European Economic Community (EEC). Thus, the GDR had underhand access to the European markets in the EEC. Furthermore, West Germany never officially recognized East German citizenship. Although the GDR had passed its own Law of Citizenship in 1967, the official West German position remained that there was only one German citizenship for all Germans. Refugees from the GDR thus automatically were entitled to a West German passport upon entering West German territory. In the refugee crisis in the fall of 1989, this entitlement was a strong incentive for East Germans to cross the border to West Germany, thus initiating the beginning of the end of East Germany.

2. The adherence to the unity of the nation required further permeation of the Wall separating peoples from East and West Germany. Fostering inter-German travel and contacts between people in East and West, family reunions, cultural, academic, and technological exchange were of special importance in the operationalization of the principle of national unity. Germany had once been a *Kulturnation*, a nation predominantly defined by its common culture, language, and by its history.[21] The sense of commonality could not be kept alive under conditions of separation; therefore, communication between people in East and West had to be improved to keep alive the idea of the German nation as a necessary minimum for a policy of national unification.

3. To keep the German question open was not only a legal obligation, but also a moral one. The legal dimension was embodied in the Basic Law, the decision of the Federal Constitutional Court, and the residual rights and obligations of the western allies for Berlin and Germany as a whole. The moral dimension was best captured by the phrase that the German question would be open as long as the Brandenburg gate was closed; in other words, human rights became part of the German question. The delicate question if the West German government would be prepared to trade full democratization and liberalization of the GDR for a full recognition of the GDR and an unequivocal renunciation of unification lingered, but never surfaced to the full. The dual dimension of the German question had been recognized early on; Adenauer once was tempted to propose to

untie the two dimensions: a solution to the German question similar to the "Austrian way," by which the GDR would be separate from West Germany but would be democratic. Adenauer never seriously pursued the idea, but it occasionally resurfaced in the West German political debates.

4. The Europeanization of the German question widened the conceptual framework of the West German approach to *Ostpolitik* and the relations with East Germany. The German question became embedded in the policy of détente. The division of Europe and the division of Germany were seen as two sides of the same coin; thus a solution of the German question independent of the larger European context was not conceivable. The German question could only be solved in a pan-European peace settlement, in which the division of the European continent would be overcome.[22] The Europeanization of the German question also served to alleviate fears of Germany's neighbours. It became a credo of German politics that the settlement of the German question could not be achieved against or without Germany's neighbours.

Business as Usual?
Shifting Paradigms in the 1980s

At the end of the Social-Liberal Coalition in 1982, the high-flying hopes of the beginning 1970s had vanished. A change through rapprochement did not materialize, the East German regime pursued a policy aimed at hedging off contacts between people in the two German states, while at the same time being cooperative on an official level. The normalization of relations between the two German states had not come about. Egon Bahr, the main architect of the *Ostpolitik*, had commented after the signing of the inter-German agreement that an era with no relations between East and West Germany was followed by one of bad relations.[23] This assessment still held true in 1982. The East German government had enforced its policy of seclusion during the 1970s, well aware of the fact that the *Ostpolitik* of the FRG, as beneficial as it might be for East Germany, could be a Trojan Horse for the stability of the regime itself. Erich Honecker, secretary general of the ruling communist party *Sozialistische Einheitspartei Deutschlands* (SED) (Socialist Unity Party of Germany) in East Germany, had raised the stakes in inter-German relations in 1980 when he demanded a full recognition of East Germany, including the exchange of ambassadors and the termination of Bonn's practice to issue temporary passports to East German citizens while staying in West Germany. In October 1980, the obligatory minimum exchange on entering the GDR was raised to DM 25 per person per diem, thus creating artificial financial obstacles for visits to East Germany. Moreover, the prevailing mood of détente in East-West relations had deteriorated in the second half of the 1970s. The Soviet invasion of Afghanistan in 1979 and the election of the staunchly anti-communist Ronald Reagan to the presidency of the United States marked the end of détente on the global level for the time being.

The end of détente overshadowed a summit meeting of Erich Honecker and the German Chancellor Helmut Schmidt in December 1981. Schmidt undertook to convince Honecker that the improvement of relations between the two German states should continue even though the superpowers embarked on a more confrontational course. Honecker pleaded with Schmidt about the West German government's support of the NATO dual track decision that would allow for stationing of American intermediate nuclear weapons in Germany, provided that no previous agreement on nuclear arms reductions could be reached. The final communiqué reflected the aim of both sides to support actively the policy of détente in Europe and to contribute to a stable development of the international situation, but these rather lofty declarations were immediately brought down to reality by the imposition of martial law in Poland to crush the Solidarity movement. Schmidt found himself in an awkward position. His decision to continue the visit was an indication that inter-German relations had emancipated themselves from the intricacies of East-West relations in general. The criticism that Schmidt faced from the opposition at home and the western allies underlined the difficult balance between political necessities in the Federal Republic's relations with the West and opportunities in its relations with the East. In the second phase of the Cold War at the beginning of the 1980s, the two German states were not longer outposts in the conflict, but sought to exploit the advantages of inter-bloc cooperation, hoping for a spill-over effect on East-West relations in general. Both German states had stakes in their relations which they did not want to see compromised by the strategic international environment. Did the special inter-German détente, as critics were quick to point out, foreshadow a neutralization of both German states? Was there a hidden agenda to shield inter-German relations from changes in East-West relations and to opt out of them in the long run?[24] Those allegations were certainly groundless since Schmidt always emphasized the European and transatlantic foundations of West Germany's foreign policy. But the very existence of these allegations and suspicions indicated that the division of Germany was not considered to be the natural state of affairs by West German allies and that West German efforts to manage the consequences of the division were interpreted as an attempt to establish strong intra-German ties at the expense of West Germany's western orientation.

The new conservative government under Helmut Kohl managed to put some of the fears to rest although Kohl did emphasize the continuity of West Germany's *Ostpolitik*. Yet Kohl strongly accentuated western integration as being the *raison d'état* of the FRG and his resolve to adhere to NATO's dual track decision. Schmidt's position had become increasingly precarious with the deterioration of support for his security policy by his own party. Kohl's firm commitment to the Atlantic alliance dispelled suspicions of an impending German self-neutralization and sent a strong signal to the Soviet Union and East Germany that their attempt to drive a wedge between the FRG and the allies would not succeed.

The operational continuity in Kohl's approach to *Ostpolitik* and relations with East Germany was supplemented by a harsher rhetoric. More strongly than before did the West German government emphasize the unity of the nation and the conflict between liberal democracies and communist regimes. Yet the emphasis on the irreconcilable basic positions did not prevent the new government from continuing the politics of negotiation with East Germany and to attempt to shield inter-German relations from the turbulence in the East-West relations in general.[25] Kohl declared in his inaugural address that his government would stand by the inter-German treaties and would employ them to further an active peace policy. After the German parliament took the decision to station American missiles in Germany in 1983, the West German government spoke about a "damage limitation" (*Schadensbegrenzung*) and the "community of responsibility" (*Verantwortungsgemeinschaft*) of both states for European peace. Taking up Honecker's phrase of a "coalition of reason" (*Koalition der Vernunft*), the West German government indicated that it also tried to avert the onset of an ice age in inter-German relations following the deployment of the missiles in Europe. Now it was East Germany that was regarded with suspicion by its own allies because Honecker seemed to have his own political agenda. Especially the bank loan to the GDR in

1983, amounting to one billion DM and guaranteed by the West German government, attracted international attention. Yet the West German side clearly linked the loans with political goals, such as the lifting of travel restrictions.[26] This reflected the West German belief that national unity could only be maintained from below, with the support of the people. In the five years following the loan, inter-German travel dramatically increased, and the relations between East and West Germany proliferated in other areas. Partnership agreements between cities, cultural exchanges, technological cooperation, and agreements in technical and financial questions indicated a normalization of relations.

The intra-German summit in 1987 thus seemed to reflect the good relations between both German states that had emerged since the inception of the new *Ostpolitik* in 1969. Euphemistically labeled a "working visit," Honecker's first official visit in the FRG seemed to resemble the normalcy of international relations rather than the special relations which the West German side was always quick to emphasize. Previous plans for a summit had been foiled by objections from the Soviets, but with the accession of Mikhail Gorbachev to political power, the East German government gained additional international leeway. Honecker seemed to have achieved full diplomatic recognition when he returned from the summit. To be sure, Kohl had condemned the shoot-to-kill order at the inter-German frontier, had complained about the lack of freedom and human rights in East Germany, and had also underlined the FRG's interpretation of the national question. But many observers concluded that the summit marked the final recognition of the German division.

Was this interpretation correct? The FRG did have to take the realities of Germany's division into account. National unification was at best an expectation for the long term, an expectation that had abated over the course of the years. Especially the younger generation, raised with the reality of German division, did not attach the emotional and political importance to the subject of unification as the older generations had. The day-to-day relations with the GDR seemed no different from relations with other countries, the question of national unity was seen by many as a compulsory exercise without any bearing on political realities.[27] Until 1989, a unification of Germany not only seemed as realistic as a fairy tale, but to some it also seemed undesirable because it would upset the balance of power in Europe. The premises of Adenauer's policy of unification had been outdated for a long time, and so ostensibly was the goal of unification.

What justification could the objective of a national unification have in the process of European integration where states relinquished traditional features of statehood? Was it still unification that was at the core of the national question or did, as Peter Bender suggested, the German question change its character and demanded communality more than unity, overcoming separation more than overcoming division?[28]

Forty years after the foundation of two German states, the unification of Germany seemed more remote than ever. But the GDR did not live to see its forty-first anniversary. In hindsight, the long political stability of East Germany seems to be more peculiar than the sudden collapse. But it was exactly the GDR's stability that determined West German politics, because the stability of the GDR seemingly was in the interest of the West German goal to alleviate the living conditions of people in the GDR and in the interest of European security. The swift destruction of the East German regime by a double protest movement of exit and voice[29] immediately revolutionized the context of the relations between East and West Germany.[30]

The West German government was not prepared for the radical changes in East Germany. Two basic considerations determined its immediate reaction: to avoid an escalation of protests into a crisis that might turn violent and to push for democratization and liberalization in the GDR. West Germany's offer to cooperate with East Germany were thus frequently accompanied by the urgent request to establish conditions in East Germany that would allow people to stay in their country.

Managing Unification

The fall of the Berlin Wall did again change the political context. The rapid decay of the communist regime, the continuing flow of resettlers to West Germany, and the demonstrations first against the regime, later for national unity, aggravated the crisis and called for a political strategy to come to terms with this new situation. In a speech on 28 November 1990 Kohl proposed a Ten Point Plan for the unification of Germany. He adopted an idea proposed by East Germany's Prime Minister Hans Modrow on a treaty community between the two states, and added that the FRG was prepared to "take a further decisive step, namely, to develop confederate structures between the two states in Germany with a view to creating a federation."[31] This was the first time that the West German government had opened an operative perspective for the unification of Germany. It was a cautious perspective since Kohl mentioned no particular time frame and emphasized the international context of German unification.[32] The Ten Point Plan fulfilled an important psychological task; people in the GDR were offered a concrete perspective that could meet their expectations and would help to stabilize and channel the developments in East Germany. The long-term aim of German unification was coupled with a West German promise of immediate and comprehensive aid, provided the GDR leadership would initiate fundamental and irreversible changes in the political and economic system. Moreover, the western allies had to realize that the German question was on the international agenda now. To leave no room for suspicion, Kohl immediately emphasized FRG's commitment to western integration and a pan-European peace and security system.

The Ten Point Plan marked a turning point in Germany's postwar history. Its basic principles remained of central importance for the process of unification:

- the principle of free choice in Germany's domestic and international affairs. The unification of Germany required free elections in East Germany first. Only with a freely elected government in East Germany could the constitutional obligation be met "to achieve, by free self-determination, the unity and freedom of Germany." By the same token, the principle of free choice also implied that a unified Germany could choose its position in the international system. The free choice of alliances was not explicitly mentioned in the Ten Point Plan, but seemed to be a matter of course since Kohl had always emphasized Germany's western ties as its *raison d'état*.

- the linkage between the German and the European dimension. The division of Europe and the division of Germany were seen as two sides of the same coin. The development of inter-German relations had to be embedded in a pan-European process, and Kohl particularly emphasized the role of the CSCE as a "central element of the pan-European architecture."

Those two principles were easily recognizable as the guiding principles of the West German government to cope with the German question since Adenauer and Brandt, respectively. The Ten Point Plan thus did not represent a revolutionary concept, but a recombination of traditional principles and their application to a changed international environment. Moreover, Bonn did not demand German unity, but carefully fostered the thrust to unity and tried to channel developments in the GDR and in West Germany as well. The few voices that opposed German unity remained isolated, although the procedural aspect of German unification became a contentious issue in Germany and among West Germany's allies.[33]

It was of crucial importance for the West German government to assure the support of its western allies for the process of unification. For years and decades, the western alliance had formally endorsed Germany's quest for national unity, but now the allies had to live up to their rhetoric. The British government in particular seemed to be uncomfortable at the prospect of German unification because it was feared that Germany would come into a position where it could dominate the European continent.[34] The position of the United States proved to be decisive. One observer noted that the American policy on German unification seemed to have anticipated the events rather than reacting to them[35] and, indeed, the US government took into account the possibility of German unification early in 1989 and subsequently played an active role in the unification process. The Bush government supported the process of German unification from the outset, but attached the condition that Germany would have to remain a member of NATO.[36]

This condition was not easy to meet. Soviet leader Mikhail Gorbachev had agreed to German unification in principle following Kohl's visit to Moscow in February 1990, but did not agree to a NATO membership of Germany as a whole until the famous Caucasus meeting with Kohl in July 1990. In the meantime, the process of German unification on the international level had already progressed. The so-called Two-Plus-Four Negotiations, where both German states negotiated the international aspects of German unification with the four former allied powers (United States, France, Great Britain and the Soviet Union), were well under way. The Treaty on the Final Settlement with Respect to Germany, signed in September 1990, fixed unified Germany's international status.[37] It defined the German territory as comprising the territories of the FRG, the GDR, and Berlin as a whole and stated that the united Germany would have no territorial claims against any other states. The two German governments reaffirmed their renunciation of the manufacture and possession of nuclear, biological, and chemical weapons and agreed to reduce the personnel strength of the armed forces of the united Germany to 370,000 within three to four years. Germany would remain a member of NATO, and Soviet troops would withdraw from East Germany within four years. The four powers terminated their rights and responsibilities to Germany as a whole and Berlin; the united Germany was to become fully sovereign.

As a peculiarity, the treaty was concluded by two German states binding a not yet existent united Germany. But this did reflect the way things stood between both German states, which, in a parallel effort, negotiated the terms of German unification on the interstate level. In the East German elections on 18 March 1990, the pro-unification *Allianz für Deutschland* (Alliance for Germany) had scored the majority of the votes on the basis of a promise to speed up the process of German unification. The establishment of an economic, social, and monetary union between the two states on 1 July 1990 was a major step on this path. It introduced the West German DM as the sole currency in East Germany, establishing an exchange rate of 1:1 of wages, salaries, rents, pensions, leases, and savings up to a certain amount; financial debts and claims were converted at a rate of 2:1. The West German social insurance system was introduced in East Germany, and the East German government agreed to far-reaching provisions concerning their budget and finance.[38] The treaty on economic, social, and monetary union preceded the unification of Germany, just as the currency reform in 1948 had preceded the formation of two German states in 1949. In the preamble of the treaty, both German states agreed to achieve national unity in accordance with Article 23 of the Basic Law, which provided for an accession of "other parts of Germany" to the FRG. The Unification Treaty between the Federal Republic of Germany and the German Democratic Republic, signed on 31 August 1990, outlined in 46 paragraphs and almost 1000 pages of annexes the provisions of German unification.[39] When the treaty came into effect on 3 October 1990, the German people had, as the new preamble to the Basic Law maintained, "achieved the unity and freedom of Germany in free self-determination." With the first all German elections in December 1990, which brought a solid majority for the incumbent Christian-Liberal coalition, the unified Germany had for the first time in almost 60 years given itself a freely elected national parliament and government.

In hindsight, German unification was achieved with astounding speed. In less than one year after the Wall had come down, Germany was unified. But it is even more astounding that the events leading to German unification caught almost every one in Germany off guard. The remote possibility of German unification suddenly became actual reality, and neither the West German government nor the public were prepared for it. No operational planning for unification existed, and the process of unification was more characterized by improvisation than by deliberate planning. This nonpolicy on the question of German unification prior to 1989 reflected the prevalent mood in the West German public that unification was a dead issue. History had seemingly passed a final judgment not only on the German nation state, but on the idea of nation states in general. Much of the troubles of the unified Germany accrue from the lack of planning, the improvised and sometimes chaotic circumstances of unification.

What caused the events of 1989? What caused the unification of Germany? A word of caution seems appropriate when talking about causation. Historians and political scientists always have to deal with a multitude of explanations and cannot offer a convenient cause-effect model. Moreover, historical events of the magnitude as the revolutions of 1989 are always subject to interpretation and even political casuistry, even more so when the events are still part of contemporary history.[40] But some of the causes that lead to German unification can be identified, even though we do not have the chronological distance historians prefer.[41]

First of all, the German question had always depended on the East-West Conflict. Once the conflict gradually disappeared, the German question came to the fore. Ever since Gorbachev had initiated his reform policy in the Soviet Union, there had been concerns about the effects which those reforms would have on the Soviet Union, the Warsaw Pact, and the German question. Those concerns were realistic. The East-West Conflict was solemnly declared terminated in 1990, only some weeks before the unification of Germany; one year later, the Soviet Union was dissolved. Gorbachev may have aimed at reforming the Soviet Union, but the unintentional and inevitable consequence was the reorganization of the European system as it had evolved after the Second World War.

The West German government may not have believed that unification was a realistic political goal, but its policies inadvertently contributed to achieve unification. The recognition of the GDR may indeed have paved the way for its destabilization. Since the inception of Brandt's *Ostpolitik* in 1969, the West German government never pursued an active strategy of unification. Moreover, relations with East Germany were based on a contractual level, and it was in West Germany's interest to have a stable partner who could live up to the contractual obligations. This intricacies of recognition, stabilization, and destabilization were never publicly discussed, but it may well have been the absence of an active unification policy that facilitated the unification.

The East German government lacked legitimacy and East Germany's stability ultimately rested on Soviet guarantees. Once the protective shield of the Soviet Union was withdrawn, the East German government was drawn into an abyss by a self-perpetuating, two-pronged opposition movement, voicing discontent either publicly by protest or by simply leaving the country. Once the movement had gained momentum, it toppled the already shaken and disheartened government. East Germany collapsed into national unification because once the socialist regime had been ousted, the rationale for an independent East Germany had vanished.

The West German government did not bring about unification, it did not cause the events of 1989, but it took the opportunity when it offered itself. The faint promise of national unity and its legal ramifications influenced and channeled the process of unification. After the unification of the two parts of Germany, the second part of Brandt's vision waits to be fulfilled—that the Germans, having been separated for more than four decades, will grow together again.

NOTES

1. Declaration Regarding the Defeat of Germany and the Assumption of Supreme Authority by the Allied Powers, Berlin, 5 June 1945, in *Documents on Germany, 1944–1985*, United States Department of State Publication 9446 (Washington, DC: US Government Printing Office, 1985), p. 33.

2. For the origins and the early history of the East-West Conflict see Wilfried Loth, *The Division of the World, 1941–1955* (London: Routledge, 1988).

3. On German foreign policy see Wolfram F. Hanrieder, *Germany, America, Europe: Forty Years of German Foreign Policy* (New Haven: Yale University Press, 1989), and Christian Hacke, *Die Außenpolitik der Bundesrepublik Deutschland. Weltmacht wider Willen?* 3rd ed. (Frankfurt/Main, Berlin: Ullstein, 1997).

4. Convention on Relations Between the Three Powers and the Federal Republic of Germany, 26 May 1952, As Amended by Schedule I of the Protocol on Termination of the Occupation Regime in Germany, Signed at Paris, 23 October 1954, Article 2, in *Documents on Germany*, pp. 425ff.; 425.

5. Convention on Relations 1952, Article 7, II.

6. Cf. Konrad Adenauer, *Memoirs 1945–1953* (London: Weidenfeld and Nicolson, 1966), pp. 35ff. Adenauer's life and his political career has been extensively analyzed by Hans

Peter Schwarz, *Adenauer,* vol. 1, *Der Aufstieg, 1876–1952* (Stuttgart: DVA, 1986) and vol.
2, *Der Staatsmann, 1952–1967* (Stuttgart: DVA, 1991); and Henning Köhler, *Adenauer.
Eine politische Biographie* (Frankfurt/Main, Berlin: Propyläen, 1994).

7.   Cf. Rolf Steininger, *The German Question: The Stalin Note of 1952 and the Problem of
Reunification* (New York: Columbia University Press, 1990), pp. 21ff. Steininger's thesis
that the Stalin note was a missed opportunity for German unification is highly controversial.

8.   For a vivid depiction of the events surrounding the building of the Berlin Wall cf. Willy
Brandt, *People and Politics: The Years 1960–1975* (Boston: Little, Brown and Company,
1978), pp. 13–41. For the background see Robert M. Slusser, *The Berlin Crisis of 1961:
Soviet-American Relations and the Struggle for Power in the Kremlin, June-November
1961* (Baltimore: Johns Hopkins University Press, 1973); Honoré M. Catudal, *Kennedy
and the Berlin Wall Crisis: A Case Study in U.S. Decision Making* (Berlin: Berlin Verlag,
1980).

9.   For a US perspective see Henry Kissinger, *White House Years* (Boston: Little, Brown
and Company, 1979), pp. 97ff.

10. From the vast amount of literature on the *Ostpolitik* the following are especially useful:
Peter Bender, *Die 'Neue Ostpolitik' und ihre Folgen. Vom Mauerbau bis zur Vereinigung*
(München: Deutscher Taschenbuch Verlag, 1995), pp. 155ff.; A. James McAdams,
Germany Divided: From the Wall to Reunification (Princeton: Princeton University
Press, 1993), pp. 70ff; Timothy Garton Ash, *In Europe's Name: Germany and the
Divided Continent* (London: Jonathan Cape, 1993), esp. chap. 2–4.

11. Treaty Between the Federal Republic of Germany and the Soviet Union, 12 August
1970, in *Documents on Germany,* pp. 1103–5.

12. Letter from the Federal Republic of Germany to the Soviet Union Regarding German
Unification, 12 August 1970, in *Documents on Germany,* p. 1105.

13. *Documents on Germany,* pp. 1215ff.

14. On the treaty see Ernest D. Plock, *The Basic Treaty and the Evolution of East-West-
German Relations* (Boulder, CO: Westview Press, 1986).

15. Declaration of the Bundestag of the Federal Republic of Germany Containing the
Mutual Position of the Parliamentary Groups on Foreign Policy and Inter-German
Relations, 17 May 1972, in *Documents on Germany,* pp. 1188–90.

16. *Documents on Germany,* pp. 1285ff.

17. On the CSCE process see Alexis Heraclides, *Security and Cooperation in Europe: The
Human Dimension, 1972–1992* (London: Cass, 1993); Wilfried von Bredow, *Der
KSZE—Prozeß. Von der Zähmung zur Auflösung des Ost-West-Konflikts* (Darmstadt:
Wissenschaftliche Buchgesellschaft, 1992).

18. Cf. Clay Clemens, *Reluctant Realists: The Christian Democrats and West German
Ostpolitik* (Durham: Duke University Press, 1989).

19. Basic Principles Underlying the Ruling of the Federal Constitutional Court On the
Validity of the Treaty of December 1972, repr. in extracts in *Politics and Government in
Germany, 1944–1994,* ed. C.C. Schweitzer et al. (Providence, RI: Berghahn Books,
1995), pp. 65f.; 65.

20. Those paradoxes are expounded with a mildly ironic annotation by Garton Ash, *In
Europe's Name,* pp. 162ff.

21. For the notion of *Kulturnation* (cultural nation) and *Staatsnation* (nation state) see
Friedrich Meinecke, *Cosmopolitanism and the National State* (Princeton: Princeton
University Press, 1970), pp. 9ff.

22. See Garton Ash, *In Europe's Name*, pp. 20ff.

23. Cf. McAdams, *Germany Divided*, p. 96.

24. A useful summary of those sentiments is provided by Eberhard Schulz and Peter Danylow, *Bewegung in der deutschen Frage? Die ausländischen Besorgnisse über die Entwicklung in beiden deutschen Staaten* (Bonn: Deutsche Gesellschaft für Auswärtige Politik, 1985).

25. This becomes clear not only by the official statements of the West German government, but more so in the government's contacts with the East German regime. Protocols from high level contacts between East and West German officials have been published by Heinrich Potthoff, ed., *Die 'Koalition der Vernunft'. Deutschlandpolitik in den achtziger Jahren* (Munich: Deutscher Taschenbuch Verlag, 1995). For an analysis of the *Deutschlandpolitik* of the Kohl government see Matthias Zimmer, *Nationales Interesse und Staatsräson. Zur Deutschlandpolitik der Regierung Kohl, 1982–1989* (Paderborn: Schöningh, 1992).

26. Garton Ash, *In Europe's Name*, p. 156.

27. With an accusatory touch, Jens Hacker, *Deutsche Irrtümer. Schönfärber und Helfershelfer der SED—Diktatur im Westen* (Berlin, Frankfurt/Main: Ullstein, 1992).

28. Peter Bender, *Deutsche Parallelen. Anmerkungen zu einer gemeinsamen Geschichte zweier getrennter Staaten* (Berlin: Siedler, 1989), p. 189.

29. A.O. Hirschman, "Exit, Voice and the Fate of the German Democratic Republic: An Essay in Conceptual History," *World Politics* 45, no. 2 (January 1993): 173–202.

30. A good survey of the events from the refugee crisis to unification is given by Konrad H. Jarausch, *The Rush to German Unity* (New York: Oxford University Press, 1994); for an atmospheric account see Robert Darnton, *Berlin Journal, 1989–1990* (New York: W.W. Norton, 1991); Documents relating to German unification can be found in Konrad H. Jarausch and Volker Berghahn, *Uniting Germany: Documents and Debates, 1944–1993* (Providence, RI: Berghahn, 1994).

31. Kohl's speech is reprinted in Harold James and Marla Stone, eds., *When the Wall Came Down: Reactions to German Unification* (New York: Routledge, Chapman and Hall, 1992), pp. 33–41.

32. For a background on the origins of the Ten Point Plan and reactions to it cf. Horst Teltschik, *329 Tage. Innenansichten der Einigung* (Berlin: Siedler, 1991), pp. 42ff.

33. Opposing unification Günter Grass, "Don't Reunify Germany," in *When the Wall Came Down*, ed. James and Stone, pp. 57ff.; sceptical about the procedural aspects Jürgen Habermas, "Yet Again: German Identity—A Unified Nation of Angry DM-Burghers," in *When the Wall Came Down*, ed. James and Stone, pp. 86ff.

34. See in particular Margaret Thatcher, *The Downing Street Years* (New York: Harper Collins, 1993), pp. 789ff.

35. Stephen Szabo, *The Diplomacy of German Unification* (New York: St. Martin's, 1992), p. 22.

36. See James A. Baker III, *The Politics of Diplomacy: Revolution, War and Peace 1989–1992* (New York: Putnam, 1995), pp. 158ff. In a broader context Philip Zelikow and Condoleezza Rice, *Germany Unified and Europe Transformed: A Study in Statecraft* (Cambridge, MA: Harvard University Press, 1995).

37. Reprinted in Szabo, *The Diplomacy of German Unification*, pp. 129–34. Details of the negotiations in ibid., pp. 67ff.; from a West German inside perspective Frank Kiessler and Richard Elbe, *A Round Table With Sharp Corners* (Baden-Baden: Nomos, 1996), and Hans-Dietrich Genscher, *Erinnerungen* (Berlin: Siedler, 1995), pp. 709ff.

38. Text of the Treaty in *The Unification of Germany in 1990: A Documentation*, published by the Press and Information Office of the Federal Government, Bonn 1991, pp. 13–29. Further economic details in Gerlinde Sinn and Hans-Werner Sinn, *Jumpstart: The Economic Unification of Germany* (Cambridge, MA: MIT Press, 1992), pp. 51ff.

39. The background of the negotiations is described by Wolfgang Schäuble, *Der Vertrag. Wie ich über die deutsche Einheit verhandelte* (Stuttgart: Deutsche Verlags-Anstalt, 1991).

40. The events of 1989/1990 seen from the perspective of a still staunch believer in the communist cause would, of course, vary considerably from the "official" interpretation of those events; see e.g., Erich Honecker, *Moabiter Notizen* (Berlin: Edition ost, 1994). See in broader context Matthias Zimmer, *German Unification in Historical Perspective*, Occasional Papers in German Studies no. 1, October 1994 (Edmonton: University of Alberta, 1994).

41. For a first orientation Hans Joas and Martin Kohl, eds., *Der Zusammenbruch der DDR* (Frankfurt/Main: Suhrkamp, 1993); Antonia Grunenberg, *Aufbruch der inneren Mauer. Politik und Kultur in der DDR 1971–1990* (Bremen: Edition Temmen, 1990) focusses on the domestic developments within the GDR; Jeffrey Gedmin, *The Hidden Hand— Gorbachev and the Collapse of East Germany* (Washington, D.C.: AEI Press, 1992) emphasizes economic reasons; David M. Keuthley, *The Collapse of East German Communism: The Year the Wall Came Down, 1989* (Westport and London: Praeger, 1992) blames the economic shortcomings of the East German economy and the lack of identity.

Political Culture in Germany and the Legacies of the GDR

GERT-JOACHIM GLAEßNER

When, at midnight on 2 October 1990, the national anthem rang out in front of the Reichstag in Berlin and the flag of the Federal Republic of Germany was raised, a long cherished dream became reality—if one is to believe the official statements of the politicians. A people that, for 45 years, had been divided by an insurmountable border was united again in one nation-state. The victorious allies of the Second World War had renounced their reserve powers regarding Germany as a whole and, thus, opened the way to unification. When interpreting the events which led to German unity, there is a recognizable tendency to lend historical developments a certain logic and inevitability; to interpret them, in other words, with the benefit of hindsight. But such an approach is misguided. The simple truth is that, until the end of 1989, neither the Federal Republic of Germany (FRG) and the western powers nor the Soviet Union pursued an active policy aimed at unifying Germany, even though it was evident that a lasting peace in Europe was inconceivable without a solution to the "German question." In spite of all efforts to achieve a "new thinking" in international relations, fear of the consequences of ending the postwar order was greater than the knowledge that this order was already rotten to the core.

Foreign observers saw more quickly and more clearly than the Germans that the revolutionary changes in Central Europe and the upheavals in the German Democratic Republic (GDR) represented a problem for the FRG's own sense of identity. It took the Germans a relatively long time to recognize that the unification of the two German states had suddenly become possible. After political unity had been achieved, it became obvious that the many difficulties which have to be overcome if the two German societies are to grow together had been underestimated in the euphoria that prevailed in 1990. Politicians in the FRG had acted without giving heed to the scepticism expressed by many intellectuals regarding the problems to be expected in uniting two entirely different states *and* societies.

Germany Divided

Both founded in 1949, the two German states had been outposts of two opposing political systems and social orders. In its early years, the FRG could be regarded as a classic example of a "penetrated system"—a country regulated and controlled by external actors. Until the attainment of sovereignty in 1955, when the FRG joined NATO, it was, in the words of Peter Katzenstein,[1] only a "semi-sovereign state," over which the Western Allies had a major influence. The last remnants of the Allies' rights, concerning Berlin and a solution to the German question, remained in place right up to the unification in 1990 and the arrangements made in the "Two-Plus-Four Treaty" between the two German states and the four wartime allies. Yet this limited sovereignty was the result not only of external compulsion. At its foundation in 1949, the temporary constitution of the FRG, the *Grundgesetz* (Basic Law), deliberately renounced some of the rights of a sovereign state. The Basic Law came into force at a time when cooperation between the defeated Germany and its victorious western neighbours seemed scarcely conceivable. Nevertheless, it showed the constitutional readiness of the FRG to learn from the experiences of National Socialism and to develop a future political order for Germany as a whole and as part of the emerging European order.

The especially remarkable quality in the development of the FRG is that it has changed from being a "penetrated system" into an "integrated system." Ever since the FRG joined the process of European integration, national rights of sovereignty have gradually been handed over to supranational institutions. From initially being a restriction imposed from outside, semisovereignty became part of Germany's own deliberate policy of voluntarily restricting her sovereignty—and not only in foreign policy. Against strong criticism, Konrad Adenauer, German chancellor from 1949 to 1963, broke with traditional German anti-Western politics by embedding the FRG into the Western liberal democracies. For him, European unity was meant to overcome old animosities between "archrivals" France and Germany. The GDR, in contrast, became an integral part of the Soviet bloc, the first "workers-and-farmers state on German soil." In 1955, when West Germany became a member of NATO and East Germany joined the

Warsaw Pact, the prospect of uniting Germany seemed more remote than ever. Over more than 40 years, the two German states developed distinctly different political, economic, and social systems and two distinct political cultures.[2]

| Political Culture in Postwar Germany

In 1949, when the two German states were created, they were both faced with the task of establishing a new political culture. Neither of them could simply adopt the traditional patterns of politics, neither of the Bismarck time, the Wilhelminian Reich, nor the Weimar Republic. The FRG, founded as a democratic political system under the tutelage of the Western Allies, had to cope with antidemocratic and authoritarian traditions in German society and politics. Democratic norms and beliefs were not deeply rooted in German political culture. It took more than two decades before the West German people became dedicated democrats and not only "democratic opportunists"—a type that dominated in the 1950s.[3]

The Cold War, which led to the foundation of two separate German states, integrated both into opposing political camps and very soon made them frontline states of their respective political and military alliances. Anticommunism and antitotalitarianism became the primary binding force behind the new democratic system in the FRG. It made possible the integration of former supporters of the Nazi regime without causing doubts as to the impact this kind of reconciliation would have on the new democratic political order. Political strife between social groups was avoided. Inclusion became the catchword of the time. The attempt not to exclude former Nazis from political and social life had some side-effects. Until the early 1960s, the FRG had no serious discussion of the Nazi past. West German political culture flourished and was, at the same time, put permanently in doubt by a collective amnesia. While democracy in the 1950s often meant no more than the formal procedures of electing political elites, of decision-making, and the division of powers, the 1960s brought a "liberal revolution" in West German society. The new postwar generation called for an expansion of liberal rights and personal freedoms, for greater political participation and more opportunities for marginalized groups of society. The second basic principle underpinning the West German political system and political culture was European unity. In the FRG, European integration was meant as a decisive instrument for overcoming the devastating consequences of modern German history and of two world wars.

In stark contrast to the political culture of West Germany, the German Democratic Republic has been an "occupation regime"[4] until its very demise in 1989. Even after the country gained formal recognition of sovereignty from the Soviet Union, the ruling socialist party in the GDR—the *Sozialistische Einheitspartei Deutschlands* (SED) (Socialist Unity Party of Germany)—depended on the Soviet Communist Party for political decisions and on Soviet tanks for its grip on power. Its political culture has been a specific mix of the traditional German authoritarian state (*Obrigkeitsstaat*) and Soviet-style Marxism-Leninism combined with elements of old working-class culture. The GDR took the path of an "antifascist democratic revolution" and thus brought about a radical break with the political past of pre-1945 Germany. The profound social and economic changes such as land reform, the expropriation of large industries, and the transformation of education created the preconditions for launching a new era of development toward a socialist society, one oriented toward the Soviet model. The radical rupture with the past concealed the extent to which the "revolution from above" failed to eliminate the many links to traditional German political culture. Any attempt to analyze the traditions of political culture in the GDR faces an obvious contradiction: an authoritarian political system invoked traditions in political culture that had been unable to put down roots at any time in German history before 1945.

The Historical Legacies of the GDR

The existence of the GDR was linked directly to the Soviet Union's determination to support and defend its satellite politically and militarily. The Soviets did bring in their tanks during the crisis of 1953. This was not the case, however, in 1989. The first political proclamation of the *Kommunistische Partei Deutschlands* (KPD) (Communist Party of Germany) in June 1945, which was written in Moscow, did not even mention socialism or communism. Instead, it stated that Germany should become an "antifascist democracy" with all civil rights and freedoms provided to the German people. It took only two years to transform the Soviet occupied zone into a Soviet-style political system. It was in 1948, in the wake of the controversies over "Titoism," that the SED, founded in 1946 by the forced unification of the Communist Party

and the Social Democrats in the Soviet zone, openly endorsed the fundamental principles of the Stalinist transformation concept. It proclaimed
itself a "Party of a New Type," thus accepting the narrowing down of the
Leninist vanguard concept to the leading role of the Party, a concept where
the historical role of the proletariat is reduced to the fulfillment of tasks set
by the Party. In setting out such tasks, the SED was not able to rely on the
broad consensus or active support, nor even on the revolutionary experience or actions of the proletariat. But while increasingly negating the social
democratic tradition, the SED followed the Leninist tradition only to the
extent of accepting the Stalinist type of Leninism, which was in stark
contradiction to the firmly anchored democratic traditions of the German
workers' movement, even of the KPD, insofar as the tradition referred to
Karl Liebknecht or Rosa Luxemburg. This tradition had not been
destroyed by the "bolshevization" of the KPD during the Weimar Republic
or even by the suppression of the workers' movement during the fascist era.

By the time of the SED's second party conference in 1952, the tone had
changed radically. Walter Ulbricht's report spoke of the division of the
world into two camps, "the camp of peace, democracy and socialism, and
the camp of imperialism." The national peculiarities of the development of
socialism in the GDR were not mentioned; instead, the leading role of the
Soviet was accepted without any reservations. But in contrast to the
Communist Party of the Soviet Union (CPSU), the SED was not able to
claim that it had come to power as a result of a revolutionary upheaval and
that it now had the task of transforming society only in the spirit of such a
revolution. Developments in the Soviet occupied zone even led large
sections of the bourgeois parties to hope that a democratic evolution was
possible. The first economic measures taken by the new administration—
expropriation of large enterprises, land reform, and the reform of the
education system—were fully endorsed by the population. But this
support began to dwindle as the SED, backed by the potential of the occupying power, began to formulate to hegemonic claims and demanded to
determine alone the pace and orientation of the process of social transformation. The space originally left open by the admission of bourgeois
parties to the political arena and the alliance policy pursued by the SED
was gradually narrowed down and finally reduced to a dead letter.

The political and administrative methods used to establish a new
society led to the disappearance of the last remnants of the political
consensus in the Soviet zone of occupation, manifested in the referen-

dums on the expropriation of big land ownership in 1946 and, even, in the position of sections of the bourgeois parties towards the nationalization of large-scale enterprises. The transformation of the East German society according to the Soviet model, the "planned building of socialism," as decided at the second party conference in 1952, but started earlier, proceeded as a "revolution from above." The increasingly close adherence to Soviet concepts also contributed to the abandonment of the notion of a specific German road to socialism. Broad sections of the population, including the working class, understood this turn of events as an act of final subordination to the will of the occupying power.

The workers themselves were hit much more by the abandonment of the constantly invoked democratic principles than other parts of society organized in liberal or christian parties. The numerous, immediate postwar independent forms of working-class organization, were phased out. The form used to establish the SED as well as the increasing suppression of the social democratic element within the SED meant that the organizational endeavours of the working people were channeled exclusively to a single party and to a trade union entirely dependent on that one party with an increasingly entrenched monopoly on opinion-forming and decision-making at the level of the party leadership. The party leadership, backed by the occupying power, now had full authority to suppress deviating views by using physical coercion.

The adoption of Soviet planning and management methods in the two-year economic plan of 1949 and 1950, and the reconstruction of the economy giving precedence to heavy industry after the second party conference in 1952, marked the essential stages of the acceptance of the Soviet model of development in the GDR. The workers' uprising of 17 June 1953 cast severe doubt on the popular support of this model. For the first time, the Soviet military intervened to protect the achievements of socialism in one of the countries within its hegemonic sphere.[5] This date, nevertheless, marks the beginning of a development in which—especially after the twentieth CPSU Congress in 1956—the SED turned its attention to the expansion, tightening, and improvement of the newly established political and social structures. The SED also began to replace gradually its transformation concepts originally enforced by coercive methods with a strategy of social, political, and economic reforms.

The year 1955 marks a crucial point in the history of the GDR. The signing of the Warsaw Pact Treaty in May, the formal recognition of full sovereignty of the GDR by the Soviet Union, the first appearance of the GDR at an international forum with a delegation of observers at the abortive conference of the foreign ministers of the four victorious powers in Geneva were a turning point in postwar German history. It became clear in 1955 that the "achievements" of socialism in the GDR would not be sacrificed on the altar of nation-state unity. The SED proceeded from the premise that the GDR was developing as a firm component of the world socialist system and that it was to reinforce the increasingly close alliance with the Soviet Union and other socialist states. The question of administrative structures, the improvement of planning and management methods, and the Party's political, economic, and social objectives all acquired a new significance against this background.

The attempts at reform started in 1955 and 1956 were stopped immediately after the Soviets intervened in the Hungarian uprising in the fall of 1956. The events in Hungary and social unrest in Poland were blamed on "revisionist deviations" within the party leadership and among party intellectuals, and they triggered fears in the GDR that renewed actions by the workers could jeopardize the SED's grip on power. The SED reacted by stopping all plans for reform and expressing its determination to smash all attempts at its power. Referring to Hungary and Poland, the SED attempted to silence the discussion after the twentieth CPSU Congress, which, it believed, had gone beyond admissible limits.

Coercion, economic crisis, a growing number of people seeking refuge in the West, and fading hope for a better future, all led to a fundamental crisis in the political system which was eventually solved by the erection of the Berlin Wall on 13 August 1961. Amazingly enough, this event provided the basis for the only consistent far-reaching reform of the political and economic system in the history of the GDR: the *Neues Ökonomisches System* (NÖS) ("New Economic System") of 1963. The reforms of the 1960s were a reaction to the end of the revolutionary era in GDR society. Extensive growth had been replaced by intensive growth, the transformation of the social structures had been concluded, and the achievements were now to be consolidated. Surprised by the events of 17 June 1953, driven by a policy of de-Stalinization, wary of the crises in the system in both Hungary and Poland, and conscious of opposition among the "new" intelligentsia in 1956 and 1957, the SED had to admit that it was no longer in a position to function as a united centre of action and, from this position, to guide society in all its aspects. Economic, scientific, technical, and social developments, as well as the spreading differentiation and diversification in social processes and structures, compelled it to reconsider its own role.

Following a phase of experimentation, lasting roughly from 1954 until 1963, the SED drew up the NÖS from ideas it had previously condemned as revisionist. It had to concede that the GDR, like all other economically advanced countries, was facing a new situation: it had to be capable of standing up to the challenges of the second industrial or scientific and technical revolution if it did not want to forfeit its future. At the end of the 1950s, the SED learnt that these challenges could not be met by the established organizational concepts, excessive bureaucracy, and centralization. But since it was neither willing nor able to overcome the other impeding factors—in particular, the system-dependent restrictions of organized individual or group interests—its endeavours at reform remained of a purely technocratic nature. The allusion to Lenin's "New Economic Policy" of the 1920s was no coincidence. The experiment had to be modified after Nikita Khrushchev's fall from power in 1964, and was abandoned at the time of the next crisis in the years 1968 and 1969. The space for experimentation tolerated by the Soviets had become narrower and narrower. Under different conditions, NÖS could have become a model for technocratic reform in the socialist system.

In the mid 1960s, Walter Ulbricht's government also developed autonomous policy ideas in a variety of areas, independent of Soviet positions and no longer adhering to the utopian premise that communism as the final stage in the development of socialist societies was just around the corner. The idea of a "socialist human community," a conflict-free socialist society, took the place of utopian expectations. On closer inspection, the attempt to replace utopian, ideologically defined goals—which could be reached only by force—with new goals attainable during the lifetime of the present generation was a means to deny the existence of the real conflict and contradictions of society. The SED was certain that it could build up a "developed socialist system" with the help of scientific methods derived from cybernetics and systems theory. The building of socialism appeared to be the task of technocrats and specialists, and not of ideologues or Lenin's "professional revolutionaries."

There are Western parallels to this line of thinking: for example, in the writings of the West German sociologist Helmut Schelsky. He proclaimed the obsolescence of democracy in the wake of the technical inventions for "steering" a modern society,[6] while the GDR's Georg Klaus presented a cybernetic model of socialist society that no longer required the leading role of a Marxist-Leninist party.[7] The party soon caught on to this fatal flaw in the cybernetic discussion and put an end to it. Aside from the techno-cratic reflections, however, few voices demanded political change in the GDR of the 1960s—unlike in Poland, Hungary, and Czechoslovakia. One of the few, and most vehement, was Robert Havemann in a series of lectures at Humboldt University in East Berlin.[8] The violent suppression of the reform movement in 1968 in Czechoslovakia and the termination of the reforms in the Soviet Union initiated by Khrushchev in 1968 and 1969, put an end to all experimentation and returned socialism in the GDR to another two decades of the old, centralist political control.[9] For the GDR, Ulbricht's fall and replacement with Erich Honecker in 1971 was the end of the experiment, even though it opened the doors to the realistic coopera-tion of the SED with the West. It also created the preconditions for basic changes in economic and social policy that, again, had unmistakably inde-pendent features.

The eighth SED party congress in 1971 suggested introducing a social policy to solve these economic and social problems. For a long time, social policy had been considered utterly out of place in a socialist society. The congress started an explicit liberalization in cultural policy (and only there), and involved the emerging political and social organizations—mainly the trade unions—in major decision-making processes. This remarkable change of course was dictated by the realization that there was no identity of the interests of the individual, social groups, and society as a whole. Social policy was regarded as a counterpart and corrective to economic policy. Unity between economic and social policy became the basic precept of the SED. Social policy was meant to right the negative social consequences of economic policy and make sure—through social planning—that any disadvantages did not even emerge. In this respect, social policy in the GDR necessarily embraced virtually all other spheres of policy making: demographic development, industrial labour organization, the supply of consumer goods and services to the domestic market, housing, urban and regional planning, health policy, social security, leisure and recreation, social relations in "socialist combines," and other work-places. The unity of economic and social policy implied a revision of the former policies of the SED. It included the admission that even a socialist economy could create social diversities and imbalances which had to be

addressed by a paternalistic socialist welfare state. In the early 1970s the
SED succeeded in setting new accents on its economic and social policy
and again increased respect among its people for the new paternalism.[10]
Unfortunately, the worldwide energy crisis of the 1970s foiled its ambitious
plans.

In retrospect it is easy to forget that the SED pursued a remarkably
independent foreign policy during the years Brezhnev held power in the
Soviet Union. This led to an increase in recognition from abroad as well as
greater acceptance of the GDR as a legitimate state by its own people. The
SED also managed, during the years of escalation in the East-West conflict
in particular in the early 1980s, to salvage relations between the two
Germanys to their mutual benefit. In the area of cultural policy, the SED's
quest for greater legitimacy caused it to vacillate between liberalization
and an improved cultural climate at home.[11] In striking contrast to these
accomplishments, the SED regime appeared helpless and uncompre-
hending when faced with the changes in personal and social values and the
new social movements that raised new issues such as environmentalism,
pacifism, and the quest for individual autonomy among the youth in the
GDR. There had long been a need for reform and many informal groups
and associations emerged in the 1980s. Under Ulbricht, any such attempts
at forming autonomous groups would have been quashed from the start.
Yet these internal developments by themselves would never have led to the
overthrow of the SED regime had the Soviet Union intervened as on the
earlier occasion of 1953 to stop the liberal groundswell by force.

The Political Culture of the GDR

The political culture of the GDR was built
on four traditions. First, the traditional authoritarian state (*Obrigkeitsstaat*)
that had been particularly prominent in Germany—a country without
established democratic traditions. Second, the political system of the GDR
had incorporated elements of the old workers' culture into the dominant
political culture. Third, the SED assumed the right to exercise power as
the representative of a movement committed to a political and cultural
revolution. It also aimed to establish a communist society as the definite
answer to all human problems suffered since the early days of mankind.
Finally, the political culture of the GDR differed from that of the other
countries in the socialist bloc because it was affected by national specifics,
i.e., the division of the German people into two states and societies. From

the 1970s on, the GDR was also significantly affected by being confronted with the cultural and political beliefs of the "new" social movements in the West. These groups derived from a fundamentally different historical tradition of protest movements, and were readily dismissed by the SED as either antiprogressive, petit-bourgeois, romantic, or radical left. These influences, however, played a key role in facilitating the emergence of a protest movement in the GDR.

Authoritarianism had traditionally exerted a formative influence on German political culture. It established the principle of the division of state and society, and the notion of the impartiality. The state was conceived not as the result of a social contract, but as the highest expression of authority, an independent institution endowed with its own undelegated power. The *Beamter* (civil servant) was expected to be neutral in matters of party interest, owing loyalty to the state only. This authoritarian tradition was also reflected in the political virtues of the subjects: deference, obedience, and political absenteeism.[12] The GDR made an indisputable radical break with many of these beliefs. State and society were seen as one unit: society was organized by and through the state and its future was formed by central state planning. The state was not impartial but the instrument of the party. It was empowered by the historical mission of the party to build socialism and communism. State servants were party cadres who defended party interests in the state administration. Finally, citizens were expected to contribute to the construction of a socialist society.

The Soviet-style revolution from above, which took place in the GDR from 1948 on, left three central pillars of the authoritarian state intact, putting it into the service of the Marxist-Leninist party. The origins and justification of state authority were not based on the consent of the governed. State and society remained united, but the citizens had no voice in the determination of the goals of either one. Neither this nor the fact of being an instrument of the party ever diminished the role of the state as the highest authority vis-à-vis the citizenry. Political absenteeism, however, was not seen as a virtue, but as a violation of the moral code of a socialist society. In its place, there arose the mobilization of the citizens for the goals of party and state, and criticism of the state inevitably led to punishment. To a remarkable degree, Prussian authoritarianism and traditional modes of behaviour, rather than socialist ones, structured the political and social system of the GDR.

The culture of the workers' movement—the second traditional element of GDR political culture—had its roots in preindustrial, peasant, artisan, and urban-plebeian traditions. It was made up of manifold organizations including political and social organization within parties and trade unions, but also a variety of leisure and sports groups—singing clubs, nature societies, the different sports associations, cultural and educational initiatives—cooperatives, and mutual aid or self-help associations. The SED, however, adopted only certain aspects of these traditions. While, after 1945, the social democratic branch of the workers' movement increasingly lost sight of a future dictated according to their beliefs and views, the communists considered themselves the guarantors and executors of these "historical laws of development." They directed the working class, in whose name the SED believed it acted, to pursue the goals put forth by the party. The workers themselves had no role in the formulation of party goals. However, old forms of workers' solidarity, such as had been developed during the long struggle for social and political rights, particularly in the factories, survived in the GDR. The SED carefully cultivated many of the rules of labour law, the stress on the workers' ethos, and the significance of work traditions. Later, the regime attempted to develop further these aspects of working life and adapt them to different social conditions. For instance, "worker's honour" was a politically narrow and instrumentalized concept in the 1940s and 1950s. Later, it meant a new self-image of "leading class" in a technical, scientifically informed socialist society.

The GDR saw itself squarely in the tracks of the communist world revolution and the tradition of the Leninist cultural revolution. Communist revolutions, however, had been minority revolutions led by a revolutionary elite whose ideas about the future were shared by the majority only in exceptional cases and on passing occasions. Yet an educational dictatorship was required to realize the revolution and to overcome the traditional state of mind of the "uninitiated" masses. Education, not experience, had to create the new socialist person. In the 70 years following the Russian October Revolution of 1917, and in the 40 years of the GDR, the elite's time horizon of the realization of the communist society and the practice of life in a socialist society could never be reconciled. Achieving the communist society was a distinct, yet distant goal, but the day-to-day struggle was more concerned with prevailing over the many economic, social, and cultural problems—not to mention the risks to internal and external security from the forces of counterrevolution—for which the party could no longer offer ready solutions. The SED hid more and more behind the ritual incantations of the great goals and ideals of socialism without being able to deal with escalating economic, ecological, social, and cultural crisis.

Like the other socialist countries, the GDR was a teleological political culture which had lost sight of its final purpose over the years. After years of dynamic social and political development, it had finally arrived at the problem of maintaining and securing its own achievements. Everyday life was characterized by new political attitudes and modes of social behaviour that were no longer structured by utopian socialism and the goal of communism, but rather by "real socialism": both the political leadership and the citizenry had settled into living in the here and now. This was unlikely to succeed in the long run, however, because the old institutional structures became fetters of the newly developing lifestyles. The socio-political structures for planning and directing the system remained and continued to impose their goals and the ideological legitimation of the regime authoritatively from above. The system had survived the death of the utopian faith. Clearly, the SED never espoused the idea of a *citoyen* as a part of the developed socialist system. Its hierarchical, authoritarian ideas of society placed narrow limits on the self-realization and autonomy of individuals and social groups. It insisted that people understand their own experience according to the official templates of interpretation. However, the citizens' feelings, attitudes, views, and personal interpreta-tions of their everyday experiences conflicted more and more with the official political culture and procedures of Marxism-Leninism. When the "old faith" died, the naked authoritarian power of the system became painfully visible.

Unlike in the other socialist countries, the political culture of the GDR was affected by the special situation of a Germany divided between East and West. Its very emphasis on being a different kind of Germany sepa-rated by ideology and politics from the FRG—the presumable hotbed of fascism, capitalism, and NATO imperialism—tended to highlight the stan-dards of comparison between the two countries. The everyday life and politics of the GDR's citizens were determined, even distorted, by the perpetual comparison with the FRG. The GDR leadership never tired of stressing the security in which its citizens could live in contrast to the unemployment, material want, and other problems—such as crime and drugs—of a capitalist society. Many GDR citizens were continually comparing their situation with that of the FRG. Their comparison rested on West German television, which could be received in most parts of the GDR, and on the accounts of Western visitors since the borders had been opened to West German visitors in the early 1970s. Most GDR citizens had no opportunity to see Western life in person until after the fall of the Berlin Wall in November 1989. Imagine the collective shock, then, when they saw the other "promised land," prosperous, clean, and orderly, and without political fear.

Observers of the political and social developments in the GDR had long noticed the growing contradiction between the official political culture, with its tiring rituals and slogans on the one side, and the everyday culture of the people on the other. The first West German representative in the GDR, Günter Gaus, coined the phrase *Nischengesellschaft* (society of niches) to describe how individuals had withdrawn from the impositions of the regime to the few private spaces they could create among friends, family, and nonpolitical groups.[13] From the beginning of the 1980s, more and more people sought the "niche" of the church and became engaged in various new causes. It is important, however, to be aware of the marginal position of these groups in GDR society up until the summer of 1989 and of their return to the margins within six months after the "great implosion."

Before 1989, there had been no political opposition to speak of, a fact that distinguished the GDR from the other socialist countries. Certainly, from the late 1970s on, various informal groups had existed usually working in the protected space of the churches[14]—and which were not immune to infiltration by the Stasi, as we have learned since. From about the mid 1980s on, a "second public" emerged in the various forms of semilegal and illegal publications, but there was no organized opposition comparable to Charter 77 in Czechoslovakia or Solidarity in Poland. There were also no personal or ideological links to the opposition figures of the first three decades of the GDR, who tended to be marxist dissidents. While the earlier opposition attempts following the destruction of bourgeois forces had come from dissidents within the party, the new informal groups tended to be characterized by their subcultural nature and a lack of formal organization.

Another important difference from the other socialist countries was that socialist ideas and concepts still played a decisive role in the democratic opposition in the GDR. There was a consensus among the democratic opposition—that lasted throughout 1989—that the roots of socialism in East German cultural history, its part in fighting fascism, its interest in peace, and especially the protection of values of equality in a political utopia would all remain after the collapse of the communist regime. By the fall of 1989, the small revolutionary groups had become the vehicle of opposition and hope for democratic renewal.[15]

A New German Political Culture of Discontent?

The events of 1989 and German unification in 1990 formed a political and cultural constellation unprecedented in living memory: the incorporation of a socialist society in an established democratic system which itself, 41 years before, was inaugurated by foreign occupation forces and imposed on a people that had, in the most part, actively supported or passively tolerated the most criminal dictatorship in contemporary history. The political order of the FRG originated from the experience of the failure of democracy in the Weimar Republic, and assimilated the lessons of the traumatic events of the Third Reich. After 1989, the West German political system and political culture had to digest not only the results of democratic revolution in the East, but also experiences of more than 40 years of SED dictatorship in the GDR. Fundamental differences between the Western and Eastern political cultures are the main obstacles to uniting the two parts of Germany socially and culturally in the foreseeable future.

As important as differences in economic performance in East and West, different unemployment figures, West German financial transfers, or East German structural problems all may be, the cultural cleavages are more significant than anything else and will probably last much longer. This difference of political cultures in East and West is due to the years of the division of Germany into separate states and societies in antagonistic political and social systems. When the East German regime collapsed in 1989, only the octogenarians there could remember democracy. In the revolutionary euphoria of autumn 1989, many in the GDR believed that the seeds of a completely new political culture were beginning to bear fruit: the desire for justice, democracy, peace, and the protection and preservation of nature were the driving force for the civil rights movement. However, East Germans had no genuine working knowledge of parliamentary democracy, democratic institutions, autonomous interest articulation, and civil society.

The end of the GDR brought in its wake the collapse of the institutional structure of official political culture. The people heaved a liberated sigh of relief and believed that they had rid themselves of everything which had oppressed them for so long. They only gradually realized that they could not get rid of their past so quickly and that they had been more profoundly influenced by the old system than they had previously thought.

Ironically, it was Karl Marx who, in *The Eighteenth Brumaire of Louis Bonaparte*, used a poetic image to describe the lasting influence of inherited beliefs in a society which had set about building something altogether new and unique in history:

> The tradition of all the dead generations weighs like a nightmare on the brain of the living. And just when they seem engaged in revolutionising themselves and things, in creating something that has never yet existed, precisely in such periods of revolutionary crisis they conjure up the spirits of the past to their service and borrow from them names, battle cries and costumes in order to present the new scene of world history in this time-honoured disguise and this borrowed language.[16]

Although the majority of East Germans wanted the end of the old system—as was evident not least in the results of the first free elections on 18 March 1990—they now faced obvious difficulties in letting it go for good. This is not surprising since the people in the GDR had been transported unprepared into a new social reality which they knew only from hearsay and Western television. Nonetheless, there were some in the East who believed that the GDR offered an opportunity for the creation of a new, socialist society. Despite decades of disappointment, hope for an alternative to capitalism was stronger in the GDR than in any other socialist country. The collapse of "real socialism" nurtured the hope that this goal could now be reached at last.[17]

Both reform-minded SED members and the citizens' movements were left clutching at straws. Some among them hoped to realize a long-cherished dream, others were inventing new ones. Both groups sought to build a genuine socialism, a truly just society on the rubble of old-style socialism. But their view of the FRG shared indisputable similarities with the image propagated by the Marxist-Leninists whom they had never believed. Still others succumbed to the delusion that by adopting the Western economic order the major problems would be rapidly, if not immediately, resolved. On 18 March 1990 the East German electorate voted for rapid change. This meant more than just getting their hands on the Deutschmark, as many

Western observers were wont to remark with a mixture of ignorance and arrogance. The electorate's decision represented the desire to speed up a radical break with the cultural, social, economic, and political past, and to introduce as soon as possible a life in political freedom and economic prosperity similar to that of the Germans in the West. It was only later that many people recognized the risks and disadvantages that this would also entail, such as the obligation of the state to protect people from all the hardships of life, which had been taken for granted in the GDR.

Citizens of the former GDR only gradually realized that they had committed themselves to the most radical transformation of their entire lives. Like many dictatorships before it, the authoritarian welfare state of Erich Honecker protected the population from the vicissitudes of the world economy by means of separation (*Abgrenzung*) and the ruthless, unchecked exploitation of natural and human resources. The full extent of the price paid in terms of the exploitation of the environment, the near total destruction of the country's industrial infrastructure, and the consequent and serious undermining of its industrial future came to light only after the fall of the SED.

In the long term, even without revolutionary change, the barely concealed economic and environmental crisis would have inevitably precipitated a social crisis. The fact that the social crisis now accompanies the process of democratization after the fall of the socialist regime and the integration of the former GDR into a market economy is not without its problems.[18] It is often too readily forgotten that the transition from authoritarianism to democracy is not the cause of the crisis. By the same token, the initially naïve trust in the power and will of politics on the part of the East Germans could only turn into disappointment, resignation, or apathy. The hopes and expectations in the spring of 1990 were quickly dashed. When, in the summer and early autumn of 1990, the economic situation again became bleak, and currency union did not produce the anticipated short-term improvements, but, instead, an escalation of the economic crisis, the initial mood of optimism finally gave way to deep resignation. There was a danger of regressing into old attitudes, summed up in the saying "things are taking their socialist course." In other words, it was not worth getting involved, for it would only cause problems and create difficulties. It will probably take years before these deep-seated beliefs and patterns of behaviour can be overcome.

There was a widespread feeling among the people in eastern Germany that the dependency of the past has been replaced by another. This is not unusual in the context of transitions from dictatorship to democracy. However, in the case of the coexistence of the German people in one united polity, this feeling of having exchanged one dependency for another has assumed a problematic dimension because of the special situation that the new order was inherited from the West as opposed to having been developed by the people of the eastern *Länder*.

The politically prudent, if not—in view of the international political situation—imperative choice of accession of the GDR to the FRG under Article 23 of the Basic Law has produced some serious side effects. It inevitably meant that familiarity with the political system would not be preserved and that a degree of alienation would have to occur. Entirely new norms, procedures, and modes of behaviour were introduced overnight. This distinguishes the transition process in the GDR from that in all of the other socialist countries in Eastern Europe. As a result, behaviour codes, social forms, experiences, and qualifications of an entire population were invalidated *en masse* and replaced by new ones which could not be learned so quickly. An entire society had to go back to school and learn what its counterparts in the West had known and practiced for a long time.

The fact that East German society's own experience could have been drawn upon to instruct change did not occur to the majority of Westerners. The last GDR Prime Minister, Lothar de Maizière, alluded to this problem in introducing his government's programme in spring 1990: "Wherever we became used to the custody of the state and passivity we shall have to grow up as a society—independent and active. This is as true for each citizen as it is for parliament, government and the entire life of society."[19] A new social character was indeed required in the new German *Länder* where, formerly, both party and state expected unwavering obedience in return for social stability and modest prosperity.

The initial and continuing exposure of the all-pervasive character of the GDR's instruments of oppression, especially the zealous state security apparatus, the Stasi, appears, at first, to confirm the simple image that a ruling elite oppressed an entire society. Yet this image is misleading. The fact of the sheer number of people from all levels of East German society who played a role in monitoring and reporting on their compatriots rather proves the complicity of the majority of the population in its own oppression. The official world view and ideology propagated by the SED had a far deeper effect on the thoughts and actions of East Germans than many were at first prepared to admit. With some resignation, the writer Peter Schneider draws a historical parallel to this situation:

> Today we can see that hardly anyone in the GDR had his heart or at least his fist in communism. The whole GDR must have been a day clinic for ideologically abused adults. And we can now see that the SED and the other Bloc parties—just like the NSDAP in its time— were training grounds for clandestine resistance fighters who in fact worked with such secrecy that hardly anyone noticed anything until the end...The exercise I describe is by no means restricted to the GDR. It is passionately pursued on both sides of the border.[20]

The collective suppression of the past cannot succeed. New and ongoing revelations from Stasi documents reveal the complicity of many politicians and numerous citizens in the injustices of the past. It was not easy to break with the modes of behaviour in which people had been drilled for a number of decades. The inherited norms and behaviour patterns of the citizens of the former GDR, despite their efforts to conform, remain incompatible with their new compatriots in the West. Indeed, only the collapse of the communist system was able to reveal that there was an independent social character emerging in the GDR. The longer the SED-dictated political and social system remained in place, the greater the success the SED had in implanting its vision of a society of rela- tive equality. In comparison with Western societies, the GDR was, in relative terms, indeed, a society with egalitarian social structures. Nevertheless, a closer inspection of statistical data now available shows that the "society of equals" was little more than an ideological construct. Differences in income, social circumstances, working conditions, between urban and rural areas, and between the north and south had been widening since the 1970s. But the most important factor in the make-up of GDR society was the unequal distribution of power. The rule of the SED was reminiscent of "a patrimonial rule operating in the realm of free, traditional despotism"—a form of rule which the German sociologist Max Weber called "sultanistic rule."[21] Until September 1989, however, there had been no indication that the party patrimony of the SED was a Colossus on clay feet. Consequently, it should be not surprising to us to learn that the majority of people in the GDR led a double life: in public they adhered unerringly to the dictates of party and state, while in private they sought to fulfil their own understanding of individuality.

At the same time, there were attempts to withstand the difficulties of the transition process that were reminiscent of attitudes in countries which have undergone a similar experience. As problems multiply, a sense of nostalgia for the old leaders and the old ways is cultivated.[22] In eastern Germany this nostalgia, even among those who had previously called for a rapid end to the GDR, was born out of memories of a difficult, but more easily predictable time under the authoritarian regime. Only a very small number of the social and political experiences of the GDR's citizens can be understood by people in West Germany. Two social orders with antagonistic political, economic, and social systems, and 40 years of separate culture and history are growing together at breakneck speed since 1990. Only now are people beginning to realize that highly diverse and fundamentally different social characteristics have developed in both parts of Germany and that these differences could not simply be merged harmoniously under one set of laws and political institutions. One could be polemical by saying that the events of 1989 and 1990 have brought Germany state unity and social division. Before 1989, the majority of the German people were probably convinced that only politics and politicians were preventing them from living in a common polity. Since 1989, there has been a great reluctance to admit that more than 40 years of separation has produced social and cultural divisions. Now it seems as if the two German societies are drifting apart again as differences and problems persist. It will certainly take more than one generation to overcome these divides. Instead of being answered by the events of 1989 and 1990, it appears that the "German question" is writing another chapter.

NOTES

1. See Peter Katzenstein, *Policy and Politics in West Germany: The Growth of a Semi-Sovereign State* (Philadelphia: Temple University Press, 1987).

2. There is a vast amount of literature on the GDR; see inter alia David Childs, *The GDR: Moscow's German Ally*, 2nd ed. (London and Boston: Unwin Hyman, 1988); Gert-Joachim Glaeßner, *Die andere deutsche Republik. Gesellschaft und Politik in der DDR* (Opladen: Westdeutscher Verlag, 1989); Hermann Weber, *DDR. Grundriss der Geschichte, 1945–1990*, expanded and revised edition (Hannover: Fackelträger, 1991);

Mary Fulbrook, *Anatomy of a Dictatorship: Inside the GDR, 1949–1990* (New York: Oxford University Press, 1995).

3. See Gabriel A. Almond and Sidney Verba, *The Civic Culture: Political Attitudes and Democracy in Five Nations* (Princeton: Princeton University Press, 1963); Gabriel A. Almond and Sidney Verba, eds., *The Civic Culture Revisited* (Newbury Park, CA and London: Sage, 1980).

4. See Samuel Huntington, *Political Order in Changing Societies* (New Haven, CT: Yale University Press, 1968).

5. See Arnulf Baring, *Uprising in Germany: June 17, 1953* (Ithaca, NY: Cornell University Press, 1972).

6. See Helmut Schelsky, *Der Mensch in der wissenschaftlichen Zivilisation* (Cologne and Opladen: Westdeutscher Verlag, 1961).

7. Georg Klaus, *Kybernetik und Gesellschaft* (East Berlin: Deutscher Verlag der Wissenschaften, 1964; 3rd ed., 1973), and *Kybernetik—eine neue Universalphilosophie der Gesellschaft?* (East Berlin: Akademie-Verlag, 1973).

8. Rober Havemann, *Dialektik ohne Dogma. Naturwissenschaften und Weltanschauung* (Reinbek: Rowohlt, 1964).

9. See Andrzej Korbonski, "The Politics of Economic Reforms in Eastern Europe: The Last Thirty Years," *Soviet Studies* 41, no. 1 (1989): 11.

10. See Sigrid Meuschel, *Legitimation und Parteiherrschaft in der DDR. Zum Paradox von Stabilität und Revolution in der DDR 1945–1989* (Frankfurt/Main: Suhrkamp, 1992).

11. See Ian Wallace, "Die Kulturpolitik der DDR 1971–1990," in *Eine deutsche Revolution. Der Umbruch in der DDR, seine Ursachen und Folgen,* ed. Gert-Joachim Glaeßner (Frankfurt/Main: Lang, 1991), pp. 108–25.

12. See Martin Greiffenhagen, "Vom Obrigkeitsstaat zur Demokratie: Die politische Kultur in der Bundesrepublik Deutschland," in *Politische Kultur in Westeuropa. Bürger und Staaten in der Europäischen Gemeinschaft,* ed. Peter Reichel (Frankfurt/Main: Campus, 1984), pp. 52–65.

13. Günter Gaus, *Wo Deutschland liegt. Eine Ortsbestimmung* (Hamburg: Hoffmann und Campe, 1993).

14. See Reinhard Henkys, "Thesen zum Wandel der gesellschaftlichen und politischen Rolle in Kirchen in der DDR in den siebziger und achtziger Jahren," in *Die DDR in der Ära Honecker, Politik - Kultur - Gesellschaft.,* ed. Gert-Joachim Glaeßner (Opladen: Westdeutscher Verlag, 1988), pp. 332–53; Detlef Pollack, ed., *Die Legitimität der Freiheit. Politisch alternative Gruppen in der DDR unter dem Dach der Kirche* (Frankfurt/Main: Lang, 1990); and Jörg Swoboda, ed., *Die Revolution der Kerzen. Christen in der Umwälzung der DDR* (Wuppertal and Kassel: Onkenverlag, 1990).

15. On parties and political groups in general Michaela W. Richter, "Exiting the GDR: Political Movements and Parties Between Democratization and Westernization," in *German Unification: Process and Outcomes,* ed. M. Donald Hancock and Helga A. Welsh (Boulder: Westview, 1994), pp. 93–137.

16. Karl Marx, *The Eighteenth Brumaire of Louis Bonaparte,* in Karl Marx and Friedrich Engels, *Collected Works,* vol. 11 (London: Lawrence and Wishart), pp. 103–4.

17. See Konrad H. Jarausch, *The Rush to German Unity* (New York: Oxford University Press, 1994), pp. 75ff.

18. Cf. Helmut Wiesenthal, "East Germany as a Unique Case in Societal Transformation: Main Characteristics and Emerging Misconceptions," *German Politics* 4, no.3

(December 1995): 49–74; Fred Klinger, "Der Transformationsschock. Wirtschaftliche und soziale Entwicklungen nach der 'Wende,'" in *Das wiedervereinigte Deutschland. Bilanz und Perspektiven*, ed. Ralf Altenhof and Eckhard Jesse (Düsseldorf: Droste, 1995), pp. 163–90.

19.   *Volkskammer der Deutschen Demokratischen Republik*, 10. Wahlperiode, 3. Tagung, 19 April 1990.

20.   Peter Schneider, "Man kann ein Erdbeben auch verpassen," *German Politics and Society* 20 (special issue *Germany: From Plural to Singular*, 1990): p. 2.

21.   Max Weber, *Wirtschaft und Gesellschaft* (Tübingen: Mohr, 1972), p. 134.

22.   Lothar Fritze, "Identifikation mit dem gelebten Leben. Gibt es eine DDR—Nostalgie in den neuen Bundesländern?" in *Das wiedervereinigte Deutschland*, ed. Altenhof and Jesse, pp. 275–92.

5 Party System in Transition

STEFAN IMMERFALL
and ANDREAS SOBISCH

West German[1] political parties are regarded as some of the most successful political forces in postwar Western democracies. These parties presided over and shaped the successful transformation of a defeated and devastated country into a prosperous market economy with high social standards, helping to create one of the most stable and ideologically moderate democracies in Western Europe.

To understand the specific historical conditions that influenced these developments, as well the potentially serious problems challenging German parties today, requires an examination of the history of the German party system. Although the main parties have been very successful, the weaknesses and shortcomings of the "German Model" of party politics need to be discussed to evaluate the transitions the party system is facing.

Germany shares with other European countries a party system that has developed from similar circumstances. In addition, certain peculiarities have come to characterize the country's party system, such as the regional diversity of the party system, its considerable stability and high concentration, the political moderation of the major parties combined with a continuous commitment to the ideology of their respective party family, and the major parties' dominant position within the German political system.

These four characteristics are explored, first by examining the historical roots of the contemporary system, second by providing an account of the central role of political parties, third by analyzing the individual parties, and fourth by discussing current developments. Finally, the future of the German party system in transition will be speculated on.

Historical Background

As in other European countries, political parties in Germany have long historical roots.[2] Events and conflicts that took place long before the advent of universal suffrage and modern party politics influenced the form and content of the emerging parties and are still relevant today.

As Lipset and Rokkan[3] pointed out, four major conflicts have proven decisive for the development of the European party system. The "center-periphery cleavage" pitted the central elites against minorities who resisted the standardization of laws, languages, and customs. A second clash emerged between the state and the church, especially about the control of education. A third conflict, the "rural-urban cleavage," concerns differences of interests and lifestyle between rural and industrial classes or, more generally, between the countryside and the city. Finally, the class cleavage embodies the manifold conflicts between workers and the owners of capital.

In Germany, the religious and class divisions have been the most persistent ones. The rural-urban cleavage was resolved to a certain extent during the Second German Empire (1871–1918) by a compromise between landholders and industrialists through which the former received high tariffs on grain imports and the latter the same on industrial products.[4] The importance of the "center-periphery" cleavage has varied over time. Most of the time it has been dormant, but with unification it may well have acquired new relevance.[5] Also, the emerging partisan forces among the varied members of the *Deutscher Bund*, the loose federation of German *Länder* (states) between the Congress of Vienna (1815) and the founding of the Second Empire, may be understood in these terms. Whereas the conservatives sided with the autocratic government, the opposing liberals campaigned for a more democratic constitution.

After unification in 1870/71, the liberals split into "national" and "democratic" wings. The national liberals were willing to compromise with the government in order to achieve national unity, while the more progressive wing continued to demand democratic reforms. This split of the liberal forces continued into the Weimar Republic, with the *Deutsche Demokratische Partei* (DDP) (German Democratic Party) on the left and the *Deutsche Volkspartei* (DVP) (German People's Party) on the right. Even after the unification of liberalism into a single party at the beginning of the Federal Republic, this historical rift within the *Freie*

Demokratische Partei (FDP) (Free Democratic Party) remained evident. One wing tends to favour economic liberalism, that is fiscal austerity and minimal state intervention, whereas the other is more concerned with protecting and extending individual rights. As in most Western European countries, the importance of political liberalism has declined in Germany over the course of the twentieth century. This decline in electoral support for the FDP is now beginning to threaten the FDP's traditional strategic importance in the German party system.

Two other important political forces took shape in Imperial Germany. The first was the organization of political Catholicism. With the Reich's foundation under Bismarck, Catholics suddenly found themselves both numerically and culturally in a minority position. Catholic political groups were being treated with increasing contempt by Bismarck. His measures to suppress their influence, however, failed and the catholic *Zentrum* (Center party) continued to be one of the persistent political forces throughout the Empire and into the Weimar Republic. While conservative on most issues, the Center party, in contrast to the conservatives and the liberals, also included many workers among its supporters.

One of the most important events in German party history took place after World War II, when leaders of the conservative and the catholic camps agreed to form a biconfessional party, the *Christlich Demokratische Union* (CDU) (Christian Democratic Union). For the first time in Germany, protestant and catholic conservatives found a political home in one party. The experience of the Nazi period was important for this bold step as many of the CDU's new leaders had spent time in Nazi prisons or concentration camps. This common experience helped them overcome their deep-seated animosities toward each other.

The CDU still reflects a combination of conservative and Roman-Catholic strands, the latter usually being more socially oriented. Therefore, the CDU is clearly to the left of the "pure" conservative parties in Scandinavia or Great Britain. This moderate stance sometimes attracts the scorn of radical conservatives, but it is highly successful with middle-of-the-road voters. Another feature of the CDU is its continued regional diversity. As a matter of fact, its Bavarian ally, the *Christlich Soziale Union* (CSU) (Christian Social Union), continues to maintain a proud and, from the point of the CDU, sometimes annoying independence.

Finally, to complete the historical account, in 1863 and 1869 two working-class parties were formed out of which the *Sozialdemokratische*

Partei Deutschlands (SPD) (Social Democratic Party of Germany) evolved. In terms of members and voters the SPD soon became the largest party in Imperial Germany, although not until 1912 was this reflected in parliamentary seats. Due to the authoritarian structure of the Empire, the SPD's political influence was limited. Between 1878 and 1890 the party was even banned. The discrepancy between votes and seats was due to the double-ballot majoritarian electoral system of the Kaiserreich. The class conflict was so intense that even if a Social Democratic candidate received a plurality of the votes in the first round, the bourgeois parties would usually unite and defeat him in the ensuing second ballot.[6]

At the end of the First World War, the party opted for parliamentary democracy instead of a Soviet-style republic. During the Weimar period (1919-1933), the SPD was the ill-fated republic's staunchest defender. It participated directly in six of the 19 cabinets and tolerated two others, thus considerably helping to stabilize an otherwise highly volatile polity brought forward, in part, by the purely proportional system of representation. The SPD remained the strongest party until nearly the very end, only in the last two elections, in July and November 1932, finally being overtaken by the *Nationalsozialistische Deutsche Arbeiterpartei* (NSDAP) (National Socialist German Workers' Party), as the latter garnered 34.7 and 33.1 percent of the vote, respectively.[7] On 30 January 1933 Adolf Hitler was appointed chancellor. Five months later, all parties except the NSDAP were outlawed.

The SPD's turn toward pragmatism during the Weimar Republic infuriated its radical minority, which broke away to form the Soviet-style *Kommunistische Partei Deutschlands* (KPD) (Communist Party of Germany). In the Federal Republic, the Communist party has been of little significance, even before it was banned by the Federal Constitutional Court in 1956. In East Germany, however, the communists ascended to power with the help of the Soviet Union and the Red Army. Under the name of the *Sozialistische Einheitspartei Deutschlands* (SED) (Socialist Unity Party), they ruled until shortly after the breakdown of the Berlin Wall in November 1989.

The Emergence of the Party State

The historical lessons from the Weimar Republic and the experiences in the anti-Nazi resistance influenced the founders of the Federal Republic. This included the belief that multiparty instability, radicalism, and demagoguery had contributed greatly to the rise of Hitler. If the new democracy was to fare better than its predecessor, its main political forces would have to be predictable, moderate, and respon-sive. This could be achieved only through large, cooperative, general-interest parties. By refusing to license radical and marginal-interest parties, the Western Allies considerably helped in the quest for moderation and stability.[8]

The authors of the Basic Law, as the new constitution was named, in particular wanted to insure that parties would fulfill their roles in the new democracy in a responsible manner. This desire led them to conceive of Article 21 of the Basic Law that officially recognizes political parties and their role in "forming the will of the people." It further states that German parties have to conform to democratic principles and must serve democ-ratic aims. Several right and left extreme parties have been banned by the Federal Constitutional Court for failing to meet these requirements. In these decisions the Court has asserted that the Federal Republic is a "mili-tant democracy." The constitution is not "morally neutral, but grounds itself on certain central values, takes them in its protection and gives the state the task of protecting and guaranteeing them." These central values include such principles as human rights, world peace, justice, and popular sovereignty. The concept of the militant democracy clearly underscores the strong qualitative difference between the political system of the Federal Republic and those of its predecessors, including the Weimar Republic.

West Germany's party system came to be known as a "two-and-a-half" party system because of the presence of two large parties (CDU/CSU and SPD) and one small party (FDP). Yet, the success of the two large parties, which coincided with the success of the Federal Republic as a stable democracy and as a prosperous economy, could not easily have been fore-seen. In the very beginning the new party system displayed characteristics similar to those of the Weimar system, including a high level of fragmenta-tion and the presence of "anti-system" parties at both ends of the political spectrum. The first national election in 1949 saw 11 parties win seats to the *Bundestag* (the federal parliament), and the largest of them, the CDU/CSU, won only 31 percent of the vote. However, by 1957 the number of parties represented in the *Bundestag* had dwindled to three (CDU/CSU, SPD and FDP), and from 1961 on these three parties captured well over 90 percent of the national vote. This pattern lasted until 1983, when *Die Grünen* (the Greens), with 27 seats, became the first new party to enter the *Bundestag* in more than 20 years (see tables 5–1 and 5–2, p. 128). This continuity and concentration of the German party system is all the more remarkable because Germany has a proportional electoral system with lenient registration requirements for new parties. The "five percent clause," which came into being at the federal level in 1953, is only one factor in the winnowing-out process described. This clause requires that in order to claim any seats in the legislature, a party must obtain at least five percent of the national vote or, alternatively, win three single-member constituencies. Another important factor was the continuing impressive economic growth rate, which reduced the protest potential and helped in the transformation of the two major parties into broad based "people's parties."

Over the years German parties have come to play such a pervasive role in the political system that Germany has often been characterized as a "party democracy" or even a "party state." To this day political parties virtually monopolize the selection and nomination of candidates for elective office, the staffing of high political and administrative positions, and the initiation of legislative proposals and constitutional amendments. There is a distinct lack of opportunities for direct citizen input into the political process, which dates back to the considerable mistrust in direct democracy on the part of the framers of the constitution. This mistrust may have been justified in the early years of the Republic because of the Nazi and Communist misuse of referenda in the Weimar Republic. But when the constitutional commission in 1993 passed on the chance to inject a careful dose of direct democracy into the Basic Law—which had to be adjusted because of unification—it appeared to be out of the unwillingness of the established parties to share power.[9]

One should not overlook, however, the considerable provisions for direct citizen input at the local and state levels. German federalism also serves as a strong countervailing force to the centralizing tendencies of the party system. As one of only three federal systems in all of Europe (Austria and Switzerland being the other two), the German political system is more decentralized than those of the other major European democracies. While this German version of checks and balances makes the pursuit of coherent policies more difficult, it also inhibits radical policy changes and fosters the appearance and diffusion of incremental policy innovations.[10]

Federalism is not just a constitutional provision, it has been a constant feature of German history.[11] This is true for parties as well. Parties have behaved quite differently in the many historical regions of Germany in terms of electoral performance and political predominance, and they have differed with regard to their social bases, internal organization, leadership, and programs.[12] This continues to be the case despite the decline of regional inequalities over the years.[13] In 1990 German unification has added a new dimension to the territorial tapestry.

The Main Parties

If postwar Germany's parties are early examples of the catch-all model, than it is the CDU to which the laurel of being the pioneer belongs. Its transformation occurred not only earlier but also more radically than that of the SPD. Unlike the SPD, the CDU is a genuine postwar creation, even if its roots reach well into the last century. The CDU has often been described as the first "people's party" because it has been able to integrate diverse constituencies without giving up its core of devoted religious supporters.[14] Consequently the CDU has been the dominant party of the (West) German party system for most of the period since 1949.

By being able to attract both middle-class conservative and catholic workers, the CDU enjoys a structural majority. Only once, in 1972, has it been surpassed by the SPD. By 1997, the CDU had been in control of the federal government for 35 out of the 48 years since the founding of the Federal Republic. Only between 1969 and 1982 was the party in opposition, a role to which it submitted only grudgingly. However, these 13 opposition years turned out to be crucial because they allowed the party to redefine itself and to implement a much needed organizational modernization program.

Initially, the CDU had been relatively slow to adopt a national party organization based on a mass membership. It had been founded primarily as a party organized around local and regional notables. This was advantageous initially, given the heterogeneity of its supporters and Germany's federal structure. During the 1950s and 1960s the national office did little more than coordinate the federal election campaigns. This also explains the CDU's nickname of *Kanzlerwahlverein* (committee to elect the chancellor) during those years. Beginning with the creation of the office of General Secretary in 1967, the CDU initiated a massive modernization program to upgrade its organizational structure. When it emerged from 13 years in opposition in 1982, it was in many ways a different party. The party apparatus at all levels had been professionalized and technologically modernized, party membership had more than doubled to slightly over

700,000, and mechanisms to insure greater coordination among the various constituent groups had been installed. Moreover, since 1973 the party has had in Helmut Kohl an energetic and capable chairman, who has ruled the party with little serious internal opposition. Like the other parties, the CDU experienced an erosion of membership beginning in the mid 1980s. In September 1996, it had about 651,000 members, about 15 percent of whom lived in the new federal states.

Its roots in Catholicism prevented the CDU from ever converting to the radical conservatism of, for instance, the Thatcherite type. In fact, the CDU was the main architect of the German welfare state. From the outset, the CDU's policy stances were characterized by a heavy dose of pragmatism. This flexibility has served the party well while in government, although it has left it open to attack as unprincipled and indecisive. However, the lack of ideological fervour should not be equated with a lack of firm principles. The main pillars of the CDU's program are as valid today as they were in the 1950s: (1) the "social market economy" (*Soziale Marktwirtschaft*), Germany's unique blend of free markets and a strong welfare state; and (2) its western orientation (*Westbindung*). The latter has meant that the CDU has always strongly supported Germany's membership in both NATO and the European Community. In fact, during the 1980s Chancellor Kohl was the principal force in moving the Community (now Union) out of its period of relative stagnation and into its current phase of the Single Market and the Maastricht Treaty.

The CDU's Bavarian sister party, the CSU, had even earlier embarked on a course of organizational modernization. Although organizationally completely independent from one another, CDU and CSU have maintained a joined *Bundestag* caucus since 1957 and are cooperating very closely, both in and out of government. In fact, their association is so close that, at times, they are considered a single party. This, however, is not the case. The CSU has consistently sought to put its own stamp on the combined CDU/CSU federal platform, and it sees itself as the promoter of Bavarian regional identity and interests in the politics of the Federal Republic.

Much like its sister party, the CSU was founded with the goal of integrating under a single banner the various regional, social, and religious currents. However, in the case of the CSU this was an especially tricky undertaking because well into the 1950s Bavaria was a predominantly agricultural state, with a deeply entrenched rural, predominantly Catholic, farming sector. This sector stubbornly resisted integration into the rapidly emerging cosmopolitan, industrial economy of Bavaria and the Federal Republic at large. The "Free State" of Bavaria had always enjoyed a certain degree of regional autonomy, and a party wishing to be successful there could ignore this only at its peril. The CSU's main rival in the early days of the Federal Republic, the Bavarian Party (BP), tried hard to cultivate this backward looking sector, very much in the tradition of the old Bavarian People's Party (BVP) of the Weimar Republic. However, by 1957 the CSU had achieved a position of predominance that it has maintained to this day.

Its virtually unassailable position in Bavaria has given the CSU a very strong base from which to influence the politics of the Federal Republic. It tends to be more right-wing and conservative than the CDU, but in terms of party organization and industrial policy it also pursues a vigorous modernization program. Today, former agricultural Bavaria is economically one of the most advanced regions in Europe, rivaled in Germany only by neighboring Baden-Württemberg.

It is the CSU that claims (and deserves) credit for this rapid transformation. The CSU has obtained an absolute majority of the votes in federal and state elections without interruption since 1957 and 1970, respectively. It is extremely well organized at all levels of government in Bavaria, and it possesses some 3,000 local offices, which employ a full-time staff of about 300. It maintains excellent connections to many important groups in society, in particular the Catholic church and small business as well as farm associations. Unlike the other major parties of the Federal Republic, the CSU's membership has remained relatively stable since the early 1980s. In 1996 it had about 180,000 members, down only slightly from its all-time high of 186,000 in 1990. The party organization is hierarchical and intraparty democracy is de-emphasized. This was true in particular under the more than 25-year leadership of Franz Josef Strauß, who skillfully mixed staunch conservatism with a generous dose of populism. Strauß was also the long-time rival of CDU leader, and chancellor, Helmut Kohl. Their troubled relationship came to an end only with Strauß's death in October of 1988. During and after Strauß's reign, the CSU became embroiled in a series of kickback allegations but, so far, this has not undercut its love affair with the Bavarian voters. In the last *Landtag* (state) election, the CSU under its new prime minister, Edmund Stoiber, again took more than half of the votes (52.8 percent), while the SPD, even with its popular leader Renate Schmidt, trailed badly with 30.1 percent.

While the enlargement of the country through unification reduced the CSU's share of the nationwide vote, from its strong Bavarian home base the CSU continues to play an important role in German politics. Actually, the CSU has tried to compensate for its diminished status by attempting to establish a sister party in eastern Thuringia. However, this experiment failed, once more underlining the fact that the CSU can be successful only within the confines of Bavaria.

Both CSU and FDP vie for influence with the larger coalition partner, with the CSU being more conservative and the FDP more liberal in outlook. This frequently puts them into serious conflict. The CSU's dislike of the FDP is exacerbated by the fact that, relative to its size, the FDP is the most influential of the German parties. Though rarely obtaining more than ten percent of the vote, the FDP has served in all but two national governments during the postwar period, more than any other party (see table 5–3, p. 129). The party owes its strength to the pivotal role it plays as "king maker" in the German party system. Since the big parties, CDU/CSU and SPD, alone are unable to win absolute majorities in the *Bundestag*, they need the centrist FDP in order to form a coalition government.

The FDP's program emphasizes the traditional pillars of classical liberalism: civil rights, a free market economy, and anti-clericalism. This orientation distinguishes the party equally from both Social and Christian Democrats. However, the "national" wing within the FDP has always seen itself as primarily anti-socialist, whereas the "social" wing has generally been more hostile to the sometimes harsh conservatism of the union parties, particularly the CSU.

By putting a different foot forward from time to time, the FDP has been able to shift coalition partners when necessary, while carefully retaining its distinctiveness within each coalition. During the 1960s the party developed a preference for conciliation and detente with the countries of the communist block, including East Germany. This strained its relations with the CDU/CSU, paving the way for the eventual coalition with the SPD in 1969. During this period the FDP's social wing also gained the upper hand, most notably with Walter Scheel and Hans-Dietrich Genscher. Whereas Scheel became president of the Federal Republic in 1974, Genscher, as foreign minister, dominated German foreign policy for 20 years until his retirement in 1992. During its 13 years the SPD-FDP coalition initiated a number of important social reforms in such areas as divorce, abortion, and education, which would scarcely have been possible in a coalition dominated by the CDU/CSU.

As in the early 1960s, tensions gradually built up within the coalition, culminating in a bitter quarrel over how best to tackle the economic downturn. Finally, in 1982, the FDP again switched partners. In the new coalition with the CDU/CSU the FDP once again fought hard to maintain its identity, gaining concessions on a number of important social and economic issues during the 1980s and 1990s. The FDP has been particularly keen to lower taxes, to reduce government subsidies to industry, and to cut down on excessive regulations and bureaucratic red tape, while always catering to its core clientele, the so-called three "A's" (*Ärzte, Apotheker, Anwälte*—medical doctors, pharmacists, lawyers).

Like the CDU, the FDP was founded as a regional party, and for the first decade of its existence the FDP's organization was extremely loose and heterogeneous. To a certain extent this is still the case today, although its electoral weakness at the state and local levels has increased the importance and influence of the national organization and leadership. In particular, the FDP is highly dependent on its high profile federal office holders. Compared to the big parties, the FDP also possesses a very low organizational density, with just over 2,000 local offices. The FDP's full-time staff is small (only about 30 at the federal headquarters), and, compared to the big parties, it has a much lower ratio of members to voters. As of 1996 the party had about 76,000 members, up from about 65,000 before unification, but down from about 110,000 in 1992. The latter figure reflects a short-lived boost through the acquisition of the FDP's East German counterpart(s). But here the decline in membership was particularly dramatic, from 114,000 (1990) to 27,000 in April 1995. In contrast, the FDP is a more democratically structured party than either SPD or CDU/CSU. It is much more open to both grass roots influence and newcomers than either of its big rivals.

The old and tradition-rich SPD is the other large party in German politics. After World War II the SPD leadership consciously sought to rebuild the party in its Weimar image, calling for the socialization of large industries and for economic planning. With the credit of staunchly having resisted Adolf Hitler, and with the tide of times seeming to point to "democratic socialism," the first *Bundestag* election of the new republic was disappointing. Frustration grew when in subsequent years the SPD fell even further behind the Union parties. Eventually, the party adapted to the new realities by giving up its Marxist rhetoric and by dampening its working-class appeal.

The "Bad Godesberg Program" of 1959 expressly embraced the social market economy and Germany's western orientation. These innovations made the SPD more attractive to the middle class and, in effect, transformed it too into a *Volkspartei* ("catch-all" or people's party). Final respectability was won as a junior partner in the Grand Coalition with the Christian Democrats between 1966 and 1969. In 1969, Willy Brandt became Germany's first Social Democratic chancellor since 1930.

The "Small Coalition" with the FDP was a period during which many important reforms were passed in both domestic and foreign policy. But it was also a period during which the SPD experienced a dramatic internal transformation. Beginning with the student protests in the late 1960s, a new challenge arose in the form of the "New Left." It affected the SPD both from the inside (party members) and from the outside (electorate). Made up largely of young and well-educated individuals of middle-class background, the New Left demanded more opportunities for direct participation, pushed for greater attention to environmental problems, and, later on, questioned Germany's membership in NATO and its commitment to nuclear defense.

The SPD successfully integrated large parts of the student movement and its followers. In doing so, the party contributed substantially to the liberalization of the Federal Republic, which was still displaying authoritarian features left over from the Adenauer era. But, the new, well-educated, and white-collar party members, many of whom were employed in public service, differed from the traditional working-class constituency in lifestyle and political orientation. To this very day, the SPD has difficulties reconciling its left-libertarian wing with its traditional "Old Left" wing. It would be wrong, however, to assume a conscious subversion form the New Left. Rather, the SPD's changing party structure reflects a changing of Germany's society at large. But increasing diversity makes life particularly difficult for a party that drew so much of its strength out of a vital sense of solidarity.

Today the SPD continues to be a mass membership party, relying more than any other German party on membership dues as its main source of income. However, the SPD's membership, like those of other parties, has been declining steadily since the mid 1970s, when it exceeded one million. As of 1996 its membership stood at about 798,000. Similar to the Greens, the party was unable to build a viable party organization in the eastern part, with memberships stagnating around 27,000. At the same time, the party's constituency in the West has become older, reflecting in part the strong competition for the young generation from the Greens. Only about a quarter of SPD members are women. In order to become more attractive to them, the party has imposed a strict mandate upon itself, namely that by 1994 40 percent of all SPD office holders will be women. With 28 percent, the SPD can pride itself on a larger part of its membership being women than any other party with the exception of the Greens.

Although this history exemplifies the never-ending success story of the main parties—and up to a certain point, it actually is—nothing fails like success. The German parties have not been spared the challenges resulting from social change as well as from new competitors. The five junctures of the German party system's recent history that challenge the stability and success of the main parties are the emergence of the Greens, the dilemma of social democracy, the impact of unification, the rise of right-wing protest, and the general disillusionment with political parties.[15]

❚ Challengers and Challenges

As in other Western democracies, forms of political participation began to change in the mid 1960s. Citizens' movements criticized particular local problems, and large scale demonstrations were staged against the Vietnam war, the old-fashioned university system, and the passage of the Emergency Laws.[16] Subsequent targets were, in the 1970s, the construction of nuclear power plants and, in the early 1980s, the deployment of new nuclear missiles in accordance with NATO's 1979 "double track" decision. This decision turned out to be the single most divisive issue for the SPD during the 1980s. It called for the modernization of intermediate range nuclear missiles, most of them to be stationed in Germany, unless the Soviet Union abandoned its own plans for upgrading its weapons aimed at Western Europe. Ironically it had been SPD Chancellor Helmut Schmidt who had initiated NATO's decision in the late 1970s, and, therefore, the SPD's parliamentary leadership was firmly committed to it. The division within the party over this issue contributed significantly to the demise of the SPD-FDP coalition in the fall of 1982 and to the concomitant rise of the Greens.

By that time the protests had already diversified themselves into a broad stream of social movements of which the women's, the peace, and the ecological movements were the most prominent ones. The emergence of these multifaceted forms of protest and dissent reflected a growing self-confidence of many citizens in their ability to participate in politics. While critical of established institutions and their decisions, the vast majority of protesters were supportive of democracy itself and thus not a threat to the political system, although they were sometimes portrayed as such. Much of the thrust was initially captured by the SPD, but after 1974, as Chancellor Helmut Schmidt had to resort to austerity policies in the face of economic recession, the integration of the New Left became increasingly impossible. It is doubtful, however, if any other Social Democratic leader could have achieved this task since most participants in new social movement activities were critical of parties anyway. It is thus paradoxical that these critics would eventually form their own party, the Greens, which after years of trial and error became an accepted and established party in the German party system. The aversion against party organization in favour of more direct forms of participation is still evident in the fact that of all parties the Greens have the lowest member/voter ratio. In 1995 the Greens had just over 40,000 members. Even if this figure is almost ten percent below the peak in 1988, it means that the Greens are the only German party not losing members in the 1990s.

The Greens first arrived on the political scene in the late 1970s as nothing more than a loose and ideologically quite heterogeneous electoral representative of various environmental and alternative groups, including some remnants of the student protests. After some early fits and starts, the decision was made to form a national organization in order to contest the 1979 elections to the European Parliament. With 3.2 percent of the votes this first national Green alliance achieved an unexpected result and, more importantly, became eligible for over 4,000,000 marks in government subsidies. The association now had the financial resources to set up a formal party organization and contest the 1980 federal election. It actually made it into the *Bundestag* in 1983.

The transformation of an umbrella organization of movements into a full-fledged party[17] was not taken lightly, however. Great pains were taken to prevent the Green party from becoming a "normal," that is, in the eyes of Greens, a bureaucratic and nonresponsive party. Over time many of the measures adopted by them to prevent this have proven to be impractical, and the Greens have adjusted accordingly. For instance, they no longer require their members of parliament to step down halfway through their term in order to make room for other party members. The Greens also moderated politically, and many radicals left the party. Nonetheless, the Greens continue to display special traits in terms of party organization and policy goals. For example, they have kept their strict quota system according to which at least half of all offices have to be occupied by women.

No other party merged more slowly and democratically with its eastern counterpart than the West German Greens. It was not until May 1993 that they formally joined forces with the East German Greens (founded in November 1989) and the East German Alliance '90 (founded in February 1990) to create the Alliance '90/The Greens (*Bündnis 90/Die Grünen*). Yet the Greens remain very weak in the eastern part of Germany, where the enormous task of reconstruction overshadows postmaterialist policies. These economic problems, combined with different cultural legacies, undermine any left-libertarian "milieus" that have been so favourable to the Greens in the western part. But it its fair to say that the Greens have become an established party that will remain a force to be reckoned with in the German party system. They get high marks on ecological issues even from nonsupporters, and the possibility of the Greens participating in a national government no longer scares the electorate.

In light of their moderation in recent years, the Greens present an increasing strategic problem for the SPD. The Greens not only compete for the SPD's young New Left constituency, they also offer themselves as an alternative to those voters who are put off by the SPD's attempts to capture moderate voters from the Free and Christian Democrats. If the SPD tries too hard to lure the left-libertarian voter, it is bound to alienate its traditional working-class core. The best direction for the SPD would be to leave the New Left to the Greens and concentrate on centrist voters in order to combine enough votes for a Red-Green coalition. So far this strategy has been prevented by the presence of too many left-libertarians within the SPD. The middle elite of the SPD continues to be more post-materialist than both the leadership and the rank-and-file.[18] As a result, the party constantly wavers on key issues, trying to please both wings. Throughout the 1980s the SPD struggled to blend ecological and postmaterialist issues with its traditional emphasis on economic growth in order to form a coherent platform.

The SPD's 1989 Berlin program, which was touted as the successor to Bad Godesberg, is an example of the party's troubles. Since the demise of

Keynesianism in the 1970s, which served as the intellectual foundation for postwar economic policy, the party no longer had a convincing platform on the basis of which it could mobilize electoral support. The Berlin program emphasized left-libertarian concerns at the very moment in which German unification called once more for the priority of "old politics," that is, industrial reconstruction in the East and financial curtailment in the West. The SPD's response to the fall of the Berlin Wall was symptomatic of its internal state in the late 1980s and early 1990s. Whereas the CDU/CSU, led by Chancellor Kohl, quickly recognized and responded to the desires of East Germans for rapid unification, the SPD hesitated and during the 1990 campaign continually emphasized the negative side of unification (i.e., the high costs). Even if proven correct in the end, this stance did not endear the party to East Germans, who were left with the impression that the SPD did not want them in the country. This led to an electoral catastrophe for the SPD in the East in 1990 from which it is still trying to recover.

The plight of the SPD is somewhat tempered by its strong presence at the state level. By early 1996, the party participated in 14 of Germany's 16 state governments. Yet, its desire to take advantage of Chancellor Kohl's narrow *Bundestag* majority through the leverage of the *Bundesrat*, the Federal Council of the *Land* governments through which most legislation must pass, is doomed to failure. The *Land* prime ministers have to attend to their states' interests first. Party discipline plays only a minor role. This is especially true for the so-called *Länderfürsten* (regional barons), strong and regionally entrenched prime ministers who, like Lower Saxony's Gerhard Schröder, even govern with an absolute majority. More often than not they are regarded as rivals by the party leadership. In fact, personal rivalries considerably added to the SPD's demise. The German public was partly amused, partly stunned by the way the SPD's leaders treated each other after the 1994 election defeat. Oskar Lafontaine, who toppled hapless Rudolf Scharping in a semi coup d'etat at the Mannheim convention in November of 1995, is no less than the fourth party chair after Willy Brandt retired in 1987. Ironically it was Scharping who had been elected via a postal ballot among all party members in 1993 in an effort to promote greater dialogue, participation, and grassroots influence within the party.

Because of the predominance of heavy industry in the East, it was at first assumed that the SPD would profit from unification. But when the Berlin Wall crumbled in November of 1989, no party was better positioned to take advantage of this development than the CDU/CSU. Recognizing in early 1990 that the overwhelming majority of East Germans desired unification as quickly as possible, Chancellor Kohl used both the advantages of incumbency as well as the indecisiveness of the opposition parties to present himself and his party/government as the vehicle through which unification could be achieved most quickly and with the highest benefit at the lowest cost. The result was a landslide victory for the "Alliance for Germany," the eastern allies of the CDU/CSU, in the first and last free national election of the German Democratic Republic.

Perhaps the biggest irony of German unification concerns the fate of the small East German opposition groups, which had formed in the last year prior to the fall of the Wall.[19] It was largely these groups that openly challenged the communist regime and thus deserve the main credit for bringing about its collapse. But these groups were ill prepared for what followed. Desiring initially to preserve the country and to reform it via a "third way," between capitalism and communism, they were completely out of step with the rapidly changing political climate and the aspirations of their own compatriots. Yet, there is one "Eastern" party that has survived unification, the *Partei des Demokratischen Sozialismus* (PDS) (Party of Democratic Socialism).

The PDS[20] is the reconstituted, and partly reformed, version of the *Sozialistische Einheitspartei Deutschlands* (SED) (Socialist Unity Party), the former East Germany's ruling party. Under the capable leadership of the reform-minded Gregor Gysi,[21] the PDS was able to cultivate a new image as the party standing up for the interests of East Germans during (and after) the unification process with West Germany. By skillfully exploiting the fears and apprehensions of many easterners, the PDS has, against the predictions of many experts, been able to establish a relatively solid base of voting support in the five new states and especially in the eastern part of Berlin. Its core constituency comprises less of those who suffered most from unification in any objective sense but rather the relative losers of unification who lost privileges, morales, and lifetime security. The PDS's strong showing makes it the third party in the East, a role otherwise occupied by the FDP or, increasingly, the Greens.

The PDS still can build on a potent organization and a strong presence in local politics. Of course, the PDS could not retain all of the members it inherited from the SED (2.3 million out of population of 16 million). Nevertheless, the PDS membership still reached 123,000 in early 1995, almost all of which comes from the eastern part. The most notable characteristic of the party's membership is its highly unfavourable age structure. Since the party is unable to attract support in the western part of Germany, both in electoral and in membership terms, its survival in the *Bundestag* will depend on winning at least three direct seats in the East, which would override the five-percent threshold. It is uncertain for how long the PDS will be able to accomplish this. Nevertheless, for the foreseeable future the PDS is likely to remain a viable regional party. And as long as the PDS is beyond the pale, coalition building will be extremely difficult in the Eastern state parliaments.

The parliamentary presence of the PDS and the moderation of the Greens has affected the FDP, too. The "two-and-a-half" party-formula no longer works because the formation of an SPD-FDP government is arithmetically impossible. A SPD-FDP-Green coalition, while arithmetically feasible, is ideologically questionable, at least for the time being. The FDP therefore no longer plays the pivotal role as "king maker" to either a left-center or a right-center coalition government, and its fortunes are thus more than ever tied to the Christian Democrats. However, because it lacks a reliable regional or social base of support, the FDP's survival depends on its ability to make itself functionally indispensable by acting as a "moderate corrective" to overly conservative (CDU/CSU) or socialist (SPD) tendencies within its respective coalitions.

In order to maintain its distinct profile, it is vital for the FDP to be in government. In opposition, it tends to get lost in the rivalry between the big parties. The FDP has played this role at both national and state levels, although it has been much more successful in the federal arena. In autumn 1993 the FDP had been represented in all of the 16 state parliaments, in spring 1996 in a mere four. In fact, between 1992 and 1995 the Free Democrats have failed to achieve the five percent necessary for parliamentary representation in 12 of out of 15 state elections, including all five new states. If this trend continues, the political viability of the FDP is in serious jeopardy.

In the mid 1980s it looked as if the CDU/CSU would face as serious a challenge from the right as the SPD had been facing from the left. "The Republicans" (REP) party was founded in Munich in 1983 by three CSU renegades, among them the colourful Franz Schönhuber, a former talk-show host who had been sacked because of his boasts about having been a member of the Nazi Waffen-SS.[22] After a minor success (3 percent) in the Bavarian state election in 1986, the REP achieved a number of spectacular results in 1989, most notably 7.5 percent of the vote in the elections to the Berlin state parliament and 7.1 percent (nationwide) in the elections to the European Parliament. After a protracted slump in 1990 and 1991, the party experienced a comeback in 1992 and 1993, winning over ten percent of the vote, and 15 seats, in the state election of Baden-Württemberg. However, the REP has so far been unable to duplicate its 1989 success at the national level, falling well short of the five-percent hurdle in both the 1990 and the 1994 *Bundestag* elections. Two older and more unambiguously extreme rightist parties, the *Nationaldemokratische Partei Deutschlands* (NPD) (National-Democratic Party) and the *Deutsche Volksunion* (DVU) (German Peoples Union), also experienced short-lived boosts in their electoral fortunes. The Federal Republic had not witnessed such a resurgence of the Far Right since the late 1960s.[23]

Like other European radical right parties, the public rhetoric of the REP is nationalistic, xenophobic, and populist. By far its most important rallying cry is to turn back all asylum applicants, refugees, and other foreigners seeking to make Germany their permanent home. Common REP themes further include the supposed deterioration of public morality, the "selling out" of Germany's national interests through European integration, the decline in national pride, and the corruption and mismanagement among political elites. Because of the party's far right ideology, its initial successes created considerable domestic and international attention. With a dramatic increase in violent racist attacks in 1992, many observers predicted the rebirth of German fascism.[24] Actually, Germany is one of the very few West European countries with a strong left-libertarian and a weak right-wing populist party at the same time.[25] Therefore, it is the relative failure rather than the REP's limited success that has to be explained.

Some observers link the REP's decline primarily to the severe tightening of Germany's liberal asylum law in May 1993. As suggestive as this explanation may be, it seems rather improbable. France, for instance, also restricted asylum and naturalization laws without, however, affecting the National Front's electoral fortunes. It seems more likely that Germany's past still causes many voters to have second thoughts about casting their vote for a far right party. Moreover, one must also consider the REP's internal state of affairs and its positioning in the party system. With respect to the former, an important element seems to be the permanent leadership quarrels beleaguering the party, which have caused Franz Schönhuber to be deposed as party leader several times. Second, the party was unable or unwilling to disassociate itself categorically from the extremist fringe, many of whom were drawn to the party. This prevented the REP from taking on a more acceptable public image. It was also unable to overcome the fragmentation and disunity of the far right. The party's potential was further limited by the strong stand of the CDU/CSU. Unlike many other conservative parties in Western Europe, the CDU/CSU plausibly made it clear that it would refrain from any coalition with the REP. However, these factors cannot be taken for granted; one should not assume that there is no voting potential in Germany for a unified and more cleverly acting far right party.

Politikverdrossenheit (disaffection with politics)[26] is certainly a factor that contributed to success of right-wing parties in the late 1980s and early 1990s. Party membership, party identification, vote share of the major parties, and the electoral turnout rate are all in decline and may be seen as further indicators of the disenchantment with politics. Even more important may be the conspicuously negative image of parties and politicians as regularly reported in representative surveys.[27] In fact, *Politikverdrossenheit* is a misnomer since there is as much interest in politics as ever. Terms like *Parteienentfremdung* (weariness of parties) and even *Parteienverdrossenheit* (alienation from parties) are more to the point. Given the pivotal role played by parties in German politics, rising discontent with the established parties (including the Greens) once again raises concerns about the future stability of German democracy.

Usually, political scandals are blamed for this development. Indeed, such scandals and the generous allowances for parties and politicians have certainly tarnished the reputation of political parties. But there have been scandals before. It seems rather that the public is now less willing to tolerate the misbehaviour of the political class. In part this may be due to the fact that the protracted economic difficulties have made it more difficult for politicians to "dish out goodies" to their constituents. Beyond that, they sometimes seem helpless in the face of economic globalization as they are unable to influence crucial processes outside the national borders.

Part of the political malaise is perhaps explainable as a "normalization effect" from the heydays of the 1970s, when trust in the problem solving capacity of politics was at its highest level. To the extent that it reflects the structural transformation of party politics, parties and politicians will never again enjoy such deference. A main reason is the transformation of the catch-all party into what Richard Katz and Peter Mair have called the "cartel party."[28] The catch-all party, as we saw above with SPD and

CDU/CSU, buried much of its ideological baggage and vied for electoral support with little regard for voters' social affiliation. The new type of party no longer attempts to encapsulate its members; immediate electoral concerns override long-term political objectives.

The advent of the cartel-party represents a further push in that direction whereby social identity and policy distinctiveness become even less meaningful. As ideological and social differences between parties wane and almost all parties have access to office, parties increasingly anchor within the state. Parties, as "semi-state agencies," have access to many resources independent of voluntary contributions. Through this arrangement they are insured against electoral misfortunes and need to rely less on activists to campaign and communicate on their behalf.

The model of the "cartel party" fits the German case particularly well. From the very beginning, West Germany's parties were well positioned to take advantage of state revenues. The party privilege has led to, among other things, a very generous system of public finance. It has been interpreted by many, not the least by the parties themselves, as giving them extensive authority over many aspects of public life, including policy making, the civil service, the judiciary, broadcast media, education, and even the military. German parties and party-related foundations receive a substantial, continuous, and increasing flow of public money.[29] International comparisons are notoriously difficult, but it seems that German professional politicians are among the best paid in the democratic world. Of particular annoyance are general revenues, pensions, and *Übergangsgelder* (interim allowances) once politicians retire or fail to be re-elected.[30] It is perhaps no coincidence that the new German *Bundestag*, with its 672 members,[31] is the largest of all free parliaments in the world.

Prospects

The party system of the Federal Republic of Germany has long been regarded as a model of stability. However, since the early 1980s the entry of new parties into the federal parliament, the substantial loss of prestige of the established parties in the eyes of the German public, and the repercussions associated with the unification of the two German states in October of 1990 have upset this traditional stability and brought in new dynamics. Yet, our basic conclusion is that while the German party system is changing, reports of the death of the German catch-all party are premature.

Of all parties, the future of FDP is the most uncertain. It represents itself as a party without topics nor leaders capable of mobilizing voters. It is true that the FDP has faced alarming prospects before, most recently between 1978 and 1983, and it managed not only to survive, but to prosper. But this time the situation is even more alarming as the party has lost its king-making quality. This is extremely dangerous for a party that relies to a large extent on the strategic support of voters from other parties who want their preferred coalition to win. Opportunities are now quite limited for the FDP. If it stays with CDU/CSU, it may lose its independence; if it switches to the SPD, it will have to put up with the Green since there is no SPD-FDP majority in sight. It is even possible that some in the FDP will attempt to adopt a "Haider strategy," that is, pursuing a right-wing populist course that has worked so well for the Austrian *Freiheitliche Partei Öster-reichs* (FPÖ) (Freedom Party of Austria). If that were to happen, however, it would lead to the break-up of a party with already limited personal resources.

A second question concerning the development of the German party system arises out of the protracted weakness of the SPD. The party's inability to offer personal and programmatic alternatives to an apparently exhausted governing coalition stalls party competition and contributes to the disenchantment with politics. To date, Chancellor Kohl has accrued personal power to an extent that is probably unhealthy for a working parliamentary democracy. The *Richtlinienkompetenz*, the chancellor's right to formulate the general policy guidelines wherein the ministers conduct the affairs of their department, has, as in Adenauer's time, turned into a full-fledged "chancellor democracy."[32]

Finally, a certain disaffection with political parties will continue to be a structural feature of German democracy. Technological changes, differentiations in the social structures, and rising educational levels do not permit political organizations to go back to the former days of catch-all parties, to say nothing of the mass party model. Nevertheless, even if party members are less important for party finance and campaigning than they were in the old days, there are reasons to believe that they still fulfill a crucial part in political communication within the democratic society. Thus, parties are well advised to cater to ordinary members and to attenuate the ties to the state in favour of a closer rapport with society.[33]

German parties are reading this writing on the wall. Concerned members of both large parties came forward with suggestions to revitalize party life, to open party positions to outsiders, and to partly retreat from patronage politics.[34] All in all, German parties are still up to their task, not the least since they have retained certain features of the older mass party model.[35] Being of a mixed type—anchored in both state and society and on their way to a modern service enterprise—will help them fend off potential protest parties while continuing to be responsive to the civil society. Political parties may no longer be the sole centers of politics as they were in the past. But, as the "normalization" of the Greens testifies, there is no alternative, especially when it comes to mitigating the middle-class bias of politics.

Table 5–1: Results for Bundestag Elections, 1949–1994

Year	Turnout	CDU–CSU	SPD	FDP	PDS[A]	Greens	Far Right[C]
1949	78.5	31.0	29.2	11.9	5.7	-	1.8
1953	86.0	45.2	28.8	9.5	2.2	-	1.1
1957	87.8	50.2	31.8	7.7	-	-	1.0
1961	87.7	45.3	36.2	12.7	-	-	0.8
1965	86.8	47.6	39.3	9.5	-	-	2.0
1969	86.7	46.1	42.7	5.8	-	-	4.3
1972	91.1	44.9	45.8	8.4	0.3	-	0.6
1976	90.7	48.6	42.6	7.9	0.3	-	0.3
1980	88.6	44.5	42.9	10.6	0.2	1.5	0.2
1983	89.1	48.8	38.2	7.0	0.2	5.6	0.2
1987	84.3	44.3	37.0	9.1	-	8.3	0.6
1990	77.8	43.8	33.5	11.0	2.4[B]	5.0[B]	2.1
1994	79.1	41.4	36.4	6.9	4.4	7.3	1.9

A. KDP from 1949–1953, DKP from 1972–1983, PDS from 1990 on.
B. In the first all-German elections 1990 the five percent clause was applied separately for eastern and western Germany. Thus the *western* Greens failed to gain seats as they polled only 4.8%. The PDS and the *eastern* Greens won seats by vitue of winning more than five percent in the east (11.1 and 6.0 percent, respectively)
C. DRP from 1949-1961, NPD from 1965–1987, Republicans from 1990 on.

Table 5–2: Bundestag Seat Distribution, 1949–1994

Year	Total	CDU	CSU	SPD	FDP	Greens	PDS	Other
1949	402	115	24	131	52	-	-	80
1953	487	191	52	151	48	-	-	45
1957	497	217	53	169	41	-	-	17
1961	499	192	50	190	67	-	-	-
1965	496	195	49	202	49	-	-	-
1969	496	193	49	224	30	-	-	-
1972	496	187	48	230	41	-	-	-
1976	496	190	53	214	39	-	-	-
1980	497	174	52	218	53	-	-	-
1983	498	191	53	193	34	27	-	-
1987	497	274	49	186	46	42	-	-
1990	662	268	51	239	79	8	17	-
1994	672	244	50	252	47	49	30	-

Table 5–3: Composition of Federal Government Coalitions, 1949–1994

Period	Chancellor	Governing Parties
1949–1953	Konrad Adenauer	CDU/CSU, FDP, DP
1953–1956	"	CDU/CSU, FDP, DP, GDB/BHE
1956–1957	"	CDU/CSU, DP, GDB/BHE
1957–1961	"	CDU/CSU, DP
1961–1965	from 1963:	CDU/CSU, FDP
1965–1966	Ludwig Erhard	CDU/CSU. FDP
1966–1969	Kurt-Georg Kiesinger	CDU/CSU, SPD
1969–1972	Willy Brandt	SPD, FDP
1972–1976	from 1974:	SPD, FDP
1976–1980	Helmut Schmidt	SPD, FDP
1980–1982	"	SPD, FDP
1982–1983	Helmut Kohl	CDU/CSU, FDP
1983–1987	"	CDU/CSU, FDP
1987–1990	"	CDU/CSU, FDP
1990–1994	"	CDU/CSU, FDP
1994–	"	CDU/CSU, FDP

NOTES

1. We will not consider the East German case, which was devoid of party competition due to the monopolization of power through the communist SED. We will, however, consider East German legacies when discussing the party politics of the unification process. The most thorough account of the state of the German party system is Alf Mintzel and Heinrich Oberreuter, eds., *Parteien in der Bundesrepublik Deutschland*, 2nd, rev. ed. (Opladen: Leske and Budrich, 1992).

2. For recent general histories of the German parties, see Robert Hofman, *Geschichte der deutschen Parteien. Von der Kaiserzeit bis zur Gegenwart* (Munich: Piper, 1993); Peter Loesche, *Kleine Geschichte der deutschen Parteien* (Stuttgart: Kohlhammer, 1993); Susanne Miller and Heinrich Potthoff, *Kleine Geschichte der SPD. Darstellung und Dokumentation 1848–1993*, 6th ed. (Bonn: Verlag Neue Gesellschaft, 1993); Jürgen Dittberner, *FDP—Partei der zweiten Wahl. Ein Beitrag zur Geschichte der liberalen Partei und ihrer Funktion im Parteiensystem der Bundesrepublik* (Opladen: Westdeutscher Verlag, 1987); Alf Mintzel, *Die CSU. Anatomie einer konservativen Partei 1945–1972*, 2nd ed. (Opladen: Westdeutscher Verlag, 1978); Joachim Raschke et al., *Die Grünen. Wie sie wurden, was sie sind* (Cologne: Bund-Verlag, 1993).

    Accounts on the smaller parties can be found in Richard Stoess et al., *Parteien-Handbuch. Die Parteien der Bundesrepublik Deutschland, 1945–1980*, 2 vols. (Opladen: Westdeutscher Verlag, 1984) and in Mintzel and Oberreuter.

    For a discussion of current problems of each party, cf. Warnfried Dettling, "Ende oder Wende. Was wird aus der CDU?" *Aus Politik und Zeitgeschichte* B1 (1994): 3–7; Peter Lösche and Fritz Walter, *Die SPD* (Darmstadt: Wissenschaftliche

Buchgesellschaft, 1992); Alf Mintzel, "CSU-Strategie gegen Gewichtsverlust," *Die Neue Gesellschaft* (September 1990): 828–31; Peter Loesche and Franz Walter, eds., *Die F.D.P. Richtungsstreit und Zukunftszweifel* (Darmstadt: Wissenschaftliche Buchgesellschaft, 1996); Hubert Kleinert, *Aufstieg und Fall der Grünen—Analyse einer alternativen Partei* (Bonn: Verlag J.H.W. Dietz Nachf, 1992).

3. Seymour M. Lipset and Stein Rokkan, "Cleavage Structures, Party Systems and Voter Alignments," in *Party Systems and Voter Alignments*, ed. S.M. Lipset and S. Rokkan (New York: Free Press, 1967), pp. 1–64.

4. Cf. Volker R. Berghahn, *Imperial Germany, 1871–1914: Economy, Society, Culture, and Politics* (Providence, RI: Berghahn, 1995).

5. Cf. Thomas Emmert and Dieter Roth, "Zur wahlsoziologischen Bedeutung eines Modells sozialstrukturell verankerter Konfliktlinien im vereinten Deutschland," *Historical Social Research* 20, no. 2 (special issue, ed. S. Immerfall and P. Steinbach, 1995): 119–60.

6. Cf. Peter Steinbach: "Die Entwicklung der deutschen Sozialdemokratie im Kaiserreich im Spiegel der historischen Wahlforschung," in *Der Aufstieg der deutschen Arbeiterbewegung*, ed. G.A. Ritter (Munich: Oldenbourg, 1991), pp. 1–35.

7. On the electoral basis of the Nazi-party, see the seminal account of Jürgen W. Falter, *Hitlers Wähler* (Munich: C.H. Beck, 1991). The phenomenal rise of the NSDAP continues to puzzle political scientists and laymen alike. For an interesting new attempt, see Courtney Brown, *Serpents in the Sand: Essays on the Nature of Politics and Human Destiny*, chap. 5 (Ann Arbor, MI: University of Michigan Press, 1995).

8. See Daniel E. Rogers: *Politics After Hitler: The Western Allies and the German Party System* (New York: New York University Press, 1995).

9. See issue B52/53 (1993) of *Aus Politik und Zeitgeschichte*.

10. Compare, for instance, Josef Schmid, *Die CDU. Organisationsstrukturen, Politiken und Funktionsweise einer Partei im Föderalismus* (Opladen: Leske and Budrich, 1990) and Fritz W. Scharpf, "The Joint Decision Trap: Lessons from German Federalism and European Integration," *Public Administration* 66, no. 3 (1988): 239–78.

11. Cf. Stefan Immerfall, *Territorium and Wahlverhalten. Zur Modellierung geopolitischer and geo-ökonomischer Prozesse* (Opladen: Leske and Budrich, 1992).

12. See the examples in Karl Rohe, ed., *Elections, Parties and Political Traditions: Social Foundations of German Parties and Party Systems, 1867–1987* (New York: Berg, 1990) and Dirk Berg-Schlosser and Ralf Rytlewski, eds., *Political Culture in Germany* (Houndsmills, Basingstoke: MacMillan, 1993).

13. Cf. Dieter Oberndörfer and Karl Schmitt, eds., *Parteien und regionale politische Traditionen in der Bundesrepublik Deutschland* (Berlin: Duncker and Humblot, 1991).

14. As demonstrated by Karl Schmitt, *Konfession und Wahlverhalten in der Bundesrepublik Deutschland* (Berlin: Duncker and Humblot, 1989).

15. On the state of German party sociology, see Oskar Niedermayer and Richard Stoess, eds., *Stand und Perspektiven der Parteienforschung in Deutschland* (Opladen: Westdeutscher Verlag, 1993); for a summary, see Stefan Immerfall, "Die letzte Dekade westdeutscher Parteienforschung—zur Analogie der Defizite von Parteien und Parteienforschung," *Zeitschrift für Parlamentsfragen* 23, no.1 (1992): 172–89.

16. The Emergency Laws were passed by the Grand Coalition in 1968 as an amendment to the Basic Law. Critics feared that these laws gave the state too much power in case on a national emergency.

17. See Thomas Poguntke, "Goodbye to movement politics? Organisational adaption of the German Green party," *Environmental Politics* 2, no. 3 (1993): 379–404; on the parliamentary level, Stefan Immerfall and Werner J. Patzelt, "GRÜNE Parlamentarier: Ergebnisse zweier Befragungen," *Forschungsjournal Neue Soziale Bewegungen* 5, no. 3 (1992): 93–96.

18. Hermann Schmitt, *Neue Politik in alten Parteien. Zum Verhältnis von Gesellschaft und Parteien in der Bundesrepublik* (Opladen: Westdeutscher Verlag, 1987).

19. For a general account of the new organizational landscape in the Eastern part of Germany, see Josef Schmid, Frank Loebler, and Heinrich Tiemann, *Organisationsstrukturen und Probleme von Parteien und Verbänden* (Marburg: Metropolis-Verlag, 1994).

20. Cf. Jürgen P. Lang, Patrick Moreau, and Viola Neu, *Auferstanden aus Ruinen...? Die PDS nach dem Super-Wahljahr 1994,* Interne Studien Nr. 111 (Konrad Adenauer Stiftung, 1995).

21. After allegations of having spied for the East German secret police, Gysi resigned as chair. This, however, has not diminished his influence within the party as neither has the confession of former party secretary André Brie to have worked for the East German state security for almost 20 years.

22. See Hans-Gerd Jaschke, *Die 'Republikaner.' Profile einer Rechtsaussen-Partei* (Bonn: J.H.W. Dietz, 1992).

23. Cf. Richard Stoess, *Politics Against Democracy: Right-wing Extremism in West Germany* (New York: Berg, 1991).

24. Actually, if anything, there is an inverse correlation between electoral performance of radical right parties and racist violance.

25. Cf. Stefan Immerfall, "The Future of the Neo-populist Agenda," forthcoming in *New Party Politics of the Right: The Rise and Success of Neo-Populist Parties in Western-Style Democracies,* ed. Hans-Georg Betz and Stefan Immerfall (New York: St. Martin's, in press).

26. For a summary of the burgeoning literature on Politikverdrossenheit, Stefan Immerfall: "Parteienforschung in der Parteienkrise," *Politische Vierteljahresschrift* 35, no. 3 (1994): 480–92.

27. Cf. Frank Christian, *Krise ohne Ende? Parteiendemokratie vor neuen Herausforderungen* (Cologne: Bund-Verlag, 1993).

28. Richard S. Katz and Peter Mair, "Changing Models of Party Organization and Party Democracy," *Party Politics* 1, no. 1 (1995): 5–28.

29. Klaus von Beyme, *Die politische Klasse im Parteienstaat* (Frankfurt/Main: Suhrkamp, 1993), pp. 131–55; Christine Landfried, *Parteifinanzen and politische Macht. Eine vergleichende Studie zur Bundesrepublik, zu Italien und den USA* (Baden-Baden: Nomos, 1994).

30. Recent examples can be found in Wolfgang Hoffman, "Der verbrauchte Staat. Die Versorgung der politischen Elite kostete den Steuerzahler viel Geld," *Die Zeit* (12 January 1996): 17–18.

31. See table 5–3; this includes 16 so-called excess mandates (*Überhangmandate*) based on the provision that a party can keep its district seats even if their number exceeds the number of seats based on the proportional distribution of the vote.

32. Cf. Stephen Padgett, ed., *Adenauer to Kohl: The Development of the German Chancellorship* (Washington, D.C.: Georgetown University Press, 1994).

33. Cf. Stefan Immerfall, "Politische Kommunikation von Parteimitgliedern. Eine mehrebenenanalytische Fallstudie zur Bundestagswahl 1990," *Zeitschrift für politische Psychologie* 1, no. 3/4 (1993): 247–71.

34. For references see Stefan Immerfall, "Der Präsident und die (anderen) Praktiker, die Professoren und die (anderen) Publizisten Krise der politischen Parteien," *Zeitschrift für Parlamentsfragen* 23, no. 2 (1994): 310–13.

35. See Alf Mintzel, "Auf der Suche nach der Wirklichkeit der Grossparteien in der Bundesrepublik Deutschland," in *Wohlfahrtsstaat, Sozialstruktur und Verfassungsanalyse*, ed. H.D. Klingenmann and W. Luthardt (Opladen: Westdeutscher Verlag, 1993), 66–105.

6

The Orderly and the Extremist

Understanding German Political Culture

THOMAS HUEGLIN

The old West German republic is no more, and perhaps no one is an expert on the new united Germany that is emerging. The year 1989 has been called a second European revolution (after the French one of 1789), and the two German states that existed since the end of World War II have at least geographically been at the heart and centre of it. Strangely enough, though, revolutionary change is hardly visible to the visitor of the new Germany. The consequences of 1989 appear more dramatic in Poland and Hungary, or even in Italy. Could it be that Germany is once again on a *Sonderweg*, a different path towards the future, avoiding revolutionary change as it did in the nineteenth century?

This is a difficult question, and one must sort out, preliminarily, what appears to be old and new in the new Germany. Focusing on German political culture, and narrowly on what might be extremist manifestations of it,[1] this chapter concentrates on right-wing extremism. There can be no understanding of German political culture without some reflections on the past, some analysis of transformations in institutions and governance, and some references to the changing socioeconomic environment with which Germans are now confronted.

The Legacy of Heidegger

When modern Germany became united for the first time, in 1871, it soon came to be seen as the country of blood and iron (*Blut und Eisen*). But it also carried another label, as the land of poets and thinkers. Perhaps the most influential among the latter, in the twentieth century, was Martin Heidegger. He became discredited when he put himself into the service of the blood and iron regime of the Nazis, temporarily only and early on, but had been carried by the conviction that Hitler was the revolutionary hero who would lead into a future where mere human existence could become transformed into real human being.[2]

During much of the post-World War II period, Heidegger's philosophical fame flourished undiminished in many parts of the world, especially in France, but less so in Germany, where it remained muted by the embarrassing remembrance of the past. This seems to have changed recently. A visitor to the new Germany will notice with astonishment that half of the philosophy shelves in almost any academic bookstore are filled with books by and about Heidegger. Heidegger is *in* again. How can one explain this turnabout in the land of poets and thinkers? Three possible explanations can serve as starting hypotheses for the examination of German political culture in the 1990s.

The first, most obvious, and most immediately, disturbing hypothesis is that the renaissance of Heideggerian thought goes hand in hand with the rediscovery of German nationalism. Unification happened under the banner of nationhood, and the nationalism that carried it, continues to be a genetic (*völkisch*) rather than political one. In Heidegger's philosophy, individual being is thrown into (*Geworfenheit*), and existentially surrounded by, the genetic community of the people-as-fate (*Geschick*). In one terribly time-bound sentence, Heidegger had linked the essence of individual being to the existential acceptance of a people's collective fate, and as a conscious act of *electing one's hero*.[3] However, this hypothesis does not carry very far. The new German nationalism is not one of blood and iron, and neither was Heidegger's. Nevertheless, German political culture cannot be fully understood without this continuity of genetic nationalism in German political thought.

The second hypothesis has to do with cyclical changes of cultural orientation in German society. In the nineteenth and early twentieth centuries, German intellectuals and, to a certain degree, also popular culture, had gone through a phase of romantic idealism followed by the rise of a industrial-technical empiricism which in turn, when the rational world collapsed during the social catastrophes following World War I, gave way to the rise of ontological questions about the meaning of human being, existence, action, and time. Here, then, Heidegger's star began to rise, and so did Germany's fascination with Hitler as its hero-leader into a more wholesome future.[4]

A similar diagnosis may apply at the outgoing twentieth century. After the irrational nightmare of World War II, the political and cultural discourse in West Germany was at first dominated by a lofty democratic normativism. It came to be criticized and replaced once again by a more pedestrian empiricism, which regarded human behaviour only on the basis of facts and tended to avoid asking questions that could not be measured and counted. But when the end of postwar growth and prosperity signaled a crisis of the rational-material world, questions about the nature and meaning of life began to be asked once again.[5] The organized world of modernity came to be challenged by the deconstructivist efforts of postmoderns who, as had Heidegger, denied that human existence should be understood as a rational calculation of choice in universalized subject-object relations.

The analogism of this hypothesis cannot carry too far either. The postmodern fascination with Heidegger's subject-object denial is by definition a fragmented one, aiming at a deconstructed world of difference[6] in plural life worlds. It wants exactly to break out of the people-as-fate condition that Heidegger had taken as a given environment. When the postwar epoch of exceptional affluence came to an end, dominant socioeconomic and political elites began to reassert universalized market forces as the natural and allegedly rational environment for calculated choice. They cancelled the class compromise that had for so long lent stability to the universalized regime of subject-object relations. At the fringes, extremist reactions occurred against this downscaling of personal life chances. Far from constituting any kind of organized effort, these reactions could nevertheless grow out of a public discourse in which political parties tried to regain lost ground by conjuring up, once again, the wholesomeness of the people-as-fate.

The third hypothesis turns to populism and language. It has been said of Heidegger's principal work, *Sein und Zeit* (*Being and Time* (1962)), first published in 1927, that it is not a difficult book to read unless one attempts to understand its fundamental intention.[7] And indeed, Heidegger was in his time not just a philosophers' philosopher, but a popular public figure whose complex and idiosyncratic language could serve populist interpretations.[8] At least unintentionally, his philosophically precise language pandered to a populist rhetoric loaded with deliberately imprecise meaning and sentiment. It was such rhetoric that obfuscated public discourse and helped the Nazis into power. Heidegger himself appeared caught, for a few terrible years, in his own rhetoric of folk, fate, and fear.

Similarly, it has been argued that the public discussion about nationalism, multiculturalism, refugees, and asylum seekers in the Germany of the 1990s has been carried by a populist rhetoric of "semantic overdetermination."[9] In order to stem the tide of their sagging electoral fortunes, party politicians began to appeal to popular sentiments of nation, history, and identity, once again. Foreigners, ethnic minorities, refugees, and asylants were congealed into the one fuzzy image of the *other*. That alien other was quickly perceived as threatening German jobs and exhausting German public services. Right-wing extremists soon enough turned fuzzy rhetoric into terrible deed. The point is not that the political classes condoned or even sympathized with this turn of events, but that their calculated use of populist rhetoric for the sake of political expediency turned incalculable in the hands of arsonists.

It was Hannah Arendt's brutally personal criticism of Heidegger, her one-time secret lover and lifelong intellectual challenger, that he, in his philosophical desire to redeem humanity from the meaningless banality of its existence, embraced the revolutionary destructiveness of the totalitarian movement by temporarily entering a pact between mob and elite.[10] But once again, this hypothesis can only be tested with caution. Heidegger's motivations during the early 1930s were surely those of the erring philosopher-king. And they were motivations only. He had no active part or control of the Nazi agenda and would himself be observed with suspicion soon enough. Those political classes who have been playing with the forces of nationalist resentment since the 1980s well before the process of reunification, would reopen the unresolved question of German nationhood. Resembling sorcerers' apprentices, they thought that they could utilize those forces to their own political benefit and now do not know how to call them back into the corner.

Fortunately, it is unlikely that the forces of right-wing extremism will succeed once again to march from the lowlands of disparate extremist action to the commanding heights of German politics and culture. But, as one of the most important indicators of a society's political culture is how it deals with its conflicts,[11] they cannot be ignored either.[12]

Extremism in Comparative Perspective

Before nationalism, change of cultural orientation, and populism in the new Germany can be examined further, the comparative record first needs to be set straight. Extremist and racially motivated attacks against foreigners and "asylants" in Germany attracted much international media attention in the early 1990s for obvious reasons. Germany is well remembered as the country that only half a century ago had carried racism to its most perverted extreme. Despite occasional references to the political success of Le Pen's National Front movement in France, for example, the international community tended to observe the German case in isolation. It did not pay attention to the fact that racism had raised its ugly head elsewhere and earlier in Europe.

In Britain, for example, race riots date back to the 1950s. Complaints about racist police orientations have been endemic. Even grave acts of racist violence have often found little attention in the media. Official statistics for 1991 reveal 7,780 racially motivated criminal acts of violence, a number apparently consistent over several years. The numbers for Germany, a country with 30 million more inhabitants (east and west), are 1,483 in 1991 and 2,285 in 1992. It was this increase that alarmed the international community. Comparisons, however, were for the most part duly avoided. British Home Secretary Baker argued in November 1992 that Britain had to tighten its refugee policies because otherwise violence and racism would spill over from the Continent. He did so regardless of the fact that the stream of immigrants into Britain had almost entirely ceased during the 1980s, and that Britain's immigration/emigration ratio had even turned negative during several years.[13] He also did not take into consideration that at the time, more refugees landed in Germany than in all other European countries taken together.

The comparative perspective can be extended to non-European countries as well. In Canada, a country proud of its liberal immigration and multicultural policies, there may be as many as 9,000 hate-inspired crimes annually.[14] So-called "visible minorities" continue to suffer various forms of discrimination. When Mohawk warriors and Quebec police confronted each other during the 1990 Oka crisis, rocks were thrown by white bystanders as in Rostock. Sikh turbans are regarded by many as threat-

ening the established order of society, be it in the RCMP or among
veterans. Suspicions and evidence of racist orientations in police and
justice system have surfaced time and again. Despite relatively small
numbers (37,720 in 1992 as compared to 450,000 in Germany), and despite
a general amnesty in 1986, unfinished refugee files are piling up again.
Overall, the right-wing extremist potential may be about the same as in
Germany (plus/minus 15 percent). In sharp contrast to Germany, however,
racism is publicly condemned by all political parties. Individual extremist
attitudes cannot count on public toleration in a society where electoral
success is not possible without support from minority groups.[15]

When considering the electoral record, the German case does not
appear to be particularly exceptional. In France, Le Pen, who at one point
declared that the gas chambers of Auschwitz were a minor point in the
history of World War II, persistently receives 10 to 15 percent of the
national vote. In Italy, a neofascist party has been part of Berlusconi's
government coalition, which also included the *Lega*, a northern Italian
regionalist party with xenophobic sentiments towards southern Italian
migrant workers. And in Canada, the recently founded Reform Party, in its
drive to become a national political force, had to expel openly racist candidates from its roster, but it clearly operates within a far-right ideological
spectrum that appears attractive to extremist orientations. By comparison,
the German *Republikaner*, a radical right-wing party with obvious xenophobic and racist overtones, have enjoyed electoral successes similar to
those of the National Front in France, especially in regional and European
elections, but they were all but wiped off the political scene in the 1994
federal elections. However, this may have to do more with the major
parties' tactical move to the right that absorbed some of the *Republikaner*
voting potential than with the disappearance of that potential itself.

Germans reacted to the violent attacks against foreigners and asylants
in the fall of 1992 with the largest mass demonstrations since 1945.
Hundreds of thousands of citizens in Berlin, Munich, Hamburg, and elsewhere joined in the streets holding candles in order to demonstrate their
solidarity with foreigners. And even among the much maligned punker
youth of Germany, such solidarity with fellow-outsiders seems more
common than racist resentment. Inscriptions like "racism is stupid" on
their studded leather jackets appear to be far more frequent than the
display of extremist paraphernalia.

It can be argued that right-wing extremism in Germany is and is not a particularly alarming or exceptional case. It does not seem to go beyond experiences in other countries, quantitatively or qualitatively, and there are few if any indications that it will have a chance to become a particularly German problem once again. But, it appears that the kind of extremism associated with xenophobia and racism is more deeply than elsewhere rooted in a peculiarly German tradition of "genetic nationalism," and that mainstream political parties, especially the *Christlich Demokratische Union* (CDU) (Christian Democratic Union) and its Bavarian sister party, the *Christlich Soziale Union* (CSU) (Christian Social Union), are more willing to play this card for the sake of electoral fortunes.

Nationalism and Extremism

Nationalism as patriotism or group loyalty may be a natural part of the human social condition. People feel affinities towards those living in the same place with whom they share history and culture. Nevertheless, "nation is a construction of nationalists."[16]

The French nation was constructed as a political community of citizens after the Revolution of 1789. Nationalism in France came to be based on belonging to this community of citizens, on being part of *la grande nation*. French nationalism is not primarily based on positive self-identification in terms of ethnicity or race. Racism can and does surface negatively, as prejudice against what is perceived to be outside the community of citizens, but it is not grounded in the concept of nation itself. France is a country founded on political nationalism.

The German nation was constructed differently, out of notions of genetic descendance during the nineteenth century period of romanticism. Possibly because they did not at that moment have *une grande nation*, nor could refer to a revolution establishing citizenship, German nationalists entertained the historically untenable idea that there was an uninterrupted bloodline running from the Germanic tribes all the way to modern Germans. This idea proved to become the "most persistent of all German ideologies."[17] Germany, therefore, is a country founded on genetic nationalism.

Genetic nationalism became the ideological justification for Auschwitz. For Hitler, the Jews constituted a danger for the German nation precisely because they appeared so readily assimilated into German culture and life.

It was their willingness to become members of a German political and cultural community that threatened the idea of a genetically constructed nation. And after Auschwitz, when it was a widely held position that German nationalism had forfeited its right of existence for all times to come, the newly established West German state nevertheless ordained, in Article 116 of its Basic Law (*Grundgesetz*), that only ethnic Germans could immigrate with an automatic right of citizenship. This genetic determination of citizenship accounts for Germany's unwillingness to grant dual citizenship in general (because the dual conception of genetic nationalism is logically impossible), and to the millions of migrant workers (*Gastarbeiter*) in particular. It also lies at the heart of Germany's confused reaction to the swelling stream of asylum-seekers, mostly from former Soviet bloc countries,[18] and to the periodical violent outbursts against them by isolated groups of extremists.

Because these violent attacks coincided *with* the process of unification, and seemed to occur more often in the east than in the west, they were quickly interpreted as a problem *of* unification. Especially for young east Germans entering the work force, it was argued, the social transformations after 1989 constituted a double threat. The social costs of reunification in general and job competition from immigrant-foreigners in particular were perceived as existential irritants that ultimately triggered violence as acts of emotional compensation. But such classical "blame the victim" explanations are not valid.[19] They certainly do not account for the fact that resentment against foreigners in the western part of the new Germany appears higher than in the eastern part.[20] More generally, they do not take into consideration the specific historical situation that may have led to a resurgence of genetic nationalism as a breeding ground for racism and xenophobia.

Right-wing extremism in postunification Germany cannot be understood and explained sufficiently without taking a closer look at the general political culture of suppressed nationalism that characterized both German states throughout their divided postwar history.[21] Before 1945, all Germans had lived under a totalitarian regime of extremist nationalism. After the war, two separate German states were founded on radically different political cultures that were superimposed rather than developed as a process of unlearning. In the German Democratic Republic (GDR), the very notion of a German nation was suppressed by a socialist regime of bureaucratic authoritarianism claiming that it had eradicated all links to the past, and to the other German state that insisted on the continuity of one German nation.[22] That other state, the Federal Republic of Germany (FRG), acknowledged its historical responsibility for the fascist past in principle, but in practice escaped into an unpolitical materialism embedded in western market capitalism. The student movement of the 1960s, perhaps the first stirring of a more active and participatory understanding of democracy,[23] ironically rephrased that no longer sung line of the German national anthem "Germany over all" (*Deutschland über alles*) into "Export over all!" (*Export über alles*).

As a consequence, no one in either part of Germany had for a long time asked the historical as well as cultural question about what it meant to be German. But when unification became a possibility, suddenly and unexpectedly, there was no other justification for it than that of the one German nation.[24] Thus, when the necessity arose to construct unity, it had to be done on the basis of a concept of nation that had not been part of the official or popular political culture since the end of the war. It should not be surprising, then, that the discussion about nationalism and the German nation had to begin precisely where it had been left off, within the concept of genetic nationalism and its legalistic continuity in the West German Basic Law.

It also cannot be surprising that extremist manifestations of genetic nationalism would occur when the process of unity construction did not lead to the desired results immediately. In this context one must bear in mind that this process was a one-sided takeover (*Anschluss*). The political culture of the West was superimposed upon the East. With it not only came the hope for a quick material fix of the dullness of everyday life under "really existing socialism," but also the hard realities of a western market economy that had in fact changed its tune quite dramatically already well before 1989 from the social compromise of the postwar settlement years to a harsher climate of "desolidarization" (*Entsolidarisierung*).[25] This change of political orientation in the West German polity must be considered as a broader and more general environment conducive for the growth of extremist attitudes and actions.

Extremism and Political Culture

Right-wing radical parties had accompanied political life in the West German republic for some time. In 1969, the right-wing nationalist *Nationaldemokratische Partei Deutschlands* (NPD)

(National Democratic Party) narrowly failed to overcome the five percent hurdle of the national vote that would have allowed it to enter the Federal Parliament. However, it was during the later 1980s that a new right-wing party appeared on the scene, the *Republikaner*, scoring electoral successes in Bavaria (1986), West Berlin (1989), and in the European elections (1989). Right-wing parties did not play a role in the unification election of 1990, but soon afterwards the *Republikaner* and the *Deutsche Volksunion* (DVU) (German People's Union) began to invade German parliaments at the *Länder* and local level at an alarming rate. In the April 1992 election of Baden-Wuerttemberg, the *Republikaner* scored 10.9 percent and became the third largest party, ahead of both the liberal *Freie Demokratische Partei* (FDP) (Free Democratic Party) and *Die Grünen* (the Greens).[26]

Spectacular successes in the early 1990s again seemed to link right-wing extremism to the process of unification. What could be conveniently ignored is not only that right-wing radical parties scored consistently lower in the east, but moreover had first seen their electoral fortunes rise in the west and before unification was anywhere in sight. The search for explanations therefore has to begin with the transformations of the West German state and its political orientations during the 1980s.

As has been pointed out convincingly, there has never been one particularly German political culture. Instead, there are several strands which may or may not come to the fore according to time and circumstance.[27]

A first strand is the etatistic tradition. It arose from a conservative reaction against political pluralism in the nineteenth century, and it found widespread confirmation during the Weimar Republic's chaotic experience with party democracy. It has not been a dominant tradition in the postwar West German republic, but there may still be a tendency to call for a strong(er) state in times of insecurity or challenge. Indications are the state's overreaction to the student demonstrations in the 1960s as well as the massive increase of police and surveillance practices during the terrorist years of the 1970s. A point of illustration is perhaps that while police in France may in fact have clubbed down students more brutally than in Germany, the students could count on widespread support and sympathy among French citizens in general. German citizens were more likely to side with the police and the state.[28]

A second and closely related tradition is that of the unpolitical citizen. Elections are more seen as a duty than as a participatory possibility. Politics is regarded as a dirty business that ought to be left to professionals whose authority is rarely questioned even though that in turn increases suspicions about corruption and manipulation even further. The West German state has tried to overcome this democratic deficit through school curricula as well as special institutions dedicated to political education. But it was not until the rise of the social movements growing out of the student movement of the 1960s that political participation became a more widely accepted feature of political culture.

Third, there is a lingering tradition of political idealism. It tends to judge reality against the absolute yardstick of some utopian order and consequently dismisses all pragmatic efforts of reform and improvement as insufficient or even despicable. In times of crisis in particular, it cries for a totally new order that will eliminate all instability of small political steps. The orderly citizen then becomes the extremist follower. This tradition, which obviously helped the Nazis into power, has not seriously haunted the postwar West German republic. It resurfaced temporarily, however, in the radical fringes of the student movement that tended to see the West German state as corrupt in its entirety, if not as a new fascist beginning, and it may still be discerned, for example, among members of the fundamentalist faction within the Green Party.

A fourth element arising both out of the anti-revolutionary conservatism of the nineteenth century as well as the negative experience with party competition in the Weimar Republic is a tradition of conflict avoidance. Many Germans still mistrust the regulated conflicts of government and opposition, and they tend to see ideological struggles within and between parties as a sign of national weakness. They still yearn for a utopian regime of harmonized community in which conflicts can no longer upset the established order. This led to the orderly model of social compromise on which the stability of the West German state was based during much of the postwar period. But, it also triggered extremist reactions (on the left and right) among those who wanted an ideal community immediately and instead of what they saw as a continuity of compromised ideals.

Finally, there is a strong and, for the most part, undiminished tradition of political legalism. It is in many ways the summation and consequence of all previous ones, of idealism and compromise as obviously contradictory orientations, and of a political culture in which largely unpolitical citizens continue to yearn for extreme harmony and mistrust the political process as one of orderly conflict. The result is a tendency to escape into juridical and bureaucratic formalism. The political process is often regarded with disdain, but law and order are for the most part accepted uncritically. This accounts for the fact, for example, that while many Nazis resurfaced in the political and bureaucratic institutions of West Germany, Nazism did not. The same people now administered the law and order of a democratic state. The extremist had become the orderly citizen.

One can subdivide the formation of the postwar west German republic into three phases characterized by various combinations of these cultural traditions according to time and circumstance.[29] The first phase, 1949–60, was one of unfettered capitalist reconstruction, largely unchallenged by an unpolitical general public that was happy enough to find a job and some degree of comfortable material existence. This phase ended when full employment was reached by 1960, unions gained power, and a stable postwar settlement was reached on the basis of class compromise—acceptance of market capitalism in exchange for job stability and welfare security, at times mediated in corporatist arrangements between capital, labour, and the state.

It was a phase of growing political and social respectability, but it was also characterized by conflict avoidance and a turn to statist-legalistic regulation. At the first sign of an economic downturn, the major parties (CDU/CSU and *Sozialdemokratische Partei Deutschlands* (SPD) (Social Democratic Party of Germany)) entered a grand coalition that left the role of opposition to the tiny FDP (1966–69).[30] During the left-liberal government of Chancellor Willy Brandt, all major parties and governments agreed on the infamous policy statement of 1972 about "radicals in civil service" (*Radikalenerlass*). Members of extremist parties (mainly of the left) were considered unfit for public service, perhaps as many as a million citizens were screened, about a thousand were rejected or dismissed.[31]

This phase of centrist compromise and conflict avoidance ended with the oil shock which in turn spelled the end of the postwar growth phase. After the mid 1970s, painful cuts into social spending had to be administered, first by the social democrats under Chancellor Schmidt, and then, more asymmetrically, after the neoconservative "turnabout" (*Wende*) of 1982/83, under Helmut Kohl. This is when the foundations were laid for a radical turnabout in political orientations as well. The class compromise was cancelled by the politically and economically dominant classes and replaced by crisis regulation in the best etatistic tradition.[32] Consecutive rounds of industrial restructuring resulted in rising levels of persistent unemployment. Increasingly, responsibility could be passed on to

European Community regulations adopted through intergovernmental bargaining in which Germany played the dominant role nevertheless.

In this changed sociopolitical climate two diametrically opposed reactions changed the political landscape. More and more citizens realized that the dream of the great social compromise had irrevocably come to an end. They began to reject macropolitical constructions of society and turned to a deconstructed diversity of micropolitical goals.[33] This strengthened both the emerging party of the Greens who eventually appeared in the Federal Parliament (*Bundestag*) in 1983, and some 50,000 citizens' initiatives (*Bürgerinitiativen*) and social movements, which by the end of the 1970s comprised nearly as many members as the established parties.[34] But, far more citizens became politically disillusioned and turned to conservative pipedreams of a wholesome world of simple explanations and traditional values. This meant that the large establishment parties underwent a sharp move to the right. The West German polity returned to a sociopolitical climate of mainstream individualization and unquestioned (i.e., depoliticized) subject-object relations within a deregulated market economy.

In other words, new social movements, and the societal minorities they represented, held on to a participatory idealism that challenged the mainstream vision of a vigilant state protecting an insecure society from disorder. This became the political climate of "desolidarization" (*Entsolidarisierung*), in which toleration of outsiders and losers thinned. Resentment not only turned against cultural challenges from foreigners and asylants, but also against what was perceived as the deviant behaviour of, among others, feminists and homosexuals.[35] These and other groups did not really challenge the majority in power, but they challenged the moral and symbolic order in which society could feel secure.[36]

This leads to conclusions that, initially, do not appear specifically linked to the West German state and its political culture. As the comparisons with other countries such as Britain or Canada suggest in particular, right-wing extremist attitudes tend to grow out of social conditions of polarization. This happened during the years of the Weimar Republic, and it happened again, albeit on a much smaller scale, when the postwar settlement of class compromise was cancelled and replaced with a harsher environment of individualized market relations, a "culture of dependency" and "subjectivism."[37] Attacks on foreigners or homosexuals are not an organized part of that culture, but they are stimulated by it. They may be marginal manifestations of extremism, but they grow out of mainstream social conditions nevertheless.[38] Moreover, they cannot be simply pinned down on "losers," on the *Lumpenproletariat* at the lower end of modernization and restructuring processes. Instead, right-wing extremist orientations find support in all classes[39] because the perceived threat to the moral and symbolic order by those who do not seem to fit into the mainstream cuts across all segments of society.

In the specific German situation after unification, a few more concrete observations can be added. First of all, an enormous social polarization took place in West Germany during the 1980s that cannot be denied. Between 1980 and 1989, while net corporate profits rose by 139 percent, working incomes only saw an increase of 27 percent, hardly above the rate of inflation. It is this trend that is now being reproduced in east Germany as well.[40] An entire quintile of German society (east and west) may now be living near or below the poverty line,[41] and what counts here is not so much the absolute line of where poverty begins or ends, but instead the tremendous relative differential between rich and poor in one of the wealthiest countries in the world. The trend is being reinforced by policies of social security reduction, and by the parallel privatization of insurance for those who can afford it. Disparities within each of the two parts of the new Germany as well as across them have little chance of being balanced out in the foreseeable future.[42]

For the socioeconomic relationship of the two German parts this means that new walls have gone up, borders that only open when goods and transfers move east, or when young and mobile workers move west.[43] Immediately after unification, this triggered a short-lived economic boom, averting, for the moment, a recession that had already been knocking at West Germany's door. But when all the east German savings were used up, and the west German chocolate trucks stopped rolling into the former GDR, the recession hit, in early 1992. West German solidarity with their poorer east German cousins came to a halt. West German unionized workers in particular demanded that their wage increases would no longer be restrained by further transfers. After a strike shutting down Germany's airports, the public employee union reached a 5.4 percent wage settlement. East German workers realized that they could not count on union solidarity and that the promised wage parity, which would now require double-digit wage increases in the east, was out of reach, probably for generations.

This, then, can help to explain where, in a general political climate of social polarization, the voter potential for right-wing extremist parties may come from: disproportionately from skilled and unionized workers/ employees in the west who feel threatened in their relative position of security by a rapidly growing reserve army of labour; and east German youth who feel frustrated in their relative insecurity by the growing inaccessibility of meaningful and well paying jobs. Both sentiments appear linked to the cancellation of a class and welfare compromise that has been replaced by unleashed market forces. Radical right-wing reactions among west German workers may be motivated by an attempt to force a new compromise, and among east German youth to be part of it.[44]

The focus on foreigners and asylants may also give an indication what the compromise ought to be based on: on the construction of a more wholesome and closed world in which renewed nationalist sentiments of people-as-fate are to replace the rational-material crisis of globalizing socioeconomic relations. This is precisely what the political classes of West Germany pandered to in their populist efforts to pretend the availability of nationalist solutions to international problems.

Xenophobia and the Rise of Right-Wing Extremism

The rise of racist and xenophobic tendencies in Germany's public political discourse can be analysed in three consecutive phases.[45] The first phase began in the late 1970s as a successful attempt of the Christian-conservative parties to drive the social democrats out of government. Already during the mid 1970s, the CDU in Baden-Württemberg had campaigned for a "Swiss model" of foreign worker rotation in order to bring, in the words of then Minister President Hans Filbinger, "young and fresh" workers into the country. But now, the Bavarian CSU and the right wing of the CDU started a concerted campaign that focussed on the alleged need to reduce the number of Turks and asylants. With the help of the conservative media, the negative term "asylant" was created, replacing the more positive term "refugee." By 1980, the general political climate had changed to such an extent that even Chancellor Schmidt, who generally criticized the "cynical exploitation of latent xenophobia" by Christian politicians, opposed the SPD plan of extending municipal voting rights to foreigners as deleterious to the party's electoral chances. In the electoral campaign of 1982/83, the foreigner question had become one the CDU/CSU's four main policy issues.

However, the topic disappeared from political discourse and the media when the main parties tacitly agreed to drop it. After Kohl's 1983 electoral victory, his conservative-liberal coalition did little or nothing in order to follow up on earlier campaign rhetoric. Only the liberal FDP and the right-wing Bavarian CSU battled on, without any significant result on government policy. The general public appeared to remain ambivalent about the issue during this second phase of xenophobic calm. Nevertheless, it was this phase that saw the rise and first electoral successes of a new radical party to the right of CDU/CSU. Obviously, the issue, raised by conservative politicians for electoral purposes and then dropped again when in power, had not gone away.

In 1986, Franz Josef Strauß, the charismatic populist leader of the Bavarian CSU, readily supported once again by the conservative media, launched a second campaign against foreigners before the *Land* elections of that year. It may have won him another absolute majority, but hanging onto Strauß's coat-tails, the newly founded *Republikaner* scored their first (even though insignificant) electoral result. They would soon do better, once again forcing the asylum issue into the general political discourse. The leader of the *Republikaner*, Franz Schönhuber, a disgruntled former member at the far-right fringe of the CSU, maintained close contacts to Strauß. In the words of a leading conservative pollster, the *Republikaner* emerged as "a legitimate daughter of the CSU and of Franz Josef Strauß."

This development then prepared the grounds for the third phase. First, the sudden process of unification temporarily seemed to remove negative sentiments about foreigners altogether. They neither had a place in the media spectacle of opening borders, nor in the unification election of 1990. But already one year after unification, the Christian parties and right-wing media heated up the asylum debate again. Liberal and truly Christian dissenters within their own ranks were silenced, or, as the CDU's secretary general, Heiner Geissler, ousted. The *Bild-Zeitung*, Germany's most widely read right-wing tabloid, tried to increase its circulation with a xenophobic billboard campaign. The political climate of relative toleration deteriorated, especially in the west, as the numbers of asylum-seekers did begin to escalate and serious housing shortages led to the erection of portable refugee barracks in communal soccer stadiums and middle-class suburban neighbourhoods. This in turn triggered not only the spectacular successes of right-wing radical parties in subsequent *Land* elections, but at least indirectly also those violent attacks against foreigners and asylants that stirred up international concern. These attacks were isolated incidents, for the most part carried out by young people under 20 years of age (in east and west), but they were nevertheless misguided expression of a radicalized public climate.

It was reported that during the spring 1992 electoral campaign in Baden-Württemberg, where they scored their best result of 10.9 percent, the *Republikaner* had simply photocopied and distributed articles from the *Bild-Zeitung*. The CDU, trying to stem the tide by echoing many of the *Republikaner* positions, lost its absolute majority. On the basis of similar outcomes elsewhere, it began to dawn on all major parties that their electoral strategy of populist chumming up to right-wing radicalism had begun to backfire. In December 1992, they finally agreed to concerted rearguard action, by curtailing what had arguably been the most liberal constitutional regulation of asylum law in all of Europe. The obvious hope now was that with decreasing numbers of admitted asylum-seekers, the issue would finally go away as well.

It can be argued that this late reaction of Germany's political classes lagged behind that of the German public at large. As several polls at the time showed, xenophobia and right-wing radicalism had already begun to decline dramatically in German public opinion as a consequence of the string of violent attacks against foreigners during the fall of 1992. During that time, the CSU still declined an invitation by the German President Richard von Weizsäcker to participate in a large antiviolence demonstration in Berlin. The press secretary of the federal government belittled public demands for leading politicians to participate in demonstrations of solidarity with the victims of racist attacks as a call for "condolence tourism." Only when another round of violence shook Germany even after the constitutional change of asylum law should have put an end to it, did all major political parties unequivocally join in a universal condemnation of extremism. But a certain reluctance on the part of the federal government was to be noted nevertheless. It repeatedly left it to the foreign minister to voice such condemnation—as if crimes against foreigners committed in Germany were mainly a problem of German reputation abroad, and not a problem at home.

How can one try to explain this rather unsavory behaviour by Germany's dominant political classes, and especially those who carry the label

"Christian"? Most German politicians, including the late Franz Josef Strauß, were not driven by xenophobia or any other form of political extremism. But they were prepared to play this card when it fit into their political calculations. Since the late 1970s, all western industrialized states were suffering a growing erosion of national political control in the wake of accelerating economic globalization. Questions of immigration and asylum offered a convenient avenue of symbolic nationalist grandstanding, which could deflect from the increasing helplessness in organizing other traditional national values such as security, welfare, and culture.[46]

Especially when social democratic governments in power were driven into administering budget cuts and welfare reductions, conservative oppositions had to invent other themes that could catch popular attention. As opposition leader in 1978, Margaret Thatcher began to conjure up a vision of Britain "swamped" by too many immigrants. In his electoral campaign for mayor of Paris in 1984, Jacques Chirac defined his position towards North African immigrants as "neither racism, nor laxness." And in Germany, Franz Josef Strauß demagogically played up the asylum question when he ran against Helmut Schmidt in 1980. In these cases, the exaggerated populist rhetoric was not born out by the actual numbers.[47] This was the rhetoric of "semantic overdetermination" that created the space for those with a more decidedly extremist agenda.

When in power, mainstream conservatives tended to drop the theme again, availing themselves of other national issues. In Britain, Prime Minister Thatcher battled the Falklands and the unions. In France, a newly elected President Chirac would eventually return to nuclear grandstanding. In Germany, such options were not available. Caught in the narrow confines of nationalism defined as genetic nationalism only, and by the sudden need to give national justifications for the costs of unification, German conservatives in power could not leave the issue to the radical fringe. In modified form, it had to become part of the mainstream political agenda.

In 1994, Germans as well as the international community breathed a sigh of relief. The *Republikaner* as well as the German People's Union were all but wiped from the political scene, unable to secure a single seat in eight *Länder* as well as the federal and European elections of that year.[48] Werner Weidenfeld, a prominent political science professor and close advisor of Chancellor Kohl in European and North American relations, triumphantly presented this electoral outcome as a result of Germany's asylum law restrictions, which had gone into effect in July 1993. A far less congenial interpretation appears more plausible, though.[49] The right-wing extremist parties had in fact influenced if not determined the major parties' political agenda during the election year. The entire German party system had shifted to the right. The discourse of right-wing radicalism had become implanted into the centre of German politics. The tactical defeat of extremist parties in 1994 was not a safe indicator of their electoral chances in the future.

If this interpretation is correct only in part, it casts a lasting shadow on the prospects of German political culture once again. The immigration and asylum debate may have been the tip of an iceberg only. "Desolidarization" can easily spread to other segments of society that appear to threaten the conformist mainstream, especially when that mainstream has been shaken by dramatic events and transformations. Feminists, homosexuals, or welfare mothers may be next.

However, the populist exploitation of conformist, intolerant, and callous predispositions latent in societies based on individualized competition certainly is not akin to the Germans alone. What is called a "common sense revolution" by the recently elected conservative provincial government of Ontario in Canada, for example, appears based on the populist exploitation of very similar predispositions. Doubtlessly, Canadian conservatives have been pushed to the right by the agenda-setting Reform Party, who in 1997 were given Official Opposition status. Doubtlessly, both are in turn influenced by the politics of "desolidarization" enfolding in American society south of their border. For Germany, a country more than any other embedded in, and committed to, the process of European integration, much will depend on how such predispositions are going to be handled by its neighbours as well. It is no longer a German question alone. Even the German *Sonderweg* of genetic nationalism will eventually come under European scrutiny. The question and issue of solidarity is becoming globalized as well.

A Universal Phenomenon?

In one of his most controversial statements after the war, Martin Heidegger remarked in 1949, before a private audience of liberal-conservative industrialists and merchants in Bremen, that: "Farming is now a motorised food industry; it is in essence the same as the fabrication of corpses and gas chambers."[50]

In part, this may have been Heidegger's way of explaining his own past. He had attached his philosophical yearning for a world in which real being would be purified from mere existence, to the Nazi movement because he saw in it all the trimmings of a more wholesome organization of social life based on folk, fate, and fear. He had erred, however, because he did not anticipate that this movement would more than ever fall victim to technical solutions of purification—including the holocaust, which was the most perverted form of technical determinism (*Machenschaften*).

More significantly, Heidegger's provocative comparison marked the beginning of his last philosophical phase almost entirely devoted to a critique of the modern technical world. Taken seriously, it could open paths to a more subtle understanding of extremism than the crude nationalist revisionism that surfaced in the "historians' dispute" (*Historikerstreit*) of 1986. Obviously coinciding with Strauß's second round of playing up the foreigner issue, and with the rise of the *Republikaner* to national notoriety, conservative historians had begun to question the Holocaust as a unique and uniquely German phenomenon. They opposed the view of "critical" historians and social scientists who maintained that only a permanent radical questioning of the German traditions of the past could lead to the acceptance of a new and democratic Germany. Instead, they argued that the Holocaust had been an aberration from German traditions, which should not be thrown overboard in their entirety. Of particular infamy was the attempt by Ernst Nolte, in the pages of the conservative *Frankfurter Allgemeine Zeitung*, to distinguish between a "European" and "Asiatic" tradition, claiming that Hitler's crimes had in fact been inspired by Stalin's *gulags* and therefore constituted something alien to the true spirit of European and German history.[51]

By comparison, Heidegger's insight soon after the war had located the fundaments of the Holocaust elsewhere—in the technocratic disposition of modern human existence. It was a universal phenomenon and a very German one at the same time. Universal was the disavowal of nature and human being in a reified world of formalized technology. This is what motorized agriculture and the Holocaust ultimately have in common. Both are driven by an alienated obsession with technical control and power. Extremist orientations are fed both by this obsession, and by the insecurity about the human condition that it breeds. Germany was the juxtaposition of etatistic and unpolitical traditions which, by endorsing a leadership mentality instead of civic consciousness, led to the formalistic totality of final solutions (*Endlösung*).

In reviewing the last 45 years of German history, there can be no doubt that the Germans have changed. Contrary to those who now wish to conjure up a revisionist view of the past, the vast majority of Germans has adopted a solid sense of what Habermas has called "constitutional patriotism."[52] It exists apart from whatever baggage of genetic nationalism may be carried on into the future as well. It can also be assumed that this constitutional patriotism—or civic culture—has been successfully exported into the eastern part of the new Germany as well.[53]

The fact that some 20 percent of east Germans voted for the post-communist *Partei des Demokratischen Sozialismus* (PDS) (Party of Democratic Socialism) in 1994, and therefore endorsed a party of the radical left (rather than right), does not necessarily constitute evidence to the contrary. Insofar as members of the old communist cadre live on in this party, the same argument applies as in 1945 with regard to Nazism and the Nazis: communists have survived, but not communism. Preliminary evidence, however, shows that the PDS appears disproportionately endorsed by younger and more educated voters. This can neither be explained as mere protest behaviour of losers, nor as a fall-back into older patterns of a political culture dualized between official state authoritarianism and a largely unpolitical private sphere. Instead, it may indicate the emergence of a new civic culture indeed. East Germans are learning to behave politically. They do not, on the whole, appear to hang on to the authoritarian orderliness of the old regime, but neither are they prepared to endorse uncritically the individualized extremism of the new regime.[54]

Far more troublesome appears that the disavowal of nature and human being in a reified world of formalized technological constraints more than ever marks the universal condition of the world. If political extremism is the uglier other side of that condition, then it is no longer a problem of Germany and the Germans. It has indeed long-since transcended the borderlines of German history and political culture. The *Sonderweg* has become a precarious path for all of humanity.

NOTES

1. In order to narrow down what already appears as a daunting undertaking, this article will only deal with right-wing extremism. There may be only one justification for this selectiveness. The kind of left-wing extremism and terrorism that haunted the West German state during much of the 1970s has for all practical purposes ceased to be a relevant factor in the united Germany, and likely in a post-Communist world more generally.

2. See the exceptionally thorough and carefully balanced biography by Rüdiger Safranski, *Ein Meister aus Deutschland: Heidegger und seine Zeit* (Munich: Hanser, 1994).

3. See Safranski, *Ein Meister aus Deutschland*, p. 247.

4. Safranski, *Ein Meister aus Deutschland*, esp. chapters 5–8.

5. This interpretation deliberately challenges the thesis of the so-called postmaterialist value change, which claims that the change of value orientation was a generational consequence of experienced affluence.

6. See in particular Iris Marion Young, *Justice and the Politics of Difference* (Princeton: Princeton University Press, 1990).

7. Walter Biemel, paraphrased in *Masterpieces of World Philosophy*, ed. Frank M. Magill (New York: Harper Collins, 1990), p. 544.

8. As Safranski reports, Heidegger very much enjoyed appearances before lay audiences when he was banned from academic teaching during the first years after World War II.

9. Alfons Soellner, "Von der 'multikulturellen Gesellschaft' zur 'Republik' und wieder zurück? Eine Diskussion neuerer Literatur," in *Politikwissenschaft als kritische Theorie*, ed. Michael Th. Greven et al. (Nomos: Baden-Baden, 1994), p. 302.

10. Following again Safranski's well documented and scrupulously discreet account. Safranski also reports an anecdote from the early 1930s when Heidegger came back from negotiations with the Nazis in Berlin. Alluding to Plato's ill-fated trip to the Sicilian dictator Dionysos, a colleague meeting him in the streets of Freiburg asked Heidegger: "Back from Syracuse?"

11. Thomas Herz, "Politische Kultur im neuen Staat," *Prokla* 23, no. 2 (1993): 231.

12. Surely, that goes for left-wing extremism just as well. Contrary to the situation in the 1970s, when left-wing terrorism of the Baader-Meinhof kind held the West German republic in its grip, it has been right-wing extremism that defined conflict in the late 1980s and early 1990s.

13. Dietrich Thränhardt, "Die Ursprünge von Rassismus und Fremdenfeindlichkeit in der Konkurrenzdemokratie," *Leviathan* 21, no. 3 (1993): 338–39.

14. Contrary to the numbers for racially motivated crimes in Britain and Germany, this number, based on a confidential study commissioned by the federal justice department, includes gay-bashing and other forms of hate crimes; *Maclean's* 14 August 1994, pp. 40–43.

15. See Heribert Adam, "Fremdenfeindlichkeit, Einwanderungspolitik und Multikulturalismus in Kanada und Deutschland," *Leviathan* 22, no. 1 (1994): 60–77.

16. This argument loosely follows Peter Widmann's review of theories of nationalism by Benedict Anderson and Eric Hobsbawm, "Die nationale Leidenschaft: Benedict Anderson und Eric Hobsbawm über die Nation," *Leviathan* 22, no. 2 (1994): 171–78.

17. Soellner, "Von der multikulturellen Gesellschaft," pp. 308–9.

18. The majority of those migrating into Germany, however, are ethnic Germans who receive their passports without further discussion.

19. See Thomas Herz, "Politische Kultur im neuen Staat," *Prokla* 23, no. 2 (1993): 231–50, and Alex Demirovic, "Rechtsextremismus in der Bundesrepublik," in *Rechtsextremismus und Fremdenfeindlichkeit*, ed. Institut für Sozialforschung (Frankfurt/Main: Campus, 1994), pp. 29–57.

20. See Demirovic, "Rechtsextremismus," p. 41.

21. I owe this point to Wilhelm Bleek.

22. To some extent, this was not an entirely unfounded claim. The GDR was constructed and administered by socialist-communist forces that by definition had been opposed to the Nazi regime and persecuted by it. The point was not lost on these communist leaders that in the west many former Nazis only too quickly found their way back into public office.

23. Thus Kurt Sontheimer, *Deutschlands politische Kultur* (Munich: Piper, 1990), p. 27.

24. See Hartmut Häussermann, "Über nationales Bewusstsein im neuen Deutschland," *Leviathan* 20, no. 1 (1992): 9–14.

25. See Elmar Brähler and Hans-Jürgen Wirth, eds., *Entsolidarisierung* (Opladen: Westdeutscher Verlag, 1995).

26. See Gordon Smith, "The 'New' Party System," in *Developments in German Politics*, ed. Gordon Smith et al. (Houndmills: Macmillan, 1992), pp. 100–101, and Brigitte Young, "The German Political Party System and the Contagion From the Right," *German Politics and Society* 13, no. 1 (1995): 63. During the super election year 1994, the *Republikaner* failed in eight *Land* elections as well as the federal and European elections.

27. The following is based on Sontheimer, *Deutschlands politische Kultur*, pp. 33–40.

28. As a student, the author of this chapter witnessed both, in Paris and Munich during the spring and summer of 1968.

29. See Thomas O. Hueglin, "The Politics of Limited Pluralism: West Germany as a Paradigmatic Case," *Studies in Political Economy* 28 (1989): 111–36.

30. This may account for the eventual rise of extremism on the left and right: as both major parties moved towards the centre, they alienated the radical fringe. The SPD formally expelled its radical student wing, SDS, which helped to trigger a fateful escalation of radical activism, leading from "extraparliamentary opposition" (*Außerparlamentarische Opposition*) (APO), to violence against department stores and media headquarters, and finally into the terrorist underground. The development of this radicalization can be followed in the writings of Ulrike Meinhof, 1959–69, in *Die Würde des Menschen ist antastbar* (Berlin: Wagenbach, 1994).

31. See the excellent discussion in Gordon Smith, *Democracy in West Germany*. (Aldershot: Gower, 1986), pp. 222–26. A typical case would be the one of a young historian, friend of the author, who was denied appointment as high school teacher during the mid 1970s because her car had been seen and photographed near a student demonstration with communist participation half a decade earlier, and who was not willing to swear an oath that she had not been a participant in that demonstration.

32. See convincingly Leo Panitch, "The Tripartite Experience," in *The State and Economic Interests*, ed. Keith Banting (Toronto: University of Toronto Press, 1986).

33. Compare somewhat similarly Klaus von Beyme, *Das politische System der Bundesrepublik Deutschland* (Munich: Piper, 1981), p. 93.

34. This interpretation once again modifies standard theories of postmaterialist value change. The turn to micropolitics was a change in the style and goal orientation of political activity, not just a turn to postmaterial values that had survived in the affluent 1960s

generation. Moreover, these new goals comprised both material and nonmaterial aspects of social life, which were regarded as inseparable rather than alternative choices.

35. See the empirical study of Albrecht Köhl and Roland Schürhoff, "Entsolidarisierung: Das Verhältnis der Westdeutschen zu Minderheiten und Randgruppen," in *Entsolidarisierung*, ed. Braehler and Wirth, pp. 70–87.

36. See Adam, "Fremdenfeindlichkeit," p. 67, with similar observations about Canada.

37. Thränhardt, "Die Ursprünge von Rassismus," p. 336.

38. Thränhardt, "Die Ursprünge von Rassismus," p. 353.

39. Karl-Heinz Hörning, "Das Fremde und das Eigene," in *Die Bedrohung der Demokratie von rechts*, ed. Manfred Sicking and Alexander Lobe (Cologne: Bund, 1993), p. 134.

40. See Gunter E. Zimmermann, "Neue Armut und neuer Reichtum," *Gegenwartskunde* 44, no. 1 (1995): 5–18.

41. Thus estimated by Thomas Ellwein (personal interview, August 1995). At the opposite end of the political spectrum, Hans Magnus Enzensberger came to exactly the same estimate. See Georg Kohler and Martin Meyer, eds., *Die Folgen von 1989* (Munich: Hanser, 1994), p. 22.

42. Heiner Gaussmann, "Einigung als Angleichung? Sozialpolitische Folgen des deutschen Einigungsprozesses," *Prokla* 91, no.2 (1993): 185–203.

43. On this and the following, see Peter Neckermann, "What Went Wrong in Germany After the Unification?" *East European Quarterly* 26, no. 4 (1993): 458–63.

44. See Demirovic, "Rechtsextremismus," pp. 45–46.

45. Thränhardt, "Die Ursprünge von Rassismus," pp. 339–52; all reported facts and developments in the following section are taken from his account. Thränhardt's analysis is based on a comparison of Germany, France, and Britain. It demonstrates significant similarities at least for the first and second phase. This changes in phase three when unification problems lead to more specific German developments.

46. See Michael Zürn, "Jenseits der Staatlichkeit: Über die Folgen der ungleichzeitigen Denationalisierung," *Leviathan* 20, no. 4 (1993): 490–513.

47. Thränhardt, "Die Ursprünge von Rassismus," pp. 340–43.

48. They did receive between 1.1 and 3.9 percent in those elections, but they did no longer jump across the five percent hurdle that German electoral law prescribes in order to receive any seats.

49. See Young, *Justice,* pp. 62–78; here in particular p. 63.

50. Quoted in Safranski, *Ein Meister aus Deutschland,* p. 475.

51. See the documentation *Forever in the Shadow of Hitler?* transl. by James Knowlton and Truett Cates (New Jersey: Humanities Press, 1993); a brief description can be found in Peter Pulzer, "Political Ideology," in *Developments in German Politics*, ed. Gordon Smith et al., pp. 320–21.

52. Quoted in Pulzer, "Political Ideology," p. 320.

53. This would explain why Thomas Ellwein, one of the most knowledgeable analysts of the German political system past and present, insists that serious disruptions in particular of the federal-administrative system are not to be expected (personal interview, August 1995). East Germans already have internalized the trend towards a more micropolitical orientation of political life. Especially at the communal-municipal level, their representatives emulate exactly the same behaviour as their western counterparts.

54. Henry Kreikenbom, University of Jena, presentation at Wilfrid Laurier University (September 1995).

7 "Social Market Economy" and West German Identity

DIETER HASELBACH

| "Up to now, the most successful concep-
tion of economic policy in the history of
mankind undoubtedly is the 'social market
economy,' which was implemented by
Ludwig Erhard."[1]

Under the label of "social market economy," Germany's economic order became
both very popular among Germans and the envy of other countries that had not
fared so well in economic recovery after the Second World War. It was possible to
demonstrate to the world that Germany, like the mythical Phoenix, could rise from
the ashes by using her own talents and her industriousness. The "economic
miracle" and the "social market economy" soon served as a prime source of a
renewed West German self-confidence.

In popular understanding, "social market economy" meant both a departure
from the regulated economy in Nazi Germany and from the Soviet-planned
economy. At the same time, as "social" capitalism, it cushioned its participants
from uncontrolled market forces. This popular conception was not identical with
the meaning that the "social market economy" had for the group of economists
who had invented the term and who held some influence over economic policies in
the early decades of the Federal Republic of Germany (FRG). Nevertheless,
distorted as its understanding may have been, its success was important to the
rebuilding of Germany.

To a large degree, the popularity of the "social market economy," both at home
and abroad, can be attributed to the successes that West Germany's economy
enjoyed from the late 1940s on. The postwar boom was marked by an extraordinary
growth rate and an extraordinarily fast recovery from the scattered war economy. In
the years immediately after the end of the war, for the great majority of Germans,

both living conditions and the economic outlook had been very bleak indeed. Merely returning to a bare minimum of economic functionality, in order to overcome hunger and to restore bearable housing conditions, had appeared to be beyond even the most optimistic expectations for many years to come. Given these expectations, the unexpected growth that the country experienced, leading to a moderate degree of wealth only a decade after the end of the war, looked like an economic miracle to the contemporaries.

In comparative terms, the "German economic miracle," as it was soon labeled in Germany and abroad, was paralleled by good economic performance in other postwar economies. There is something to be said for the view that the economy in the years after the war made up for the growth potential lost during the war. A more detailed analysis of the economics of the "German economic miracle" reveals that it was not all that miraculous, but can be explained by more "down to earth" factors. Doubts must be raised as to whether it really was the success of the "social market economy" policy that brought about the upturn or whether there were other more weighty preconditions that must be factored in.

Economic developments in postwar West Germany are better explained by looking at multiple facets and determinants of the fast recovery than by giving most of the credit to the concept and policy of the "social market economy." Due to the successes of postwar West Germany, the concept of the "social market economy" gained far more popularity and recognition than one would normally expect in a country's population at large regarding matters of economic policy. The "social market economy" and the excitement over matters of economic development are more fully characterized if one conceptualizes them as a West German state of mind. The "social market economy" constitutes in part West Germany's self-consciousness; it forms the specific "identity" of the West German people. In other words, the "economic miracle" and the "social market economy" constitute the founding myth of West Germany. They are—to use Gaetano Mosca's term[2]—the core "political formula" legitimizing the state of rulership and domination in postwar Germany. In this respect, more than an economic policy, the "social market economy" contributed to the amazing political stability in West Germany. It is also a factor to reckon with in comprehending some crucial features of the West German polity.

One has to recall where Germany came from in order to value the importance of this "political formula." With the end of the Nazi rule, Germans could not deny that the country had done wrong. For those who were not in a desperate mood of defiance, all chance had been lost to formulate a positive identification with Germanness and Germany's recent history. However, it is next to impossible for societies to function over an extended period of time without some such positive identification. This explains the enormous importance of the German identification with the "economic miracle." In their economic success, the West Germans could find positive identification again; the economy became a source of pride.

Another factor heightened the importance of economic performance in West Germany. After Germany's division and the formation of two states on opposite sides of the Cold War's political divide, the two countries were pitted against each other in direct competition:

> Each intended, once division was unavoidable, that its state would be a shop-window for its favored political and economic order; each assumed that it would act as a magnet for the discontented population of the other side.[3]

In terms of economic performance, the eastern German Democratic Republic (GDR) was falling behind the West already in the 1950s.[4] Thus, in the West, economic success also served as a unifying experience in competition with the East. In the East, questions of economy were crucial as well. In comparing their performance with the Western wealth, Easterners tended to put the blame for failures on the planning system, that was not capable of awakening this German industriousness (which they also felt capable of) from potentiality to actuality.

All this makes the importance of the economy for postwar Germany plausible. It also makes clear the extent to which economics became a field that substituted for disgraced politics. The substitution of politics by economics had a replay in Germany's unification after 1989: collective memory turned back on the "heroic years" of West Germany's economic success and the population of both East and West Germany expected a similar miracle to take place, once the East was liberated from the burden of a planned economy. However, this was not to happen. The discrepancy between expectations and the still bleak economic perspectives of Germany's east explain much of the disillusionment and the feeling of betrayal that has become the public mood in unified Germany.

▌ The Founding Tale

The following is an idealized version of a narrative that many Germans who have lived through the postwar period would tell in one way or another. This is even true for people who were skeptical at the time or who were even hostile toward an economic policy that clearly disadvantaged them.[5] This is the *founding myth* of West Germany.

West German history starts with an "Hour Zero" in May 1945. Whatever took place before this time is not to be conceptualized as part of West German history, since after 1945 it was claimed that the past had no more relevance for the present. Thus, it may as well be forgotten. The only heritage of the time before was that Germany's economy was completely crushed. Everyday life was characterized by misery, destruction, and hunger; people did not see much of a future for themselves. Estimates suggested that it would take about a generation's work to clear the rubble from German cities. Up to 1948, there was not much improvement; everyday life was still grim and shortages and breakdowns of an over-stretched infrastructure were legion. It is believed that the hardship was a result of both the war's destruction and the planned economy that was inherited from national socialism. This deadly mix of destruction and economic failure prevented any improvement; so it was the black market, hunger, and a lack of the most urgent consumer goods that shaped everyday life.

As in any good tale, misery is at its deepest when changes are about to appear. It was the political initiative and the vision of the genius politician Ludwig Erhard that made the misery turn into success. As a result of the currency reform of 1948 and his liberal program for a new economic policy, he put West Germany on a path of economic growth that it did not leave until the 1970s, when the lack of economic understanding of a social democratic government weakened Germany's economic performance. But even the Social Democrats were not able to entirely destroy the successful economic order. The program that Erhard had put in effect was the "social market economy" (*Soziale Marktwirtschaft*). This economic doctrine is much more than a label for a successful economic policy. The "social market economy" has saved the West German people from hunger and despair; the "social market economy" was the event that made the West German successful and thus respectable again; the "social market economy" enabled West Germany to overcome the past. Looking at this catalogue of achievements, it becomes understandable why a recent author declared the "social market economy" to be "[u]p to now, the most successful conception of economic policy in the history of mankind."[6] This was said by a marginal writer who is primarily a lobbyist for the German *Mittelstand* (literally, "middle estate") small scale businesses. However, such a statement is not more than slightly ridiculous, since it represents a widespread belief in Germany.

In the summer of 1948, on the 20th of June, was the day of currency reform. Each West German got a sum of DM 40, new money replacing the inflation-stricken *Reichsmark*. For a moment, everybody was equal. Unfortunately for the others, some soon proved to be more equal by owning assets, real estate, or other valuables beyond the initial DM 40 and the second supply of another DM 20. Although currency reform could strike one as a rather technical operation, there was more glory to the event. The highly respected French economist Jacques Rueff noted:

> The night before, the Germans were roaming the cities to get hold of scarce additional nutrition [over and above the available rations]; the day after [currency reform], their only thought was how to produce. The day before, hopelessness was drawn on their faces; the day after, an entire nation faced a future full of hope.[7]

What had happened? What was Rueff referring to? The black market had disappeared in one day. The lack of food and commodities had ended overnight. Shop windows that had been decorated with emptiness the day before were now dressed up. Everything seemed to be available. The only limitation to the craving (or, more appropriately, lust) for shopping, after the currency reform, seemed to be the limited monetary resources of the individual. After years of starvation, the currency reform looked like an economic miracle, indeed. Since then, the "economic miracle" and the *Deutsche Mark*, the name of the newly introduced currency, have become almost synonymous with the coincidence of the currency reform and the end of the postwar misery. The new currency received a healthy dose of magic, which it has not lost since then.[8]

The tale of the "social market economy," the currency reform, the extraordinary growth in the 1950s and 1960s, and Germany's position as the "world champion in export"[9] is referred to almost every day, somewhere in a German newspaper or political statement; it has become part of the national memory. Even in times of lesser successes, the economic miracle remains the frame of reference, and a restoration of the "social market economy," at every occasion, is proposed as a cure for economic difficulties.

The person responsible for Germany's extraordinary economic success was Germany's minister of Economics, Ludwig Erhard, who masterminded the miracle and who molded the first 15 years of West German economic policies. For Jacques Rueff he was something like the god of Economics, staffing the Pantheon of gods of the Latter Days:

As a result of a rare coincidence of otherwise mostly contradictory qualities, he is at one and the same time a man of reflection and of action. Whoever has heard his inspiring speeches understands full well that he knows what he wants and that he wants what he knows. By virtue of the coercive logic of his thought and his unbreakable will it was he who was first in Europe to turn the neoliberal [North American readers should read "neoconservative"] program into a success.[10]

This is, in brief, the mythical tale of the foundation of a nation that sees herself as economically successful. This myth is powerful because the events it refers to all happened as told. West Germany's postwar economic recovery and development was a success story. Germany's currency, along with the Japanese *Yen*, is still one of the most appreciated currencies in the world, even to the extent that its strength now threatens to strangle the competitiveness of Germany's industrial exports. To refer to this success story as an economic miracle might be an exaggeration, yet it is an understandable one, considering the contrast between the time before and after the currency reform, as well as the expectations of an impoverished population in the late 1940s.

Is there a lesson to be learned from the "social market economy"? Referring to the narrative presented it would be the following: a good and stable currency is the prerequisite for a successful economy. Economic recovery has to start with getting monetary things in order. Then, self-sustaining growth can and will happen, if one carefully follows the example of liberal economic policy and fine tuning, as given by Ludwig Erhard. This should be the formula for a successful economy.

Tales and Realities

But this is not the whole story. Research in recent economic history has added some shades to the picture that make the economic miracle appear less miraculous. The miracle of economic recovery becomes convincing partly because of the claim that West Germany, at the ominous "Hour Zero," started from scratch. Some doubts have to be raised here. Furthermore, the currency reform was not exactly what it appeared to be. The currency reform did not kick off recovery; it was no more then a carefully staged step in a process of putting the economy back on a path of growth. Finally, the "social market economy" is not as clear a concept and not as stringent a policy as it appears.[11]

Did Germany start from scratch? In economic terms, there was never an "Hour Zero." The economic recovery of West Germany after the war relied heavily on what had been inherited from the success of the Nazi economy. Under National Socialism, and particularly during the war, Germany's economy had been successful mainly for two reasons. First, with her military acquisitions, Germany had access to an almost limitless labour force in the occupied territories. She could redesign whole national economies to accommodate her needs and exploit raw materials she had gained access to. Second, economic planning in Nazi Germany was quite successful. The Nazis succeeded in combining the resources that were at their disposal with the initiative of the inherited economy of Germany, an economy based on private property. Economic planning under National Socialism was by no means Soviet-style central state planning; it did not rely on systematic expropriation.[12] Contrary to the Soviet economic doctrine, Nazi economic planning was performed in close collaboration with German big industry. All in all, and due to Nazi successes, a highly modern industrial stock was inherited by Germany's postwar economy. The enormous destruction which resulted from Allied bombardment and from war activities on German soil in the final weeks of the war made a big dent in Germany's economic power, but it affected housing and the infrastructure of transportation much more than it did industry proper. Much of the industrial stock was surprisingly undamaged and was up to the period's standards of technology and productivity. This gave Germany an economic advantage over countries that had to bear the brunt of fighting during the Second World War and that had not had the spare capacities to modernize their stock to the extent that the Germans had been able to.[13] In conclusion, preconditions for the later rise from the ashes were in place as a result of the Nazi war economy, despite the substantial war damage. Thus, it was not so much the policy of the "social market economy," but the heritage of what had fallen into West German possession, that explains part of the "miracle." The successes of Nazi planning also make it obvious that there is some hypocrisy in the claim later made by supporters of the "social market economy" that the planned economy in Nazi Germany had produced an economic mess.

But what about currency reform and the visible, immediate improvements of economic performance? The currency reform was only successful in 1948 because Germany was already on a path of economic recovery as early as 1947. The currency reform made the recovery visible, but it did not cause it. The precondition of this recovery was a carefully crafted policy of central allocation of scarce resources (thus, central economic planning) that had succeeded in overcoming the bottlenecks that had existed mainly in energy supply and transportation.

The currency reform was not the initial step to get Germany's economy on a growth path. Conversely, currency reform relied upon economic recovery for its success, because only a recovering economy could provide the much-needed backing for the new money. The sudden availability of merchandise that had been unavailable before, the drying up of the black market and the other things, which had appeared so miraculous, can also be explained rather conventionally.

German politicians had openly announced to the business community that a day of major economic reckoning was approaching. This gave a clear signal to both producers and wholesalers to hoard commodities for the occasion. Hoarding in the given situation made good economic sense, since the visible effects helped to convince the public at large that the new money was reliable; and this in turn helped recovery. It was only a side effect of this policy of confidence-building that the currency reform took the appearance of a miracle and that it was later remembered as the onset of the extensive growths in the 1950s. Yet, whatever it was, it was certainly good political fortune.[14]

The last central component of the mythical tale of Germany's economic miracle is the claim that the *theoretical* formula of the "social market economy" has been responsible for the success of the policy of recovery and the extraordinary growth. The economic policies of Ludwig Erhard were much less driven by a coherent theory then by an astonishing pragmatism. Although the "social market economy" would not be ill-described as a variation of market liberalism, and indeed under Erhard markets were liberalized wherever economically feasible, he did not hesitate to resort to state control and planning in fields where it seemed appropriate to him, such as in housing, coal supply, or agriculture. The letter of the economic doctrine of the "social market economy" was that markets were to be framed by institutional regulations and that only those regulations would check the self-destructive tendencies in market economies. Erhard, though, did not follow this line of *Ordnungspolitik* ("policy of economic order"), but made state action in the market proper a standard tool of his policy. Just to give one example, Erhard had never hesitated to foster capital investment through massive tax incentives. This policy violated the theoretical beliefs central to "ordoliberalism," the theory held to be the main inspiration of the "social market economy," in many ways. In particular, it violated ordoliberalism's belief that any mixed system of market incentives and state interference in the market was forcing state and society on the slippery slope down toward total planning and eventually totalitarianism. The "ordoliberal" theorist Wilhelm Röpke, although even then not totally hostile toward Erhard's economic policies, argued in 1958 that his policy, on a whole, was flawed and not up to the standards of the doctrine he believed in.[15]

What remains of the myth? There is the fact of Germany's economic success, particularly in the 1950s. It can be explained to a large degree by a set of exceptionally favourable preconditions of economic recovery and subsequent growth in West Germany.[16] This growth potential could well have been spoiled by wrong economic policies; this much credit must be given to Erhard and the West German government. But objective factors and an inherited economic strength did play a major role. There was a modern infrastructure, inherited from the Nazis. Germany enjoyed the advantages of low military spending. When the Korean boom set in, the Germans could put large amounts of manufacturing power into supplying the booming world market. For much of the reconstruction period, international trade for the West Germans received a boost from an undervalued currency.

In addition, there was a vast supply of much needed highly skilled and highly motivated labour, once the economy started to boom in earnest. The labour market was replenished by millions of immigrants and the migration into Germany kept labour costs down. First, by provision of the Allied's Potsdam Agreement, German expellees, mainly from Poland and Czechoslovakia, were moved into Germany. Later, refugees who had fled the GDR settled in the West. When this inflow stopped with the erection of the Berlin Wall in 1961, West Germany could tap into the almost limitless resources of southern European labour migrants. Again, it becomes obvious that the German economic miracle developed from a whole bundle of factors, among which the "social market economy" was certainly one, but not the most important factor.

If one is to compare the German situation with the economic transformation in today's eastern European countries, one has to stress the fact that almost all conditions prevalent in postwar West Germany do not apply to these other countries. The experience of a sluggish, if any, economic upswing in the transformation countries, even if they strictly follow a market-oriented policy, illustrates the point that it is not just a stiff dose of the market medicine which guarantees growth and economic success, but that other conditions have to be met also. Similarly, it was not so much the "social market economy" that was responsible for West Germany's success, but rather, in combination, luck, the aforementioned preconditions, and an appropriate economic policy.

A Question of Identity

Even if West Germany's postwar economic recovery was anything but a miracle, its perception as a miracle had a lasting effect on West German identity and on the country's self-perception for a long time to come. Traditional sources of identification and integration for the German people had vanished in the face of the Nazi past, with the lost war, and later with Germany's division. More than ever before, after the Second World War, German history was a contested field. How could the Germans come to terms with the genocide and war crimes they were guilty of?

> For Germans, more than for any other people in Europe, the past was a black hole and national history a liability. Their neighbors, the French and the British, and their patrons, the Americans, could construct a history that was a source of pride, a story of steady development and broadening liberty.... No one could sit down in 1945 to write a Whig version of the German past.[17]

What remained for the Germans as a source of pride and identity was, at best, an orientation toward everyday life. It was in this context that the founding myth of West Germany, her miraculous rise from the ashes, her economic success, and her new respectability as one of the main trading nations, gained its importance. For the narration of the mythical tale, it was not important that the "social market economy" is not a very well defined concept. Equally unimportant were the actual causes of economic development. The mythical tale of success was more important for its much needed emotional quality, as an uncontested source of pride and consensus in a society that had witnessed the myth unfolding as reality, no matter what the reality of the myth was. A shared belief of the Germans in the "social market economy" created consistency, unity, *gemeinschaft*. It was this quality that shaped the postwar history of both West Germany and, after unification, east Germany.

The concept of *myth* used here does not refer to the ancient religious narratives. It was the French writer Georges Sorel[18] who introduced a more contemporary use of the term. The social philosopher Hans Barth summarized Sorel's intention as follows:

> The term *social myth* is set to explain, "the way in which humans can join together to form unities that are historically effective. In this understanding a myth terminates the isolation of the individual.... It creates consensus. It is the organizing force in the center. It is the starting point of enthusiasm, which enables humans to live and attain greatness."[19]

In other words, for Sorel, social myth is a tool to solve the modern problem by means of mass politics, identity creation, orientation, and integration. In modernity, religion and tradition do not bind together members of society any more. Other ways of social formation have to be found. Where the liberal mainstream, and with it the political left, hoped for reason and a rational construction of society, conservatives feared this cure as part of the problem, rather then a remedy. In the terminology of late nineteenth century conservatism, the problem of identity formation could be called the problem of forming groups from masses. A myth is a moral message. Sorel's solution focuses on the irrational as a source of social consensus and of shared feelings of identity. In Sorel's understanding, the ultimate aim of creating a social myth was to morally rejuvenate society.

Modern myths differ from their "classical" predecessors by their "reflectiveness." They are no longer "naive" narratives that bring about their integrative potential as an unanticipated side effect. Modern myths, in the Sorelian sense, are deliberately constructed; they rely on actions, they are narratives and are purposefully put forward to bring about the desired result of social integration. The new myths come close to applied mass psychology; they are social engineering as a means of domination. They are manipulative and inherently modern as a tool of hierarchical politics, more "modern" than their supporters are ready to admit.

Although Sorel believed that his theory would represent a reformulation of revolutionary socialism,[20] the reception of Sorel's concept of a social myth has shown that it was more plausibly applicable in a conservative political framework. A founding myth, if widely believed, can be a source of social order, where sources of traditional consensus (substituting a belief in descent) have faded away or where a projection of shared aims is not obvious for a group that is to be integrated (substituting a shared will). The reception of Sorel's ideas was divided. One stream turned his concept into a strategic device of Italian fascism; Mussolini was a Sorelian as was Vilfred Pareto, the grand sociological theorist of fascism. The other stream was Anarcho-Syndicalism, a left-wing radical movement, strong in southwestern Europe in the 1920s and 1930s, that merited Sorel's strategy of the "general strike" more than his concept of myth. In much of the political left, as in political liberalism, the appeal to the irrational as a core idea in a policy of myth was never popular; it was often incomprehensible to their rationalistic frame of mind.

Myths as a resource of integration are radically different from interests or ideologies linked to interests. Integration through a myth builds on irrationality. Whoever (or whatever force) succeeds in launching a social myth establishes the irrational, rather then rational argument, as a basis for domination and social cohesion. In Germany during the 1920s and 1930s, the influential conservative catholic scholar Carl Schmitt tried to exploit this approach to finding a solution for social instabilities. Schmitt praised Sorel's concept as the nucleus of a strategy of conservative modernization of society and as a means to replace parliamentarianism by "true democracy." He argued that it was the very quality of irrationality that made myth a source of order, discipline, hierarchy, and authority. It was Schmitt's hope that this new order would be able to heal the deep cleavages and rifts brought about by economic modernity and capitalism. In the 1930s, Schmitt favoured a "national" myth to stabilize the German polity. For him, myth bears the power to initiate "grand historic activity"[21] (*große geschichtliche Aktivität*), "the ability for action and for heroism"[22] (*die Fähigkeit zum Handeln und zum Heroismus*) and with this potential, myth leads beyond the "productive mechanism" (*Mechanismus der Produktion*) with its "rationalistic determination"[23] (*Gesetzmäßigkeit*). In the same breath, Schmitt warned that myth, politically utilized in the Sorelian sense, was a concept without content. This bore the danger that a great number of competing myths[24] could arise, and that a "polytheism" of instant religions could undermine order, brought about by shaping the irrational. Ironically, this shows how the approach of using myth to heal society from modernity, is not able to escape modernity and its reflexive, rather then traditional, frame of mind. The polytheism of myths creates a market of meanings and leads into a competitive environment rather then into an order of beliefs, based in tradition and hierarchy.

Carl Schmitt, a distinctive voice in the German debate not only for his sharp rhetoric, can be seen as a mouthpiece for new conservative strategies in Germany to overcome the notorious political and metaphysical instability of the Weimar Republic. During the 1920s and 1930s, amongst those right of the political center, a desperate search was going on, not only to secure the existing political institutions, but to find political stability by overcoming the Republic itself and its liberal democratic constitution. Both from economic liberalism and from this frantic search for new sources of political stability in the old order, ordoliberalism sprang.

The World of Ordoliberalism

Ordoliberalism is a German variety of economic liberalism. Under the domination of the "historical school" (*Historische Schule*), represented by scholars like Gustav Schmoller and Adolf Wagner in the late Empire and the very popular Werner Sombart after the turn of the century, it was a widely held belief that capitalism had come to its final crisis. Werner Sombart's concept of "late capitalism" (*Spätkapitalismus*) as a capitalism without further growth potential was very influential at the time, increasingly so since the world economic crisis of 1929 could be seen as proof for all that such skepticism was well-founded. Ordoliberalism tried to hold up Western liberal thought against this obstruction, whilst admitting that conservative anticapitalist skepticism in Germany had made a valuable point as well. As dyed-in-the-wool liberals, the ordoliberals believed that open markets were the most efficient means of economic coordination and they insisted that the new devices of business cycle policies, as laid out in the economic theories of their contemporaries, should be employed to overcome the economic crisis. At the same time, they shared with conservative anticapitalism the criticism of the market as a destructive modernizing and a destabilizing social force. The market for the ordoliberals was a double edged sword. In their view, a market-oriented economy relied on inherited social stability (in other words, the traditional social order) but it destroyed this very basis through its successes, or rather excesses, in modernizing social and economic relations.

The first dimension of the crisis of modern capitalism concerned the relation of the market and the state. The question raised by the ordoliberals predates similar, yet more recent, neoconservative criticism of state intervention. In 1932, the Freiburg economist Walter Eucken conceptualized the market-state-relationship since the late nineteenth century under the heading of "structural change in capitalism."[25] According to Eucken, the relation of state and market sector had reversed. The "night watchman state" of the second half of the nineteenth century had not interfered with the economic sector. This had turned out to be very successful, as growth patterns of market economies had been impressive. Since then, the night watchman state had gone under; a new form of economic activity of the state was on the rise. According to Eucken, the change had been the *politicization of the economy*: making the economic sector an object of political fights for power and control within state institutions. Eucken called the new constellation the *economic state*. The economic policy of the economic state was interventionist and it was driven by interest groups that all competed, not in the market, but for more political influence. According to Eucken, the state interventions in the economy did not reflect an increase in economic reason, or a growing ability of the state to manage economic affairs. Rather, the opposite was true; the flip side of state intervention for Eucken was always that special interests took command of state action. State action spoiled the role of the market as a neutral institution in distributing wealth and chances. The state was harmed as well. Its neutrality, its position above society, and its responsibility for the whole, rather then for parts, was weakened. At the same time, the state was increasingly pushed into responsibility for economic performance.[26] This crisis analysis assembles all the components that decades later, in the 1970s and 1980s, were discussed under the heading of ungovernability.[27] For Eucken, this was not a crisis of government, but of the very institutional structure of the economic state. When discussing solutions, Eucken demanded nothing less then a complete overhaul of the state. He could not find relief in the right people taking over government, but blamed parliamentary democracy, the very institution of parliament, for the current crisis. In Eucken's view, parliamentarianism tended to weaken the state's power and to bring the state under the spell of the "masses." In 1932, Eucken saw the danger of the "dissolution of the state"[28] (*Auflösung des Staates*), he pleaded for a new, nonparliamentarian state.

As far as politics and constitutional questions were concerned, Eucken went along with the antiparliamentarian Weimar conservatives; when it came to opposing the Weimar constitutional constellation, the ordoliberal group and the conservatives marched on the same grounds. Differences existed only in the specifics of economic policy. But even in economic policy, there was agreement in general: the task of the time was seen in finding a way in which the new, nonparliamentarian state would withdraw from economic intervention, would, in Carl Schmitt's terminology, "neutralize"[29] the economy as a politically contested field.

The constitutional position of Eucken and Schmitt was not a Nazi position. But the Nazi program certainly shared some features with the conservative ideas and this explains why there were links between the conservative critique of the Weimar state and the Nazi program. It must be remembered that, in 1932, the state really had lost much of the control over what was going on its territory; Germany was on the brink of a civil war. This gave the critical observations, expressed in the concept of the economic state (or as Carl Schmitt had put it, the "total state") its urgency. In 1932, the ordoliberal political scientist Alexander Rüstow gave the situation the most dramatic description. He views the state as a cadaver and the special interests as a bunch of wolves: "The state is ripped apart by the greedy interests. Each special interest secures its own piece and butchers it for its own purposes."[30]

The second dimension of the ordoliberal crisis analysis brings the motive of myth back into play. The ordoliberals developed a theme that became popular again in the 1970s and 1980s.[31] Eucken argued that capitalism relies on cultural preconditions, namely traditional bonding in the social realm. Eucken points to the danger that capitalism proves to be a dead end of history: "History has led to a factual discrepancy: capitalism developed in a situation of state and society, which has been destroyed by a later historical process within capitalism: the emergence of the economic state."[32] The ordoliberals thus see capitalism destroying the basis that it is built on. In using Eucken's phrase, capitalism uses up the "resources of integration through the state."

If, as the ordoliberals maintain, capitalism undermines the social value system it relies on, a purely economic solution to the crisis of capitalism is impossible, because no such solution would address the cultural dimension of the crisis. What then were the ordoliberal proposals to solve the crisis? Here again, the postparliamentarian, authoritarian, *strong state* comes into play. The ordoliberals declared it the duty of the state to reshape the values in the society in a way that takes the threat from capitalist development. A *policy of providing meaning* was to immunize the society against the erosive power of capitalist development, against innovation and modernization. The policy of providing meaning was to create an orderly and organized society; in the widest understanding, this policy comprises what is meant by the German term *Ordnungspolitik*.

The first part of this social *Ordnungspolitik* was to restitute conditions of day-to-day life that, for the ordoliberals, within themselves bore meaning. This part of the policy of meaning was called the "policy of vitality" (*Vitalpolitik*) by Alexander Rüstow. The policy of vitality was designed to create areas of social life that were not affected by the pressures of markets and the capitalist workplace. Capitalism was to be contained to the area of the workplace and was not to expand into everyday life. The ordoliberals envisioned day-to-day-life as more traditional and calm, less dependent on the system of modern economy. In particular, proletarization was to be countered in a strategy to de-urbanize society: in other words, to reroot the population on the soil. The ordoliberals drafted plans to resettle the majority of wage labourers in the countryside. A life on a small property of arable land was meant to make families self-sufficient and thus to reduce the necessity of providing social welfare through state institutions. In this sense, the policy of vitality was another facet in a strategy to push back the economic state. The ordoliberals were hostile in principle towards social welfare as a state responsibility. They saw the build-up of a social welfare system in terms of one special interest group putting stress on both the state and the system of market economy. The policy of vitality was to offer an alternative to the welfare state and make the population independent from the ups and downs of the business cycle by creating the autonomy of evening gardeners who would survive whatever economic fate would hit them by calmly consuming their home grown leeks and potatoes.

The strong state was to use the existing irrational forces in society and in the masses to fulfill this task. A policy of meaning, tapping into the collective irrational, is exactly what was envisioned by Sorel exploring a social myth as political force, refined to a source of order, as Carl Schmitt had interpreted it.

In the 1930s, for some ordoliberals this myth was best secured in the forces of nationalism. Specifically, Alfred Müller-Armack, albeit not a member of the ordoliberal core grouping, explicitly hoped for a revitalization of liberal and entrepreneurial capitalism by stabilizing it under the roof of an authoritarian state with a distinctive nationalistic ideology.[33] No wonder that Müller-Armack was an admirer of Fascism in the early 1930s and, after 1933, had some difficulties reinterpreting his commitment to fit the doctrine of the day.[34]

During the Nazi regime, the ordoliberals who had remained in the country (Röpke and Rüstow had emigrated to Turkey; as liberals, both were threatened by the Nazi party and the Gestapo) tried to exploit the political situation to further their policies. In the programmatic first volume of the ordoliberal series "Economic Order" (*Ordnung der Wirtschaft*),[35] published in 1937, the ordoliberals suggested a division of labour to the Nazis. They claimed the responsibility for economic policy, while they expected the Nazis to provide the policy of meaning. Such flirtation with an *Ordnungspolitik* dependent on the Nazis lasted only a few years; later, leading ordoliberals were found close to the conservative conspiracy against Hitler that peaked in the unsuccessful assassination attempt of July 1944. With some fortune, the ordoliberal scholars narrowly escaped the Nazi revenge against the main conspirators.

After 1945, all ordoliberals invested their efforts to find a stabilizing myth in the upswing of religious belief, at a time when nationalism and ideas of a strong antiparliamentarian state did not match the prevailing mood very well. Otherwise, there was no modification in the ordoliberal program. Still, creating *order* in a strong state and putting out a policy of meaning, both in the sense of deproletarization and of a policy of myth, was believed to be essential. For the ordoliberals, the "social market economy" thus was a concept loaded with the expectation of an integral economic and societal policy. The "social market economy" was designed as a practical conservative answer to the question of modernity itself.

If one is to measure the success of ordoliberalism with the yardstick of results, the ordoliberals failed in their attempt to curb the destructive aspects of modernization. Evidence of this failure is two-fold. Firstly, under the label of "social market economy," Germany's economy at large was not remodeled in ordoliberal terms, but rather reconstructed along the beaten path of the capitalism of the late empire and Weimar Republic.

West Germany was again, and is to the present, characterized by a smooth corporate arrangement and consensual labour relations. Except for some spectacular dismantling of dominating industrial powers, such as the IG Farben, big industry remained dominant, and so cozy relations between big industry, big banks, and big labour organizations continued, a characteristic feature of West Germany. Most obviously in the 1950s, all ordoliberal attempts were watered down to curb the power of big corporations by introducing a stiff antitrust law, modeled after US legislation. The antitrust law, which Germany adopted in 1957, did not at all meet ordoliberal expectations. By no means was German capitalism scaled down to the extent that the ordoliberals considered crucial in order to counter the contradictions that are, according to their theory, inherent in capitalist modernization. For the ordoliberals, postwar West Germany was back on the downhill avenue toward the interventionist state, the weak version of the total state, and it had totally failed in the so-called deproletarization, the "policy of vitality."

The second aspect of ordoliberal failure is rather ironic. For postwar West Germany the economy itself was the founding myth. The pride of the people was dependent upon ongoing economic success. The very stability of West German society relied on a social myth that was dependent on the economic fate of the country. When the expectation of economic success is disappointed, for whatever reason, there instantly occurs a threat to German identity, as well as a crisis regarding the legitimacy of the state institutions. The religion of postwar Germany is economic success. Thus, economic crises are crises of core beliefs; they are crises of popular religion. Rather than finding a basis for social integration elsewhere, the West German economy was the foundation of society. The state, rather then being beyond a "neutralized" economy, was again faced with almost overwhelming expectations of its ability to "fix" economic problems; the situation of the 1920s and early 1930s, in principle, had not been overcome, but worsened. Under the spell of the myth of the "social market economy," economic failure becomes a threat to the very stability of Germany; it revitalizes the old German evils. The success of the "social market economy" as a myth indicates the failure of the policy of meaning, which was a constitutive part of the ordoliberal policy set-up.

Conceptually, the tragedy of ordoliberalism was that it did not overcome the contradiction of conservatism (although ordoliberalism is not exactly a conservative position). It found itself in the same trap as any conservative strategy. Conservatism is a very specific kind of utopian thinking. It distinguishes from traditionalism by finding the values endangered that traditionalism naively took for granted. The attempt to re-establish a system which is on the verge of disappearing is a utopian move. Referring to Karl Mannheim,[36] one could call conservatism a reflexive form of traditionalism. The dilemma of conservatism is that it wants to salvage a world that is already gone. Thus, conservatism in its real meaning is only possible as an oppositional mood. At the moment that conservatives take responsibility, their utopia is very likely to turn into pragmatism.

The dilemma of ordoliberalism mirrors the conservative dilemma in a two-fold way. Like conservatives, the ordoliberals try to build on a tradition that has no currency any more. But their motives are not conservative. The perspective of ordoliberals is a liberal rationalism that has become reflexive. Thus, for ordoliberals, pragmatism is not a downfall of their project of restoring capitalism. The ordoliberal flirt with conservatism is a strategy with rather pragmatic second thoughts. Ordoliberalism tried to synthesize an economic modernism with traditionalism in societal policy; it did not work. This is the "dilemma of ordoliberalism" and of its strategy to overcome the crises in the Western modernization process.

Another Miracle in the East?

When self-confidence and identity are reliant upon economic success, as in postwar West Germany, then the slightest stuttering of the economic engine is perceived as an attack on that self-confidence. The first to suffer from this was the father of the "social market economy" himself, Ludwig Erhard, who stumbled over a rather mild economic crisis and had to resign as chancellor in 1966. But this was only one episode, compared with what was to come later. The uniquely German identity construction showed (and continues to show) its impact in the unification process.

In order to understand the history of the turbulent unification year of 1989-90 in Germany, one has to take into account not only events, but also expectations. The disenchantment of the East German population with their state was to a large part motivated by political disagreement, as well as by the realization that the GDR was not even prepared to put in effect the comparatively moderate political reforms that were touted by the Gorbachev government in the Soviet Union. East Germans felt their imprisonment behind walls even sharper when their government increased control and repression to stem the reformist influences from Eastern European partner countries, such as the USSR, Poland, and Hungary. This made "exit," attempts to leave the country and move to West Germany, look more and more attractive and the regime fell when its repressive power was no longer sufficient to prevent that exit.

However, it was of equal (if not greater) importance that East Germans had suffered from a long period of relative economic decline in the face of the growing wealth of the West. Until the wall fell, traveling to the West was allowed only for a minority of East Germans. This restricted the possible sources of knowledge about the reality of Western life and Western wealth to television, hearsay from the few who could go, and Western visitors to the East. One need only imagine a shining new Mercedes car surrounded by Eastern *Trabbis* in the worn-down gray of Eastern cities, the expensive Western leather shoes contrasted with their more humble apparel, in order to get a glimpse of the dissonance experienced by Easterners. Whatever their social standing was in the West, due to the black market value of Eastern currency, West German visitors were rich once they arrived in East Germany.

The few pseudo-authentic images, all that East Germans could gain from the West, were transmitted by Western television stations. Both the shiny world of advertising and the refined lifestyles of television films represented a beautified image of Western success. For these and other reasons, the East harboured some illusions about the ease of Western life and the wealth of their Western compatriots. At the same time, though, East Germany's government's cautioning against the risks of Western life, against unemployment, and a less comprehensive system of social welfare, had its impact and was the source of wide spread skepticism and fear among the population during the unification process.

East Germans were generally convinced that they were able to be as economically successful as their Western compatriots. They felt deprived of living up to their full capacity in economic industriousness; they felt hindered both by the Byzantine system of central planning and by what they perceived as unequal terms of trade with the Soviet Union. The foundational myth of West Germany was believed here as it was in the West, yet it provided a different morale here. Due to the constraints of the system, East Germans felt that they were not being allowed to live up to their nature. Once these constraints were lifted, a second economic miracle was to be expected.

East Germany's population was prepared to believe in a second economic miracle. East Germans shared, after all, in the German national characteristics, and, given the opportunity, they would live up to it, as the Westerners had done, 40 years before. A distinctive East German identity, skeptical about Western capitalism, as was the political belief of the first protest groups that brought down the East German regime, was washed away by a popular exploration of a sentiment of national German pride in East Germany. The rallies in Leipzig in October 1989 gathered under the slogan "We are the people," a democratic slogan against an illegitimate government. Only a few weeks later, the dominant slogan was "We are one people," a claim for national unity. The third slogan indicates what German national unity is made of: "Either the Deutschmark comes to us, or we come to it," a slogan ironically combining what was perceived as a threat in West Germany, mass migration of East Germans, with a claim for participation in what for them best symbolized the wealth that they strove for.

West Germany's government was busy catering to such expectations. When the first and only ever free elections in East Germany were due in April 1990, Ludwig Erhard's book from 1957, *Prosperity for Everybody* (*Wohlstand für alle*), appeared newly in print, and was distributed freely in East Germany's streets. The message was obvious; now it was possible to repeat the economic miracle and to achieve in the East what had been promised to the West in the title of the book. A revitalization of the memories of the glorious days of Germany's economic successes did not end here. The West German government under Chancellor Helmut Kohl won the election for their Eastern subsidiary parties by announcing a currency reform for the summer of 1990. Who would not remember the day in the summer of 1948, when the Western miracle started? Now this seemed to be within reach for East Germany as well. The West German government had taken the slogan from the streets in Leipzig to the letter, and facing the threat of an intense migration from East to West, there was not much political choice. But it was indicative of the mood in Germany, and of the will to believe in the foundational myth of the West, that a "currency reform" as in 1948 was the right action to soothe threats of mass migration.

Some irony lies in the fact that the supposed currency reform was nothing of that sort whatsoever, but a misnomer for the technical operation of including East Germany into the territory where the well established Deutschmark became sole legal tender. For the public, "currency reform," with the introduction of the economic and social laws of the West, thus the "social market economy," appeared like a guarantee that the miracle was to happen again. Chancellor Helmut Kohl's announcement that, within a few years of social and monetary union with the West, the east would be turned into *blühende Landschaften* ("a blooming country") was plausible for meeting public expectations. A final indication of this juxtaposition of mythical tale and political reality in the summer of 1990 was the way in which the public media reported the introduction of the Deutschmark; reporters swarmed out into the East, only to find that the expectable had happened. Shop windows were dressed up with hitherto unavailable Western consumer goods; currency reform was working its magic again. For Germany, history was about to repeat itself; at least there was hope that it would.

Yet, as in the years of the economic miracle in West Germany, it was not the magic that worked but the economic preconditions, together with the economic policy of the day. Preconditions in the East were radically different from what had been the case in postwar West Germany. This alone did not allow for a repetition of history. To mention but a few facts, East Germany had an outdated industrial stock, not an advanced one; East Germany could not boost international trade with an undervalued currency but suffered from the strong currency of the West; East Germany did not find new markets, but lost her old ones. The introduction of the West German currency produced an economic boost for the West, not the East; in fact, it contributed to a sharp decline of economic activity in East Germany. All this is well described in the economic and historical literature. One could sum up the literature by saying that it was only the comparative strength of the West German economy and an enormous and ongoing transfer of wealth that kept East Germany's economy from a total breakdown, since it was fully exposed to the world market after currency reform.

In a different context Alan Kramer recently raised the question of whether there was something to learn from the economic experience in the West Germany of the 1950s:

Does the experience of the West German economy from 1945 to 1955 have any lessons for other industrial countries attempting to improve their growth rates? The answer, unfortunately, is not a simple "yes" or "no."... Countries with an outdated, undercapitalized industrial structure, with relatively low skill levels in the labour force, would first have to create the preconditions for growth. Neither a new version of the Marshall Plan nor the introduction of a "free market economy," and even less a currency reform, would under these circumstances produce an "economic miracle."[37]

In this essay, the subject is not the economics of Germany's unification but the myth of the "social market economy" and of Germany's predestination to economic success. As the expectations had been high for a repetition of the economic miracle in East Germany, waking up to reality was rather painful. Germany had founded her identity on a dream, the dream of a perpetuation of economic success. Reality since unification has showed that this dream was unfounded. There is no indication that Germany is any more successful in economic transformation from an Eastern-style planned economy to Western-style market capitalism. The only advantage East Germany has over her eastern and southeastern neighbours is that her transformation is smoothed by the wealth of West Germany. This does not make transformation less economically painful, but it takes out part of the social hardship that accompanies it in Poland and Hungary.

The effects of the dashed hopes on the sociopsychological stability of unified Germany can hardly be overvalued. East Germans had expected a miracle, and they got the joys and the miseries of transformation. Likewise, West Germans had hoped for a renewal of their miracle, and more then a few of them put the blame for the nonevent on the Easterners who supposedly had lost their industriousness, after so many decades of living in an ill-fated economic regime. The myth of a guaranteed success, coupled with the failure to achieve that success, were thus additional factors of social stress in an already stressful historical situation, and it was likely to further divide East and West Germans.

One more dividing factor between West and East is that the West had had its miracle, whereas the East failed to do so. The "social market economy" and the expectations connected to it have become part of the wedge between the two new German tribes. Even the considerable successes of East Germany's transformation up to now, the gradual recon-struction of some industry, the building of a modern infrastructure of communication and transport where there was next to nothing before, are not perceived as the successes they are, but rather as a shortfall against former expectations. One could thus conclude that during unification, Germany has lost an important part of her self-confidence. Up to now, it is not clear what will be able to replace the myth of the "social market economy."

NOTES

1.   Author's translation of Helmuth Seliger, "Alexander Rüstow—ein Verteidiger des Mittelstandes," in *Perspektive 2000*, ed. Lothar Bossle (Würzburg: Creator Verlag, 1987), p. 116: "Die bislang erfolgreichste wirtschaftspolitische Konzeption in der Geschichte der Menschheit (ist)…unstreitig die von Ludwig Erhard in die Wirklichkeit umgesetzte Soziale Marktwirtschaft…."

2.   According to Mosca, the political formula is the "legal and moral basis, or principle, on which the power of the political class rests…." Political formulas "answer a real need in man's social nature; and this need…of governing and knowing and knowing that one is governed not on the basis of mere material or intellectual force, but on the basis of a moral principle, has beyond any doubt a practical and a real importance." Gaetano Mosca, *The Ruling Class*, ed. Arthur Livingston (New York: McGraw-Hill, 1939), pp. 7of. If one were to follow Mosca's observation to the letter, one would have to conclude that such an arrangement of power and legitimacy was not very durable.

3.   Peter Pulzer, *German Politics, 1945–1995* (Oxford: Oxford University Press, 1995), p. 92.

4.   Of course, there are many reasons for the lesser success in GDR's economic develop-ment. Some of the more prominent are the much higher load of reparations extracted from there, and the outward migration of a substantive part of the population. The forced modelling of GDR's economy along the lines of Stalin's economic policy also did not help to boost performance in the east. For a brief overview on economic perfor-mance and economic policy in the GDR cf. Mary Fulbrook, *A Concise History of Germany* (Cambridge: Cambridge University Press, 1992), pp. 233–39.

5.   The changing attitude toward the "social market economy" of members of the working class is best expressed in a sentence, noted in an oral history project in the heavy industry Ruhr area. Remembering the time of recovery and economic miracle, one worker stated: "Hinterher merkt man, daß es richtig war, daß es schiefgegangen ist" ("Afterwards one realizes that it was right that everything went wrong"). This is the title of the second volume of *Lebensgeschichte und Sozialkultur im Ruhrgebiet, 1930–1960*, ed. Lutz Niethammer (Berlin: Dietz, 1983).

6.   Seliger, "Alexander Rüstow." The quotation is not a singular case. To give just one more example: In 1977 , the prominent political writer Rüdiger Altmann was not shy of

stating that "social market economy" was "die erfolgversprechendste Wirtschaftspolitik des Kontinents" ("the most promising economic policy of the continent"). *Wirtschaftspolitik und Staatskunst. Wirkungen Ludwig Erhards. Aus Anlaß seines achtzigsten Geburtstags* (Bonn: Ludwig-Erhardt-Stiftung, 1977), p. 5.

7. Jaques Rueff, "Natürliche Erklärung eines Wunders," in *Wirtschaft ohne Wunder*, Volkswirtschaftliche Studien für das Schweizerische Institut für Auslandsforschung, ed. Albert Hunold (Erlenbach-Zürich: Rentsch, 1954), pp. 204–22, 205. Author's translation.

8. Much of the current reluctance of Germans to approve of the European Monetary Union can be assessed from here. EMU would replace the Deutschmark by the new Euro, a currency that still has to gain the glory of the DM.

9. A role that Germany has lost in the 1990s.

10. Rueff, "Natürliche Erklärungen," p. 222.

11. For the following I rely on the works of Werner Abelshauser: *Wirtschaftsgeschichte der Bundesrepublik Deutschland, 1945–1980* (Frankfurt/Main: Suhrkamp, 1983); and *Die langen fünfziger Jahre. Wirtschaft und Gesellschaft in der Bundesrepublik Deutschland,* Historisches Seminar, no. 5 (Düsseldorf: Schwann, 1987), and Alan Kramer, *The West German Economy, 1945–1955* (New York: Berg, 1991).

12. This is except for the systematic expropriation of Jewish citizens which was not pursued for economic reasons, but resulted from a policy of racial hatred.

13. This is especially true for Eastern Europe, but Britain as well, despite her victory in the war, was economically exhausted and impoverished at the end of the war.

14. In the context of a recovery well under way as early as 1947, it has been argued that the help of the US Marshall Plan of 1949, well intended as it was, for Germany was more important as a political symbol of inclusion in and of recognition as member of the group of Western European countries than it was in economic terms. The upswing was already well on the way when Marshall Plan help finally arrived in Germany. For a recent controversy on this question cf. *The Marshall Plan and Germany*, ed. Charles S. Maier (New York: Berg, 1991).

15. Cf. Wilhelm Röpke, *Jenseits von Angebot und Nachfrage*, 3rd ed. (Erlenbach-Zürich: Rentsch, 1961), p. 50.

16. It must be said here that Ludwig Erhard himself was opposed to calling West Germany's economic recovery a "miracle"—he attributed the success mainly to applying the "right" policies.

17. Pulzer, *German Politics*, pp. 6f.

18. In Georges Sorel, *Reflections on Violence* (London: Collier-Macmillan, 1961).

19. Hans Barth, *Masse und Mythos. Die ideologische Krise an der Wende zum 20. Jahrhundert und die Theorie der Gewalt: Georges Sorel*, rowohlts deutsche enzyklopädie (Reinbek: Rowohlt, 1959), p. 70. Author's translation.

20. Sorel saw this renewal mainly in terms of a proletarian revolution and detected the founding myth of a morally rejuvenated society in the idea of the ultimate working class power, the "general strike."

21. Carl Schmitt, *Positionen und Begriffe im Kampf mit Weimar—Genf—Versailles, 1923–1939*, 2nd ed. (Berlin: Duncker und Humblot, 1988; 1st ed., Hamburg: 1940), p. 11.

22. Carl Schmitt, *Die geistesgeschichtliche Lage des heutigen Parlamentarismus*, 7th ed. (Berlin: Duncker und Humblot, 1991; reprint of the 2nd ed., 1926), p. 80.

23. Schmitt, *Positionen*, p. 15.

24. Schmitt, *Positionen*, p. 17.

25. Walter Eucken, "Staatliche Strukturwandlungen und die Krisis des Kapitalismus" in *Weltwirtschaftliches Archiv* 36 (1932): 297–321.

26. Eucken's deliberations represent a strange mixture of mourning the German tradition of the benevolent state, headed by an enlightened sovereign, and liberal, Benthamian, ideas of a minimalist state.

27. See, as one example for a secondary work on this topic: Joachim Heidorn, *Legitimität und Regierbarkeit. Studien zu den Legitimitätstheorien von Max Weber, Niklas Luhmann, Jürgen Habermas und der Unregierbarkeitsforschung* (Berlin: Duncker und Humblot, 1982).

28. Eucken, *Staatliche Strukturwandlungen*, p. 307.

29. For Schmitt's concept of "neutralization" and "depolitization" cf. his text "Das Zeitalter der Neutralisierungen und Entpolitisierungen" in his *Der Begriff des Politischen* (Munich and Leipzig: Duncker und Humblot, 1932), a text that is not included in the English translation (*The Concept of the Political* (New Brunswick, NJ: Rutgers University Press, 1976)). Schmitt's economic position is best expressed in his speech at the "Verein zur Wahrung der gemeinsamen wirtschaftlichen Interessen im Rheinland und Westfalen," published as "Starker Staat und gesunde Wirtschaft. Ein Vortrag vor Wirtschaftsführern," in *Volk und Reich*, no. 2, pp. 81–94.

30. His speech to the Verein für Sozialpolitik is reprinted in: *Alexander Rüstow: Rede und Antwort* (Ludwigsburg: Martin Hoch, 1963), p. 255.

31. Most prominently, the theme was explored by Daniel Bell, *Cultural Contradictions of Capitalism* (New York: Basic Books, 1976).

32. Eucken, *Staatliche Strukturwandlungen*, p. 309.

33. Alfred Müller-Armack, *Entwicklungsgesetze des Kapitalismus. Ökonomische, geschichts-theoretische und soziologische Studien zur modernen Wirtschaftsverfassung* (Berlin: Junker und Duennhaupt, 1932).

34. This is what Müller-Armack tried with the booklet *Staatsidee und Wirtschaftsordnung im neuen Reich* (Berlin: Junker und Duennhaupt, 1933). Later, after Müller-Armack had become a leading official in Ludwig Erhard's Ministry of Economics, and other than the above mentioned work, this book was not worthy of recognition, and it was erased from his bibiliography. See my book *Autoritärer Liberalismus und Soziale Marktwirtschaft: Gesellschaft und Politik im Ordoliberalismus* (Baden-Baden: Nomos, 1991), chapter 3.

35. Franz Böhm, *Die Ordnung der Wirtschaft als geschichtliche Aufgabe und rechtss-chöpferische Leistung*, Ordnung der Wirtschaft, no. 1 (Stuttgart: Kohlhammer, 1937).

36. Cf. his book *Conservatism: A Contribution to the Sociology of Knowledge*, ed. David Kettler, Volker Meja, and Nico Stehr (London: Routledge, 1986).

37. Kramer, *The West German Economy*, pp. 226f.

8 Industrial Relations in Germany

An Exemplary Model Put to the Test

THOMAS VON WINTER

Within the European context, industrial relations in the Federal Republic of Germany are seen as exemplarily stable and highly functional with regard to the regulation of work relations. In contrast to France, wages and working conditions in Germany are not settled by state intervention but, to a large extent, in the framework of autonomous collective bargaining (*Tarifautonomie*), through negotiations between associations of employers and trade unions.[1] In contrast to the British system of industrial relations, German collective agreements with a validity that usually exceeds plant and regional boundaries are very widespread.[2]

It is both typical and to the advantage of the German system of autonomous collective bargaining that not only does the state not have the burden of regulation and legitimation because of the unions' and the employers' self-regulation, but also the employers avoid an atomization and pluralization of regulations. It has been possible for both mechanisms to become effective on the basis of a certain constellation of actors and actions, which has developed especially in the period after 1945 to form a typical structure of industrial relations. Institutional characteristics of this structure are a highly concentrated system of associations and a centralized system of negotiation, factors which are based on the strong "juridification" (*Verrechtlichung*) of industrial relations as well as on the basically cooperative orientation of the industrial partners. The formation of this special arrangement of institutions and actions has been strongly promoted by the socioeconomic and political framework of the 1950s and 1960s. Stable economic growth, low unemployment rates, and the structural domination of trade and industry, as well as an effective welfare state have created favourable prerequisites not only for the processes of concentration and centralization, but also for actors dealing with each other in the way of social partners.

┃ Changes in Industrial Relations

Institutions do, in fact, lead their own lives once they are established—an autonomous life that makes them relatively resistant to changes desired by individual actors—but their survival can only be guaranteed if they are supported by the majority of the people acting within and for them. Centrifugal tendencies increase whenever the framework of the institutional arrangements changes. With regard to industrial relations this has been the case for almost all levels since the end of the 1970s. Considering the process of change as a whole, we can distinguish five dimensions:

1. Economic stagnation and an even partly declining national product result in shrinking margins for distribution purposes and make it more difficult for unions and management to find compromises in wage policy. At the same time, the continuously high unemployment rate is responsible for a shift in the distribution of power between labour and management. This is due to the fact that the increasing supply of labour results not only in reduced chances of the individual worker on the labour market, but also weakens the bargaining position of the unions in relation to the employers.[3] Furthermore, unions are forced to reorient their strategy because the goal of increasing the income of the employed workers, having traditionally had priority over other goals, must now be harmonized with the concerns of employment policy. The reconciliation of the various goals becomes more difficult the more the labour market diversifies and splits up into two segments: the core staff and the fringe staff.[4]

2. Globalization of the economic relations and, thus, also of the conditions for competition has led to a new dimension of socioeconomic change since the end of the 1980s. The formation of the Common Market in Europe, political and economic changes in Eastern Europe, and the growing presence of Southeast Asian countries on the world market account in two ways for the pressure on the German collectively agreed standards (*Tarifstandards*). The existing regulations can be undermined by shifting the production abroad, employing foreign workers, and other measures. But, national companies face direct international competition for low-level labour costs.

3. Apart from general crises and the tendency towards globalization, changes within the economic structure also influence labour relations. This affects tendencies such as the blurring of existing borders

between industrial sections and the creation of new economic sections, which both question the structure of unions—which have been arranged according to the traditional pattern of an industrialized society—as well as account for new problems such as the definition of responsibilities and the reformation of organizational units. In contrast, the structural changes also account for an increasing decentralization of companies. This results in both a more heterogeneous structure of companies and a multiplication of the items that need regulation in collective agreements.[5] The consequences of the third industrial revolution become visible here. It is this revolution that has made it possible to out-source goods and services and allow for a more flexible and diversified production.[6]

4. One further aspect of socioeconomic change that is crucial to labour relations is the change in the occupational structure. The tendency towards postindustrial society coincides with the formation of a new class of employees, who no longer represent a "natural" reservoir for unions, but has to be mobilized with great organizational effort. Furthermore, an increasing differentiation of working conditions and employment relations is taking place that is being followed by a pluralization and individualization of lifestyles and interests. Thus, society is faced with the development of an extremely heterogeneous workforce—both socially and where patterns of belief are concerned—which will hardly offer the unions any points of departure for comprehensive interest politics.

5. The most important change in the political system relevant to industrial relations was the German unification at the end of 1990.[7] In the period that followed, the industrial partners faced the double challenge of creating new association structures and establishing a working collective bargaining system (*Tarifsystem*). The expansion to eastern Germany, which organizationally was carried out effectively by the unions as well as by the employers' associations, resulted in an increase in the diversity of membership and interest structures. The primary problems in interassociation relations were lack of a tradition of social partnership and the lack of a culture of negotiation.

Due to the outlined economic, sociostructural, and political changes, the system of industrial relations in Germany has been subjected to disruptions so severe that its institutional structure seems to have become seriously jeopardized. The future of the system, however, is everything but clear. While some students of industrial relations already speak of the end of the successful German model,[8] others are convinced that the established institutions will prove appropriate not only for surviving turbulence in the social and political environment, but also for overcoming them efficiently.[9] Thus, this article discusses to what extent the German model has survived the changes or, rather, to what extent its institutional basis has already eroded.

The Four Basic Pillars of the German System of Industrial Relations

The basic pillars of the German system of industrial relations are concentration, centralization, "juridification" (an anglicization of the German term *Verrechtlichung*), and cooperation.

Concentration

One of the essential characteristics of the German system of industrial relations is the high level of concentration in the area of the corporate actors concerned. There is a small number of largely representative associations both on the employees and the employers side. From a historical point of view, this is the result of a process of harmonization in the course of which the diversification of the existing association structure, according to ideological and functional criteria, has lost significance. In both camps, the tendency of concentration was brought about by strategic decisions taken by the actors in the context of specific historical crises and by the conditions of a social and political framework that favoured the dominating actors.

On the employers' side, the concentration process had begun already at the time of the Weimar Republic. After the fusion of the two industrial associations competing up to then into the *Reichsverband der Deutschen Industrie* (National Association of German Industry) in the year 1919, which took place as a reaction to the revolutionary political situation of the time immediately following the war,[10] the division into different groups with different producer interests had been permanently overcome. However, the traditional division of the employers' side into the three parts—Chambers, industrial and employers' associations—not only remained, but even survived after 1945. This division is still characteristic of the entrepreneurial interest intermediation system in today's Germany as opposed to, for instance, the centralized system of entrepreneurs' associations in France.[11] Nevertheless, one can speak of a concentration of interest representation here because the relationship between the *Deutscher Industrie- und Handelstag* (DIHT) (German Chamber for Industry and Commerce), the *Bundesverband der Deutschen Industrie* (BDI) (Association of German Industry) and the *Bundesvereinigung Deutscher Arbeitgeberbände* (BDA) (Association of German Employers) is based on the principle of division of labour according to which the responsibility for wage policy is exclusively allocated to the BDA or its member organizations.[12] Moreover, this lead association, which is separate from industry itself, also represents the other most important areas of the economy.[13] This results in a high degree of organization that in the beginning of the 1980s amounted to about 70 percent (with respect to the companies concerned) and almost 80 percent (with respect to the number of employees).[14]

Where the unions are concerned, organizational division according to both ideological and functional characteristics was typical until the end of the Weimar Republic. First, there were the Social-Democratic unions, which had the largest number of members by far and were associated with the *Allgemeiner Deutscher Gewerkschaftsbund* (General German Association of Unions). These competed with two other unions with different ideological direction, the *Christliche Gewerkschaften* (Christian Unions) and the liberal *Hirsch-Dunckersche Gewerkvereine* (Hirsch-Duncker Unions). Each of the three groups had its own organizations for blue-collar workers, white-collar workers, and civil servants, respectively. Furthermore, each also consisted of professional associations (*Berufsverbände*) and industrial associations (*Industriegewerkschaften*) that existed side by side.[15] In view of the historical experience—notably the suppression of the union movement in Nazi-Germany—the principle of the industry-wide trade union (*Prinzip der Einheitsgewerkschaft*) became widely accepted when the unions were re-established after 1945. This principle comprised an overcoming of the former splitting according to ideological orientations.[16] Furthermore, the decision in favour of the principle of industrial associations (*Industrieverbandsprinzip*) was taken, allowing for a recruitment strategy encompassing all different social groups of workers and employees. This double organization-related decision advanced the formation of some powerful single unions (*Einzelgewerkschaften*) within the principal organization of the *Deutsche Gewerkschaftsbund* (DGB) (German Association of Unions). In the postwar period, the principal organizations of white-collar workers' unions (*Deutsche Angestelltengewerkschaft* (DAG) (German Association of White-collar Workers)) and of civil servants (*Deutscher Beamtenbund* (DBB) (German Association of Civil Servants)) were also founded again. However, the DGB became the dominant organization to which, right from its very inauguration, even a great number of white-collar workers and civil servants belonged.[17] Despite the profound changes in the occupational structure of Germany over the years which have led to a major increase in the proportion of white-collar workers and civil servants in the total number of employees, as well as to an increasing heterogeneity of status groups, the two professional organizations—the DAG and the DBB—have not succeeded in gaining any ground at the cost of the DGB.[18] Indeed, in the mid 1980s, the DGB not only increased its total number of members considerably, but it also organized far more employees and even slightly more civil servants than its professional counterparts.[19]

Centralization

After 1945, employers' associations and unions agreed upon their goal of an autonomous design for wage relations (*Tarifbeziehungen*). While they first wanted to limit state influence to a minimum, their further efforts were concentrated on establishing a formalized system of negotiation.[20] The institutionalization of industrial relations made progress insofar as the unions recognized the private market economy—this was the case by the end of the 1950s at the very latest, as a result of growing margins for economic distribution[21]—and employers were forced to make concessions in wage policy.[22] Already in 1954, labour and management reached an agreement on collective bargaining and arbitration (*Tarifverhandlungs- und Schlichtungsabkommen*), which has led to regularly re-occurring wage rounds based on a highly formalized procedure that is still practiced today.[23]

This arrangement is extremely centralized in two respects. First, because of the small group of actors involved (the member organizations of BDA, DGB and DAG), and, second, because of the mode of negotiation. The dominating form of agreement is the trade specific collective agreement (*Branchentarifvertrag*), which is mainly negotiated on a regional level, but also on a national level in smaller branches of industry.[24] Responsibility for leading the negotiations is concentrated in the hands of the associations' executives, both on the employers' and the employees' side.[25] The agreements concluded have traditionally had a strong validity and a broad scope. Plant agreements (*Betriebsvereinbarungen*)—which are possible in the dual collective bargaining system in Germany—must only set regulations for items which are not already stipulated in a collective agreement.[26] A total number of almost 90 percent of all employees has jobs in economic sectors where collective agreements are presently valid.[27] This figure is representative insofar as it is comprised not only of employees organized in unions who profit from the stipulations laid down in collective agreements, but also of others, either because companies apply those terms on a voluntary basis—which is often the case—or because the Federal Minister of Labour and Social Affairs has declared them to be generally binding—this measure being of benefit to about one quarter of all employees.[28] The centralization of industrial relations and, thus, also, the standardization of wages and work relations, have reached the highest degree within the public services sector where a single round of collective bargaining annually between public employers and unions accounts for negotiating the wages of workers and employees on the national, state, and community level. However, here, the DGB is confronted with an important competitor, the *Tarifgemeinschaft für Angestellte im öffentlichen Dienst* (Collective Bargaining Community for Employees in Public Services) which is led by DAG.[29]

"Juridification"

Even though industrial relations in Germany are largely free of state intervention, they are, however, subjected to a number of legal standards. This is true for both levels of the dual system of interrelations, that is for the plant or company level as well as for the branch level. With its combination of autonomy and regulation, the German model is somewhat similar to the system of industrial relations in countries such as the Netherlands, Austria, and Switzerland, and is clearly different from the French system of state intervention.[30]

The *Tarifvertragsgesetz* (Law on Collective Agreements), which was passed in 1949 and has stayed substantially unchanged until today, functions as the legal basis for the sectoral relations between employers and unions, yet outlines only general rules of conduct for the industrial partners.[31] Not even the possibility of declaring an agreement as generally binding, which is provided for in the law, has been able to develop towards an instrument of state intervention because the corresponding procedure requires the consent of the unions and the employers.[32] Compared to this, the regulations in the law governing industrial disputes, which is mainly case law, are relatively restrictive. Resulting limitations mainly affect the employees. According to some basic court decisions, they are bound by restrictions such as the prohibition of political and so-called "wild" strikes, i.e., strikes not organized by unions, the principle of *ultima ratio,* which allows for strikes only as a last means in collective bargaining disputes, as well as the obligation to keep the peace throughout the term of a collective agreement.[33] In contrast, courts operating under the maxim of parity of weapons, have assigned the possibility of lockout to the employers, a practice which is more common in Germany than anywhere else in Europe. The unions have never been successful with their frequently renewed claim for an interdiction of lockouts. Recently, however, they did manage to reach an agreement that allows employers to use this strategy only as a means to fight an imbalance of power on the side of the unions.[34]

Work relations at the plant and the company level are also formalized to a large extent. The juridification of work relations in the framework of the works constitution (*Betriebsverfassung*) has a very long tradition. It dates back to the German Empire, where prototypes of today's works constitution existed in the form of workers' committees founded on the initiative of the Reich government. These committees were supposed to contribute to an easing of tensions within the plant. Whereas these institutions did not meet with the unions' approval at that time, the workers' councils in the Weimar Republic, which were established on the basis of a respective law passed in 1920, soon developed into the unions' "extended arm," even though, formally, they remained independent. The basic design of the works constitution found at that time, which engenders a certain dualism between interest representation at the firm level and at the level of negotiations between the two sides of industry, was maintained in the *Betriebsverfassungsgesetz* (Works Constitution Act), which was passed in 1952 and amended in 1972. Another element of industrial relations is also rooted in the Weimar tradition, namely, the idea of social partnership (*Sozialpartnerschaft*) which has remained an essential element in the works constitution.[35] Even though the unions originally criticized the workers' councils' insufficient authority, the latter quickly developed into the centre of firm-related interest representation for employees as well of union activities at the firm level. A major reason for this can certainly be found in the high acceptance and regard the institution of the workers' councils enjoys among the workforce.[36]

On the company level, the juridification is expressed in the three different forms of employee representation on the boards of directors. Among these three, the company constitution (*Unternehmensverfassung*) in the coal, iron, and steel industries, which was established by law in 1951 and provides for true parity between the industrial partners, is the oldest and, at the same time, the most comprehensive model of codetermination in the company (*Unternehmensmitbestimmung*). The *Betriebsverfassungsgesetz* (Works Constitution Act) of 1952 (amended in 1972) and the *Mitbestimmungsgesetz* (Codetermination Act) of 1976 extended employee representation on the boards of directors to incorporated companies in other industrial sectors but without giving parity to the employee side. Whereas the Works Constitution Act only provides for a one-third parity, the Codetermination Act of 1976—which applies to large companies with 2,000 employees and more—contains at least numerical parity, which, however, to a large extent is restricted in a practical sense because of the fact that the senior executives are counted on the employee side and management holds the chair of the board of directors.[37]

Cooperation

The stability of industrial relations in the Federal Republic does not only result from specific institutional conditions and particularities in development of the interest organizations, but can also be attributed to certain tendencies of the corporate actors concerned. In this regard, the culture of industrial relations has to be seen as a condition of its own, which has a considerable influence on the institutions' respective continued existence. In particular, the formalized collective bargaining relations in the Federal Republic could hardly have developed if the employers' associations and unions had not been prepared to cooperate in principle. The unions, however, did not dispose of this readiness to cooperate from the very beginning, but developed it only gradually throughout the 1950s. The DGB's platform (*Grundsatzprogramm*) of 1949, with its clearly anticapitalist thrust, was still far away from any idea of social partnership.[38] Yet, in developing a political strategy for the implementation of the platform, union representatives already showed a certain degree of pragmatism. Fearing the growing influence of communist union members, and out of consideration for the nonsocialist groups within their own ranks, the DGB, to an ever growing extent, gave preference to conventional political lobbying over the unrestrained mobilization of its own membership.[39] At the same time, the aim of greater codetermination in companies and plants came to programmatically the fore, thus pushing further-reaching aims such as the nationalization of key industries into the background. The partial realization of this aim, which followed the introduction of codetermination at par in the coal, iron, and steel industries in 1951, in turn contributed considerably to integrating the workers and the bodies representing their interests into the market economy system.[40] Since the mid 1950s, at the latest, the unions have adopted a pragmatic strategy of striving after wage increases and better fringe benefits, and, thus, laid the foundation for a peaceful reconciliation of interests with the employers.[41] This new policy was politically endorsed in the DGB's *Düsseldorfer Programm* (Düsseldorf platform) of 1963, which was guided by a leftist-Keynesian economic policy and, thus, included the offer of cooperation with the state and with management.[42] With regard to the individual unions, however, it has to be said that they joined this programmatic re-orientation to varying degrees. The *IG Metall* in particular, and as the biggest individual union, continued to see itself as a critic of the system, and maintained its conflict-oriented strategy vis-à-vis management for a long time.[43]

In contrast to the unions, the employers' associations' policies and programs are not directed towards change, but towards the preservation of existing social structures. Therefore, it seems easiest for the employers to make concessions to the unions if these concessions stay within the given framework, i.e., if these concern social benefits or questions of distribution. Because of its adherence to maintaining the status quo, the BDA has always fiercely fought comprehensive reform plans advanced by the unions, such as the model of codetermination at par. However, at the same time, it has also showed its readiness to share the growth in the national product with the employees. For instance, the mid 1950s peaceful wage increase agreement with the unions was considerably facilitated by the rapid upswing of the economy.[44] The unions' united appearance in collective bargaining disputes further promoted the employers' willingness to cooperate.[45] Finally, the cooperative mechanisms of conflict regulation gradually developed into a good in itself, which the employers clung to even in times when they could have reached short-term advantages by applying adversarial strategies.[46]

In a process that narrowed their differences on a mutual basis, management and labour in the Federal Republic have formed a culture of social partnership in industrial relations which is founded on a consensus with regard to the principle of searching for compromises in a nonconfrontational manner. On the basis of the mutual recognition of their respective social roles, the industrial partners try to solve their conflicts of interest through negotiations. They move along the lines of a system of mutually accepted rules, which for their part have resulted from the actors' voluntary cooperation.[47]

The duration and scope of industrial disputes are, together, a reliable indicator of the general standard of social partnership, but, also, of the fluctuations between cooperation and conflict that occur in the course of time as well as when comparing the various industrial sectors. An examination of the respective data confirms the impression of the predominantly cooperative industrial relations in the Federal Republic. Both in a historical comparison with the German Empire and the Weimar Republic and when compared with other western countries, the Federal Republic reveals itself as a country with relatively few strikes.[48] However, after a longer phase of decreasing industrial disputes, the unions' and employers' readiness to fight out disputes grew considerably in the 1970s. The number of employees involved in strikes and lockouts doubled as compared with the preceding decade.[49] In contrast again, the 1980s witnessed a renewed easing of the socioeconomical climate and, consequently, a decrease in the number of industrial disputes.

Deconcentration in the System of Associations

Since the 1980s, and ever more severely in the 1990s, both trade unions and employers' associations have been confronted with rising problems in recruitment, mobilization, and integration. The organizations' claims to represent the interests of members and potential members is becoming more and more questionable. Changes in the social and economic structure are making it increasingly difficult to induce potential members to join and to gain consent from all internal interest groups for the associations' politics. As far as these problems result in the loss of both loyalty and actual members, a trend of deconcentration can be seen that affects the system of industrial relations on the whole.

With regard to trade unions, this trend becomes particularly visible when looking at the development of DGB membership in the last two-and-a-half decades. While there was strong growth in the 1970s, a crisis in recruitment became apparent in the 1980s that manifested itself in temporary fluctuations in membership.[50] As far as its present state is concerned, the DGB has gained a great deal from the unification of Germany. Its membership increased by almost half, from eight million in 1989 to about twelve million in 1991. Since then, however, figures have been falling not only in the East, but also in the West. The unions belonging to the DGB lost nearly 800,000 members in 1992 alone.[51] Whereas, in spite of temporary losses, the degree of unionization remained by and large stable in the 1980s, and the loyalty of the core membership also seemed to be unbroken,[52] the newest trends indicate a dramatic mobilization problem for the unions. According to a recent survey a strong minority of the membership—comprising about 40 percent—is considering leaving their union.[53]

The decreasing representativeness of the unions is underlined by the fact that the social structure of their membership deviates more and more from the structure of the working population. This is particularly apparent with white-collar workers who show a degree of unionization of only 20 percent in contrast to 50 percent among the blue-collar workers, although currently their share of the working population is higher than that of the blue-collar workers. The most qualified groups within the new class of employees are particularly reluctant to join a union.[54] The lack of appeal unions have for female employees results in another problem in structure. Although the rise in the gainful employment of women has been accompanied by an increasing desire to join a union, the degree of unionization among women is only half that among men.[55] Finally, another alarming development is to be found in the ever growing absence of young people in the unions. Whereas the share of young persons in the DGB in 1979 still amounted to 17 percent, it fell steadily to less than ten percent in 1993.[56] Thus, the present social structure of the unions resembles more closely that of the working population of the 1950s than that of the 1990s. The unions have remained primarily blue-collar organizations, regardless of changes in the occupational structure.[57]

By and large, the unions' organization problems derive from three interrelated and complex causes. First, the decline in membership can certainly, to a considerable extent, be explained by the incessantly high level of unemployment. Many leave the union when their employment is terminated, even though their organization, as a rule, offers them continued membership with reduced dues and fewer rights. Because unions are organizations of the gainfully employed, both in the way they see themselves and the structure of their decision-making, they only have a very limited attraction for the unemployed. The job loss usually entails the loss of contacts in the firm and ties with the union. People who were not members of a union before becoming unemployed show an even greater detachment to the unions. Though some unions have opened up to this group more recently and have granted them the option of acquiring membership with reduced participatory rights, only very few have availed themselves of this opportunity.

Second, the unions face a general problem in recruitment that is tied to the sociostructural change from a traditional society consisting of large social classes to a society of multidimensionally-differentiated status positions. Along with the trend towards the pluralization and individualization of lifestyles and interest, a general aversion against the traditional "big organizations" has spread to affect the unions to a particularly high degree. The prevailing preferences for an individual-oriented lifestyle are hardly reconcilable with integration into the organizational reality of the unions marked by traditional formal structures.

Finally, the unions' structural problems are connected with the fact that their strategies of recruitment and mobilization barely reach those groups of employees anymore who, in the course of the change to a service economy, have gained more and more importance. In contrast to the unions' core group of blue-collar workers in the manufacturing industry, which is for the most part concentrated in bigger company units, the situation of the ever growing group of white-collar workers is marked by a low degree of concentration and greater isolation, i.e., factors that cause relatively unfavourable conditions for communication for the organizational efforts of the unions. Because of the specific professional careers and the high percentage of mainly women part-time employees, white-collar workers predominantly dispose of individual, career-oriented and privatistic attitudes that pose fundamental obstacles to a collective representation of interests.[58]

After the German unification, it first seemed as if the takeover of most of the members of the single unions (*Einzelgewerkschaften*) that had been affiliated to the *Freier Deutscher Gewerkschaftsbund* (FDGB) (Free

German Association of Unions) would considerably reduce the DGB's structural problems. The DGB was not only able to increase the number of its members to a large extent and, thus, temporarily reach a degree of unionization in eastern Germany that far exceeded the western level,[59] but it also ameliorated its internal social structure on the basis of the surprisingly high readiness of white-collar workers and women to join or stay in a union.[60] However, the reversal soon to appear in this trend quickly resulted in severe losses in these groups. Due to the high unemployment of women, the percentage of women in the East German Land associations of the unions in particular decreased rapidly.[61]

Thus, the inclusion of the new east German members has contributed little to the solution of the old structural problems but has, rather, created new structural problems. First of all, the unions are now confronted with additional conflicts of interest within their memberships, since the new white-collar members are adopting a primarily instrumental attitude towards the unions.[62] Moreover, the working-class members of the east German unions do not, for the most part, dispose of that collective tendency and basic solidarity that continues to provide the unions in the west with a strong support with regard to their political strategies. Finally, the territorial expansion has lead to frictions within the single organizations and among the single unions. Reform strategies that have been developed in the west and put more emphasis on a qualitative collective bargaining policy, for instance, have met with little understanding and support in the east where people are primarily oriented towards classical questions of distribution.[63] In the mid 1990s, however, the tendencies on this point have become more alike, since, under the conditions of a severely growing rate of unemployment, employment policy has moved to the centre of attention in both parts of Germany. The organizational development of unions in east German territory has also lead to manifest conflicts among the single unions. At the beginning of the 1990s, there were fierce quarrels between the *Gewerkschaft öffentliche Dienste, Transport und Verkehr* (ÖTV) (Public Services and Transport Workers' Union) and the *IG Bergbau und Energie* (*Industriegewerkschaft Bergbau und Energie*) (Union of Mining and Power Workers), and the *Gewerkschaft Handel, Banken und Versicherungen* (HBV) (Union of Workers in Commerce, Banking and Insurance) and the ÖTV, about the question of how to delimit their fields of recruitment.[64]

Industrial relations in west and east Germany are touched by these structural problems insofar as the DGB is less and less capable of meeting the necessary requirements of its claim of comprehensive representation that derives from its self-image as one overarching trade union. Losses in membership and a considerable time lag in adapting its membership structure to the more and more tertiarized structure of the labour force have resulted in an objective loss in representativeness which, in the long run, will undermine the DGB unions' capacity to act in the field of collective bargaining policy. However, the process of deconcentration has been limited up to now insofar as it has weakened the DGB but has not led to a splitting up of the employees' side. Nonetheless, neither the union of the white-collar workers (DAG) nor that of the civil servants (DBB), which are oriented purely towards the specific professional profile and interests of their members, have been able to profit from the DGB's recruitment problems. Likewise, the foundation of special interest organizations for individual status groups has also not met with any success. It seems that, because of the primarily individualistic tendencies of the new middle class, the unions do not have to be afraid of any rivalry caused by new corporate actors, while, at the same time, however, they cannot claim to represent these groups comprehensively.

If one looks at the unions as a whole there even seems to be a tendency towards concentration rather than deconcentration. The DAG, for instance, suffers from recruitment problems caused by the job market itself, and, so, increasingly seeks to both politically and organizationally align itself with the HBV, its former bitter rival from the DGB. Meanwhile, even a merger of the two organizations does not seem impossible anymore. Mergers have already taken place or been arranged between formerly independent unions of the DGB. Within the DGB leadership there are some who regard as desirable a reduction of the number of single unions to eight or ten powerful multi-sector unions.[65] Such organizational mergers, however, do not result in a gain in power for the unions, but represent a defensive reaction to the new structural challenges.

The tendency towards the erosion of the capacity to act can also be found with regard to the employers' associations. However, the manifestations and causes of the organizational problems here are different from those of the unions. Whereas in earlier times employers only occasionally withdrew from employers' associations, an accumulation of such cases can be observed since the beginning of the 1990s. It is also particularly striking that not only small and medium-sized companies, but also ever more large companies are withdrawing from their associations. Moreover, a comparatively new phenomenon has arisen in that many newly founded companies, especially in eastern Germany, have decided not to join an employers' association at all.[66] Such an increase in withdrawn memberships and lack of new interest are relevant not only quantitatively, but also qualitatively, since they indicate a fundamental decrease in loyalty to these organizations, which seriously threatens to endanger their role as actors in collective bargaining policy.[67] Even though the majority of the member companies continues to voice a great interest especially in the "customer service" of the employers' associations, satisfaction with the associations' politics has clearly decreased on the whole.[68] The traditional solidarity of associations and quasi-automatic membership have, in many instances, been replaced by an unemotional cost-benefit analysis. During the present time of a recession and economic structural change, the far from insignificant membership fees an individual must pay is weighed against the services the respective association offers. The detection of any service deficits resulting from the modified basis of motivation directly leads to the withdrawal of an individual's loyalty to the union.

Among the manifold causes that can bring about alienation between an association and its members, the current collective bargaining policy is by far the most decisive. The collective agreements concluded by the associations and the unions have met with increasing opposition from member companies. In this very regard the wage agreement concluded in the metal industry in 1995 was widely disapproved of by the membership of the *Arbeitgeberverband Gesamtmetall* (Employers' Association of the Metal Industry) because it provided for wage increases, which many members regarded to be too high. Consequently, a few distinguished companies pointedly withdrew from their association.[69] On account of their displeasure at the BDA's conduct during negotiations, some industrial associations (*Industrieverbände*) are even seriously considering terminating their part in the traditional division of labour between BDI and BDA in order to take the collective bargaining policy into their own hands.[70] A grave consequence of this growing displeasure among member companies with the collective bargaining policy of the employers' associations can be seen in the fact that the latter no longer bear more than a limited capability to oblige their member firms to comply with the terms of the agreements concluded with the unions.[71]

In east Germany the organizational problems described arise in a joint and aggravated form. Though until the end of 1990 the BDA and its affiliated member associations had succeeded in the area-wide foundation of associations in the different trade sectors and their incorporation into the federal association,[72] the degree of organization was still considerably lower than in the west. Many companies have shied away from joining an employers' association because they do not want to be obliged to pay the agreed wage rates that they would regard as far too high, even though they urgently depend on the association's offers of service. After the so-called "graduated rate collective agreement" (*Stufentarifvertrag*) had come into being in the east German metal industry, quite a few member firms even withdrew from their employers' association again.[73] Thus, in east Germany there are some trade sectors in which up to 60 percent of the companies do not belong to an employers' association.[74]

In contrast to the unions, the processes described do not only indicate a weakening of the BDA and its member organizations, but herald structural deconcentration within the sphere of the employers' associations. For even though the latter have tried for some time to increase their appeal to the companies by improving their service and tailoring themselves to better suit the different interests of small and big companies,[75] they have not been able to reverse the trend towards withdrawn memberships and abstention from the associations. The effects of selective incentives that the associations grant in return for membership fees fall flat in view of the growth in lucrative commercial consulting and information services.[76] Therefore, the employers' associations have started to discuss ways of counteracting the erosion of their members by one of two methods: either introduce a split membership, i.e., a membership with and without the obligation to pay at rates in line with collective pay agreements, or found new organizations under the roof of the BDA without a collective bargaining mandate.[77] Even leading representatives of the BDA seem to be prepared meanwhile to accept the division of the associations in the employers' camp into two parts that would result from such measures.[78] It appears that the employers' associations can only solve the threat to their continued existence if they give up the monopoly on collective bargaining they have, for all intents and purposes, held up to now. Seeing that this monopoly is increasingly undermined by the ongoing tendencies towards withdrawn membership and disinterest in joining in any case, it seems rational to renounce the compulsory obligation to pay at rates in line with collective agreements in order to render membership in an association more attractive again for a wider circle of companies. This encompasses a considerable limitation on the traditional spectrum of the responsibilities of the employers' associations but, in return, it does reduce the probability that rival organizations with an authority to carry out collective bargaining will be able to establish themselves in addition to the BDA. Moreover, the partial shift of the responsibility of collective bargaining competence to the companies themselves is not necessarily disadvantageous to the associations affiliated to the BDA because they would be relieved of the ever more difficult task to develop a collective bargaining strategy that is equally acceptable to all types of companies.

Decentralization in Collective Bargaining Policy

The first signs of a departure from the highly centralized and standardized system of collective agreements appeared at the end of the 1960s when a shift in German collective bargaining policy from quantitative to qualitative aspects began to emerge. Whereas collective bargaining had until then be concerned almost exclusively with wage levels, the wage structure, and working hours, other issues such as work organization, labour intensity, job safety, job qualification, and participatory rights in the working process, have also, since that time, become the object of collective agreements.[79] This shift has to be seen in connection with the unions' wish to alleviate the severe social consequences for workers resulting from introduction of new technologies. Unions have had to realize that the new bargaining objects were often too differentiated to be amenable to regulations valid throughout the whole sector.[80] Unions have been under increasing pressure to shape the collective representation of workers' interests in a more firm-oriented way and, thus, much like when the consequences of rationalization intensified leading to a greater heterogeneity of employment contracts as well as greater flexibility of the deployment of labour.[81]

It was not until the beginning of the 1980s, however, that a significant step in that direction was undertaken following the unions' offensive concerning policy on working time. The turning point in this regard was the agreement concluded in 1984 that introduced the 38.5-hour week in the metal industry.[82] This collective agreement was the result of a compromise between the once diametrically opposed positions of the employers and the unions on the question of working time. This first step towards the 35-hour week was a goal of the highest priority for the unions for reasons relating to employment policy and questions of organization,[83] and the first step could only be realized at the cost of a flexible and differentiated regulation of working time at the plant level. The agreement that was reached after a fierce, six-week-long industrial dispute introduced a reduction in the average working week by 1.5 hours without any reduction in pay. However, it also enabled the individual employers to stipulate, on the consent of the workers' council (*Betriebsrat*), the variation between 37 and 40 working hours for some parts of their labour force. In this way, a step towards the destandardization of working conditions was made, but a tendency can be traced towards the relocation of the lines of authority in collective bargaining policy from the unions to the workers' councils.[84]

Although the pressure to change had existed for a long time, it has only been since the German unification that a fundamental change in collective bargaining policy has become visible. For the basic function of the area-wide collective agreement, namely the fixing of general norms and minimum standards, usually has been maintained, even though the scope of plant-related regulations has been broadened significantly in the framework of a qualitative policy in collective bargaining as well as the collective agreements that have shortened the working week. Only recently, collective agreements have been concluded that allow a deviation from these minimum standards wherever this seems necessary according to the specific circumstances in a given plant.

Whereas such new regulations have been realized only in isolated cases in west German trade-specific collective agreements,[85] in eastern Germany the decentralization and greater flexibility of collective bargaining policies have already reached larger dimensions.[86] The model case in this regard is the agreement between the *IG Metall* and the east German metal industry on a so-called "hardship clause." The agreement was preceded by a dispute of several months between the unions and the employers over the collective agreement of a graduated rate that provided for a step-by-step approximation of east German wages to the west German standard within three years.

Only one year after the conclusion of the agreement, doubts about the feasibility of its provisions were uttered by the employers in light of the rapidly worsening economic crisis in east German industry. As the ensuing negotiations aimed at revising the agreement did not lead to an immediate result and the further arbitration proceedings also failed, the employers' associations involved came to the unprecedented decision in west German collective bargaining policy to prematurely terminate the collective agreement of a graduated rate. Because of the fundamental significance attached to this case by the unions, the east German collective bargaining district became the scene of a two-week strike that was accompanied by acts of protest all over Germany and ended with an agreement that encompassed a significant modification of the collective agreement of a graduated rate. The new collective agreement does not only provide for the staggered adjustment of east German wages to western levels, but it also entails a hardship clause which, in the case of economic difficulties, entitles individual firms to fall below the level agreed upon collectively as long as the industrial partners give their consent.[87] Thus, on the one hand, the *IG Metall* succeeded in securing the practice of the trade specific collective agreement as well as the primary responsibility for the sectoral associations for collective bargaining policy, but, on the other hand, had to accept not only a general setback in collectively agreed wage levels, but also the introduction of a qualitatively new element of greater flexibility.

Whereas the possibilities of differentiation provided under collective agreements described so far constitute one form of controlled decentralization in collective bargaining policy, in that it was deliberately initiated by the corporate actors through regulations in collective agreements, a second form, "insidious decentralization," now exists that will probably prove to have more severe consequences for the future of the collective bargaining system. One characteristic of this form of decentralization is the managerial strategy of "out-sourcing." The division of enterprises is often accompanied by a change in sector-affiliation for some company units, which, in many cases, leads to working conditions within the company that are no longer ruled by uniform collective agreement but, rather, by different standards altogether. Company reorganization can, thus, prove to be an instrument for evading high standards reached by collective agreement. Furthermore, it often provokes interunion conflicts in the area of jurisdiction over the individual company units.[88] Finally, there is a deterioration in chances of the collective representation of interests at plant level, because the division of companies into smaller, and legally independent, units necessarily destroys long-established social networks.[89]

A further aspect of insidious decentralization results from changes in economic structure. The influence of the unions is diminishing automatically with the continuation of the ever increasing proportion of the tertiary sector in the national economy because they represent workers and employees to a much smaller extent in the service industries than in the manufacturing, or secondary, sector. The degree of unionization in this sector is often so small that the unions lack the power even of achieving trade-wide collective agreements. If agreements with management are to be concluded at all, then they must take the form of house agreements (*Haustarifverträge*).[90] The growing number of (predominantly smaller) service sector firms, therefore, also implies an increase in the disintegration of collective bargaining.

Finally, the modified organizational behavior of the employers, or the ever less binding nature of their role as members, has contributed to the erosion of the area-wide collective agreement. Whereas the number of withdrawn memberships from the employers' associations is still quite small and, particularly in west Germany, restricted to a few spectacular instances, this is not the case in east Germany where newly established companies have not joined the associations to begin with and, thus, have already engendered a considerable decline in the degree of organization. This has also led to a considerable increase in the number of employers who are not bound by area-wide collective agreements. Another phenomenon, that is not less significant than abstaining from the employers' associations, is to be found in the fact that a growing number of employers is inclined to behave in a way contrary to the provisions of the collective agreements. Irrespective of their membership in an employers' association, they often evade the regulations of current collective agreements either unilaterally or, even, with the tacit consent of the workers' council.

Despite these tendencies, the practice of area-wide collective agreements does not seem to be endangered in principle. There are still several thousands of collective agreements that are concluded or modified in Germany every year. In the most part, they belong to the category of area-wide collective agreements.[91] Most recently, the scope for the implementation of these agreements within the individual firms has widened considerably as far as legal matters are concerned, but the scale of the actual increased flexibility has so far remained quite modest.[92] For a large part, this can be blamed might of single unions such as *IG Metall*, which obliges its members in the workers' councils to swear to a restrictive stand on the approval of measures of greater flexibility at plant level. However, such strategy of containment by the unions can delay but never totally halt the process of shifting the responsibility of collective bargaining to the arena of the firm level as long as it takes place in the form of insidious decentralization.[93]

The further development of collective bargaining policy, and the future forms and extent of shifting responsibilities in this field to the arena of the firm in particular, will depend heavily on how the corporate actors involved will define their goals and which inner-associational interests will begin to show a benefit from the changes. The employers and the unions are unanimous only with regard to the fundamental necessity of adjusting the priorities in collective bargaining policies to meet changes in the conditions of the economy in general, and at the individual plant level, in particular. However, there is no agreement either between management and labour, or within the respective camps on how this adjustment can be realized and to what extent it requires a revision of established practices such as area-wide collective agreements.

There are particularly significant differences among the employers where the interests of one part of the associations' members concerning fundamental changes in the system of collective agreements have collided with the interests both of other groups of members and, above all, of the associations' leadership. Most particularly disgruntled are the smaller and medium-sized companies that complain about the dominance of the larger enterprises in the employers' associations and the supposedly one-sided gearing of collective bargaining practices to suit only their interests. Whereas, even under crisis conditions, the large-scale enterprises make use of concessions to labour in collective bargaining because, for competitive reasons, they are interested in trade-wide collective agreements for competitive reasons, the smaller firms no longer see themselves in position to comply with the terms of the collective agreements concluded by their associations, due to their frequent situation of small profit margins. Within their ranks, then, both a broadening of and a greater flexibility in area-wide collective agreements is much in demand. These claims are often uttered in connection with the threat to withdraw from the association.[94]

The effort to reconcile the conflicts in internal interest in collective bargaining policy has inevitably led the employers' associations into a general conflict of aims. There is the tendency to give in to the smaller and medium-sized companies' requests and restrain trade-wide regulations to the greatest extent possible in favour of greater scope for the firms, because, in this way, individual companies are given the opportunity to both react to the exigencies of international competition more readily and, in particular, limit unit labour costs. But, the erosion of area-wide collective agreements also holds considerable dangers for the employers. The disintegration of collective bargaining does not just lead to a reduction in the pressure for innovation that comes from a uniform standard in trade-wide collective bargaining, but can also engender a multiplication in selective strikes. Moreover, individual companies in industrial sectors with a high degree of unionization will probably find it difficult to hold their ground against the unions in collective bargaining disputes. An additional factor, which, from the employers' perspective, also speaks in favour of sticking to the area-wide collective agreements in principal, is the interest of the associations' leadership in maintaining its scope for formative action.

In this situation the employers adopt a dual strategy in collective bargaining policy. The area-wide collective agreement continues to be regarded as a reliable instrument of regulation that serves the purpose of keeping order in industrial relations and, in this capacity, represents an advantage to every employer that can not be replaced. House agreements, therefore, which have always existed in isolated cases, continue to be the exception.[95] At the same time, however, the scope of issues regulated by area-wide collective agreements is to be limited to core elements such as wage levels, questions of classification, and the average working week.[96] But, efforts are made to widen considerably the scope for individual employers with regard to working hours, organization of work, and wage structure.[97] In this context, employers have been trying to put special emphasis on their claims for greater flexibility by declaring union concessions in this realm to be a prerequisite for the continuation of any area-wide collective agreement.

Up to now, the unions have reacted to the new situation rather defensively by declaring, as their chief objective, the very preservation of area-wide collective agreement. Yet, at the same time, they have recognized the necessity to accommodate the ever more differentiating interest positions of the employees by shifting the responsibility for collective bargaining to the arena of the firm and also especially by increasing individual choice.[98] However, there is much wrangling within and among the individual unions belonging to the DGB as to which direction such measures of flexibility should take and how far they should go. It is mainly the workers' councils that are interested in the expansion of the scope of collective bargaining at plant level because they are the ones who feel most clearly the discrepancies growing between collectively agreed norms and the actual conditions in the firms. In addition, workers' councils can hope to profit from further decentralization by gaining more power in proportion to the unions. Moreover, the stronger presence of workers' councils reveals that such a shift in collective bargaining power could even lessen the strain on the unions because, then, the balancing of the heterogeneous interests of various members and organizations would no longer have to take place centrally. In contrast, traditional groups within the unions are very critical of any change in established practices.[99] Above all, they foresee the risk that the workers' councils could succumb to the temptation of using their new range of opportunities for formative action for the implementation of the firm-centred strategies of closing internal labour markets and further marginalizing fringe staff. From this perspective, the decentralization of collective bargaining policy would inevitably engender a much greater potential for conflicts of interests within the unions.

Whereas in the matter of greater flexibility the seeds of further internal union conflict have clearly been sown, all other parties are in total agreement that efforts have to be taken to limit the insidious decentralization of collective bargaining policy that takes the form of individual companies' withdrawing from their association and the obligation to pay in accordance with a collective agreement. The unions' priority is to prevent the situation where there is no collective agreement at all. Where companies are not affiliated to an employers' association, the unions want to conclude house agreements. In addition, one individual union, the *IG Metall*, has threatened to call permanent strikes from firm to firm if the employers actually realize the project of founding employers' associations that are not subject to the obligation to pay in line with a collective agreement. Moreover, the unions intend to respond to the employers' withdrawal from area-wide collective bargaining by launching a wage offensive targeted at the most profitable companies.[100] Thus, they want to make their opponents aware of the fact that abandoning the practice of area-wide collective agreements would entail the loss of collective goods, such as predictability, standardization, and social peace that are also much appreciated by the employers.

There are also signs of a convergence in the collective bargaining interests of management and labour regardless of the threatening gestures coming from both sides that can attributed to the present situation of economic upheaval and the uncertainties of future development. Both sides are being forced—and not least because of the new expectations of their members—to find a new balance between regulation at firm and branch level if they do not want to put the entire dual system of collective bargaining at stake.[101] In this respect, solutions that benefit only one side do not have a chance of being adopted as official associational policies. Examples of this are the unmodified maintenance of the centralized system of regulation, which is demanded by some parts of the unions, or the total relocation of collective bargaining policy to the arena of the firm, which certain companies are requesting. The employers' associations principally agree with the unions on the aim of preserving the practice of area-wide collective agreements as it is because it is particularly advantageous to large and highly profitable companies, and it promotes the continued role of the employers' associations. Trade-wide collective bargaining seems to be an instrument that grants both sides enough scope to find creative solutions, including new types of bargaining objects. An example of this is the unions' long-standing demand to do away with the separation of wage agreements for blue- and white-collar workers, which has been approved by the employers and is to be realized through the introduction of a common graduated system of classification.[102] In turn, the unions in the long term will hardly be able to resist the trend towards opening up area-wide collective agreements and reducing their comprehensiveness (*Regelungsdichte*), especially since it has turned out that their own members' wish for more flexible working hours and conditions does not necessarily conflict with the companies' efforts to establish firm-related possibilities of differentiation but, rather to the contrary, that there are common points of interest.

The High Level of "Juridification" Despite Efforts to Deregulate

Like the centralized collective bargaining system, the high level of regulation in collective and individual labour law has also come under increased criticism since the 1980s. However, whereas, in the first case, efforts are primarily directed towards a shift in the level at which regulations are established as well as towards the widening of opportunities, in the second case, attention has been given to a general reduction in the comprehensiveness of regulations. In the framework of the so-called "deregulation debate" (*Deregulierungsdiskussion*), which has been urged particularly by the employers, but also supported by certain parts of the parties in power, an increase in the range of managerial decisions has been sought through cutbacks to welfare institutions. Deliberations focussed on certain protective regulations for employees have not been directed against the high level of juridification in general, especially since this high level strongly favours the employers' interests, say, in the question of strikes and lockouts.[103] In contrast to greater flexibility in collective bargaining policy, deregulation has been met by the unions with clear and strong opposition. This has become all the more true as juridification, which, for a long time, was thought of as a corset about union policy, has turned increasingly into an instrument for institutionally safeguarding union activities.[104] Deregulation has made little practical progress within this constellation of interests so far.[105] Despite selective legal amendments, the basic legal institutions seem to be at least partly more firmly established in their function as regulators of industrial relations than at the time immediately following their introduction. This is mainly owing to the fact that the relevance of such institutions does not only depend on the stock of norms in force but, also, on the manner and extent of their embodiment in the social structure at plant level or at the level of relations between the industrial partners.

Among the few deregulatory measures in the field of labour law that have been adopted so far, the most significant one is the amendment of Article 116 in the *Arbeitsförderungsgesetz* (Labour Promotion Act). This so-called *Streikparagraph* (article dealing with strikes) sets out the conditions under which employees who are indirectly affected by a strike can claim compensation payments from the *Bundesanstalt für Arbeit* (Federal Office of Labour). It puts into specific terms the so-called *Neutralitätsgrundsatz* (principle of neutrality) according to which a certain balance of power between management and labour must not be changed to the advantage of one side as a result of measures taken by the state. Since the 1970s, regulations based on court decisions and the decrees of the Federal Office of Labour required that employees who were indirectly affected by a strike within their trade sector, but outside their collective bargaining area, ought to receive part-time payments (*Kurzarbeitergeld*) from the Federal Office of Labour.[106] This regulation, which had always been the source of contention between management and labour during an industrial dispute that lasted several weeks became the object of a fierce controversy in 1984. This argument was triggered by the fact that *IG Metall's* strategy of roving strikes in areas outside of that of the contested collective bargaining was causing an exceptionally high number of temporary layoffs. After these "former" employees had been granted claims to unemployment benefits in a few lawsuits, the employers declared that the parity of means between them and the unions was violated by the state and urgently demanded an amendment to the law in order to exclude such payouts in the future. Against fierce opposition from the unions, the governing coalition of the CDU/CSU and the FDP eventually passed an amendment in 1986 that widely accommodated the employers' demands. According to this amendment those employees indirectly affected by a strike can only claim unemployment benefits if the particular trade-specific union in their collective bargaining area makes demands that differ substantially from those made in the contested area.

For unions like *IG Metall*, which traditionally conducts collective bargaining on a regional level, the amendment to the law has brought about a strategic dilemma. Either they must decide in favour of nationwide uniform demands and, thus, accept that employees indirectly affected by a strike are not to receive any temporary payments because they can claim neither pay for part-time work nor strike pay, or they must differentiate their demands and, thus, foster a fragmentation of collective bargaining, which, in the long run, will undermine their own power. One troublesome factor, still, is that those employees indirectly affected by a lockout also cannot claim pay for part-time work, either. So, as a result, the modified law has weakened the unions' position in collective bargaining disputes. However, the Federal Constitutional Court, in a decision in 1995, declared the amendment of Article 116 in the *Arbeitsförderungsgesetz* to be, in principal, compatible with the state's duty to stay neutral in labour disputes.[107]

A second form of deregulation concerns the arrangement of individual employer-employee relation. The *Beschäftigungsförderungsgesetz* (The Promotion of Employment Act) of 1985 has curtailed the relatively comprehensive protection against dismissal that German labour law had provided as an essential point. Whereas, until then, an employment contract could only be limited in time for important objective reasons, now it is possible to limit the duration of employment contracts to 18 months without such reasons. This measure was introduced to increase the flexibility of companies' personnel management and to facilitate quicker hiring. However, experience shows that the desired positive effects on employment have largely failed to materialize and, instead, the new law has only further promoted a trend towards the transformation of previously permanent employment contracts into more unstable ones.[108]

Another way of possibly falling below previous standards has been opened up by the *Richtlinien für die Förderung von Arbeitsbeschaffungsmaßnahmen* (Guidelines for the Promotion of Job Creation Schemes) that were changed in 1994. Whereas, until then, the standard rate was usually paid in these employment contracts supported by the state, now, state assistance in the east German supporting institutions is conditioned by either payment below the standard rate or reduced working hours for the people enrolled in the program. In the west, the standard rate was kept up by legal requirement. However, in actual fact, the pay of those enrolled has fallen 90 percent, since this is the share the state provides, whereas the rest is left up to the supporting institutions who only very rarely dispose of the funds they are required to put up.[109]

In order to expedite their own plans, the federal government set up a "deregulation committee" in 1987 that was supposed to develop suitable measures for the modification of present labour law. The committee's report, which was published in 1991, discusses the measures already realized, but also mentions proposals that go much further and are aimed at quite fundamental changes. With regard to individual labour law, the committee report first suggests widening the legal authorized periods and general admissibility of loan-employment, limiting protection against dismissal for certain groups of employees, and enlarging the possibilities of limiting the duration of employment contracts. Furthermore, it proposes abolishing the monopoly of the Federal Office of Labour in the placement of labour and authorizing the introduction of private placement agencies, as well as relaxing the *Ladenschlußgesetz* (Shop Closing Times Act), which in Germany has always been rather rigid.[110]

Whatever the social consequences of each of these regulations may be, the state stays within the framework of the actor's role, which has traditionally been attributed to it in the German system of industrial relations. This would not be true for the committee's ideas on reforming collective labour law that would bring about a substantial dismantling of current law on collective bargaining and, for that matter, the freedom to collective bargaining. In this regard, the committee proposes, among other things, to limit the possibilities of declaring collective agreements generally binding, to allow agreements at firm level that fall below collectively agreed standards, and to partly repeal the "advantage rule" (*Günstigkeitsprinzip*), which prohibits an individual employee from voluntarily renouncing collectively agreed benefits.[111] The last two measures would lead to an individualization of pay conditions going far beyond the ideas of increased flexibility discussed that would certainly meet with the fierce opposition from the unions. Yet, in view of the numerous cutbacks in social policy during the last few years, which have primarily affected the employees, the government has refrained so far from further provoking the unions by such a more symbolic encroachment upon their own territory. Besides, such a far-reaching dismantling of the freedom to collective bargaining does not meet with unanimous approval among employers, either.

A uniform trend towards greater deregulation in the area of works and company constitution (*Betriebs- und Unternehmensverfassung*) is not noticeable, as becomes most evident when examining both individual labour law and long-term plans relating to collective bargaining law. There may well have been recent amendments to these laws. However, these amendments are not aimed at a general abandonment of the present high level of juridification but, rather, comprise very different measures, such as greater differentiation in the kinds of employee representation at firm level and legal safeguards for existing institutions. Codetermination at plant and company level has not, up to now, been so heavily influenced by such modifications in the law. Rather, certain societal developments have had a far greater influence, and these include changes in economic structure and technology, as well as changes in communications and the social structure in the plants.

The move that probably best fits into the context of deregulatory measures is the amendment of the *Betriebsverfassungsgesetz* (Works Constitution Act), which was passed in 1988 and, according to the intentions of the law-makers, was meant to strengthen the rights of minorities in the plants. The amendment provides for the nominations of candidates for the works councils to be valid if they are supported by five percent of the workforce, instead of ten percent as was previously the case, or a total of 50 employees in number, instead of 100. Moreover, in contrast to the old law, each union represented in the firm can submit a list of candidates even if they do not reach the quorum of signatures. Finally, a new institution in addition to the works councils has been introduced, namely the "executives' representative bodies" (*Sprecherausschüsse für leitende Angestellte*). Unlike the works councils, these representative bodies, which are only established if the majority of a firm's senior executives vote in favour of them, do not dispose of the rights to genuine codetermination, but only of the rights to observation and consultation.[112]

The general political aim of the amendment to the law was not really to reduce the rights of the works councils but, rather, to diminish the dominance which the DGB unions had up to then in the works councils. Yet, the actual consequences of the new law have proven to be a lot less far-reaching than either the government had wanted or the unions had feared. With regard to work relations, neither the executives' representative bodies nor the smaller unions hardly have played any major role up to now.

Nevertheless, irrespective of the new law, the works councils are more firmly established as an institution of industrial relations today than was the case after the first major revision of the works constitution. In the mid 1970s, only a third of the works councils that were already in place really fulfilled their function of representing independently the employees' interests. The majority of these bodies were either ignored and circumvented by the employees or extensively hindered and paralyzed by management. Conversely, at the beginning of the 1990s, conversely two thirds of the works councils were able to assert the employees' interests in relation to management by adopting cooperative or adversarial strategies.[113]

This process of change can be explained for a good part by the fact that the unions, which, originally, had always regarded the works councils to be, among other things, a competitor and, therefore, tried to limit their influence by establishing "shop stewards' committees" (*Vertrauensleutekörper*), have, in the meantime accepted precedence of the works councils at firm level. The works councils, for their part, have been able to maintain or, even, strengthen their functional autonomy with regard to the unions but, at the same time, are more closely integrated with the unions than ever. However, the growing effectiveness of the pursuits of the works councils also has to be seen as the consequence of a process of clarification with respect to their relationship with management. Whereas, previously, there had often been confrontation and much ideological position-taking in the mutual relations, this has changed, to a large extent, into a relationship based on pragmatic cooperation. In this new climate, even difficult problems, such as those regarding staff cuts, are usually overcome without major conflicts as soon as they arise.[114]

Thus, at the moment, the role of works councils is being called into question neither by legal changes nor by social relations within the firms. Rather, the institution is endangered by structural changes in the plants, like the further introduction of direct employee participation. In order to provide a social cushion to the modernization of production processes, in many cases management has chosen to give the employees concerned a share in the communication and decision processes in their areas of work. These new offers of participation compete with the traditional way of having employees' interests represented by works councils, and, thus, could lead to the beguiling loss of the latter's functions. In their endeavour to halt this process, or lessen its consequences, unions and works councils have been trying to conclude plant agreements (*Betriebsvereinbarungen*) by the way of direct employee participation with the management.[115] However, there is no telling yet in which shape, and to what extent, direct employee participation will be established. This will depend on both the quality of the participatory rights offered, and, thus, their appeal to the employees, as well as the works councils' ability to control such trends.

Codetermination at company level is a clearer example yet of how strongly the basic functioning of established institutions is influenced by developments in the structure of the economy and technology. Though legislators have intervened on several occasions to maintain the so-called *Montanmitbestimmung* (codetermination in the coal, iron, and steel industries), it will hardly be possible to stop entirely the insidious erosion of the only form of codetermination that provides true parity. An ever increasing number of trusts in this area have expanded beyond the "traditional" emphasis on coal, iron, and steel. To avoid a further erosion of the *Montanmitbestimmung*, amendments were passed in 1981 and 1988 that ruled that even companies which no longer attain more than part of their net product in this industrial sector remain subject to the special form of codetermination.[116] Yet, today, only 31 out of the original 108 companies subject to codetermination in the coal, iron, and steel industries remain.[117]

Though the *Mitbestimmungsgesetz* (Codetermination Act) of 1976 remains unaffected by changes in the structure of trade, it is, nonetheless, confronted with other challenges. There is technological development that leads to the growing differentiation and the restructuring of companies. This, in turn, engenders an increasing divergence between codetermination responsibilities and the actual control over decisions. In contrast, there is the problem of the low effectiveness of codetermination in the east German companies. Here, not only is there, in many cases, a lack of sufficient support from the workforce and works councils, but also the unions are not in possession of the organizational structures and the know-how necessary for effective representation.[118]

Like the works councils, codetermination at company level has become firmly established in the structure of industrial relations. After losing their case against the Codetermination Act of 1976 at the Federal Constitutional Court, the employers in the large companies soon came to terms with board-level worker representation. In contrast, the unions had to recognize, particularly, on the basis of their practical experience, but also, perhaps more specifically, after the legislative decision that the board of directors must be comprised of more members from the employees' representatives, that they would not be able to realize their notion of industrial democracy by using their newly won mandate.

Where codetermination at company level is applied, the resulting opportunities for formative action for the employees and unions are even more limited than had originally been assumed by the workers. Even if codetermination can be utilized to a strengthen representation at the level—which has occurred only under certain favourable conditions—the workers' representatives have to pay the price by becoming, at least partially, an instrument of management's own interests. They can only realize their influence and control over company policy if, in return, they accept the basic principles of management action and go along with the ensuing decisions.

The various modifications to labour law, which the conservative-liberal coalition has enacted since the mid 1980s, have reduced only in a selective manner the juridification characterizing industrial relations in Germany. This can mainly be explained by fact that, from the beginning, both the deregulatory measures and the plans to go beyond concentrated on and were limited to a subsection of industrial relations known as individual labour law. Institutions like the works and company constitution, which found their still currently acceptable form in the 1970s only after a long struggle between management and labour, were to be maintained in principle and only revised on account of changes in societal conditions or, more likely, political suitability. After all, they serve as an institutionalized form of class compromise which, especially under conditions of economic crisis, has proven its effectiveness with regard to the regulation of social relations at firm level and is, therefore, not questioned by any of the actors involved. Collective bargaining law has also been excepted from deregulation so far, even though the deregulation committee installed in 1987 elaborated concrete proposals for that very purpose. Intervening measures in this sector have been deferred up to now, partly out of consideration for the unions and, partly, because the employers do not regard them as being particularly urgent. Legislation which remains in place are the amendment of Article 116 in the *Arbeitsförderungsgesetz*, which restricts the unions' ability to strike, and the dismantling of protective regulations in individual labour law. The changes in the latter subsector will probably engender the most serious consequences in the long term, especially since further measures are planned. Indeed, while in former decades legislators supported and generalized collectively agreed regulations by issuing legal standards, in the 1990s there is more tendency to dismantle such regulations in order to create the conditions under which collectively agreed standards can also reduced.

The Partial Renunciation of Social Partnership

The culture of cooperation and social partnership is one of the cornerstones of industrial relations in Germany. Only select parts of this socioindustrial phenomenon have been questioned by individual actors either on the employers' side or on the workers' side. In the 1960s and 1970s, particularly the left wing of the unions endeavoured to replace the model of social dialogue with a more belligerent and syndicalistic interest policy.[119] Such ideas were to be found, above all, within *IG Metall*, self-image of which at that time was still heavily marked by the philosophy of class antagonism, and which had declared its support for redistributing income and property by developing countervailing power on the union side. However, in practice, this attitude of fundamentally criticizing the system only ever found expression in the form of a latent potential threat, which was measured mostly in careful doses to obtain greater concessions from the employers in the annual rounds of negotiations. This means that, although the choice between a cooperative and an adversarial strategy was picked up as a theme for discussion by both academics and the unions, it has never actually been on the agenda for the trade union movement as a whole. Whereas an adversarial strategy had a certain relevance for collective bargaining policy at least in the 1970s, the same can hardly be said for the 1980s. Indeed, even though the range of distribution decreased considerably, forcing many to expect a rise in the probability of industrial disputes, in actual fact the volume of strikes clearly became much smaller than in the 1970s, and the strikes took on less of an ideological look. To a large extent, this was caused by the unions' loss of power that accompanied the rising rate of unemployment, but it also certainly has something to do with the review of the unions' experiences in Germany and in other European countries.

The 1990s have heralded the start of a new epoch in the culture of industrial relations insofar as it is now the employers who increasingly call into question the basic consensus between the social partners. Collective bargaining problems in eastern Germany are the most immediate cause of the harder adversarial position of the employees. Immediately following German unification, it appeared as if the social partnership model of industrial relations in West Germany could be transferred easily to the territory of the former East Germany by the mere act of will. The social partners not only, in principle, declared their belief in the right to collective bargaining and in the well-established mechanisms for conducting negotiations and regulating conflicts but they also agreed relatively quickly on the gradual alignment of wages and working conditions in east Germany with west German standards.[120] Then, at the beginning of 1993, and under the pressure from the rapidly deteriorating economic situation, the employers' association made the decision, unprecedented in the history of the Federal Republic, to terminate the collective agreement on a graduated rate ahead of schedule and without notice.[121] In the following years it was revealed that this was not a unique step developing out of the special situation in the new federal states but, rather, the effect of an initial impulse for a new collective bargaining strategy coming from the employers. The associations affiliated to the BDA now often adopt a tougher, more confrontational stand against the unions in west Germany. This new trend is particularly apparent in that today, employers in both parts of the country make use of the previously rarely used possibility of terminating collective agreements and confronting the unions with a catalogue of comprehensive demands.[122]

The unions' reaction to the new strategies of their negotiating partners is rather restrained, especially since leaders of the employers' associations have finally proven to be more than willing to make concessions in actual collective bargaining negotiations. As can be seen from the strike activities of the early 1990s, there has not yet been a general rise in the level of conflict in industrial relations.[123] From the outside, a partial aggravation of the social climate has become visible in some collective bargaining disputes. A prime example of this is the industrial dispute caused by the employers' associations' extraordinary measure of terminating the collective agreement in the metal industry. In this case, *IG Metall* had to put into play its entire organizational potential to force the employers to retract from their position—which the union regarded as a breach of agreement—and to keep to the rules of collective bargaining, the rules of which had, up to then, always remained unquestioned.[124]

While the signs of increased confrontation between the social partners are growing, there is a continuity in cooperation which is reflected in the efficient negotiation processes going on at firm and trade level. The traditional model of peaceful agreement seems to be proving its worth above all in those cases where the employers' interest in minimizing costs and increasing flexibility matches the unions' ever more urgent interest in the safeguarding of jobs. The 1993 house agreement between *Volkswagen AG* and *IG Metall* is a prime example of just such a situation. In this agreement, the company guaranteed existing employment contracts in return for a reduction in the employees' annual income by ten percent, while fixing the working week to 28.8 hours.[125] A similar barter deal was also concluded in the chemical industry in 1994. Here, the union agreed to the experiment of setting pay for newcomers in the workforce and the previously long-term unemployed at levels below the collectively agreed rate. Likewise, in the metal industry *IG Metall* has endorsed the admissibility of plant agreements on a reduction in the working week to 30 hours in exchange for the requirement that a company renounces its right to dismissal for managerial reasons.[126]

Such arrangements are the visible effects of the social partners' readiness to look for possibilities to settle clashes of interest and to find compromises through collective bargaining even under today's more difficult economic conditions. In this very regard, round table discussions or similar discussion forums have been established in many industrial sectors during the mid 1990s to exchange information, prepare analyses, and look for perspectives to enable opponents to come to an understanding over controversial matters. These forums have also concentrated on the problem of how to maintain or, rather, improve the current level of employment in view of the given competitive conditions.[127]

As a response to the recent dramatic increase in unemployment, *IG Metall* decided at the end of 1995 to go far beyond those single initiatives by suggesting to both the employers and the state the conclusion of a so-called *Bündnis für Arbeit* (Alliance for Employment). This concept envisaged that the unions would accept pay rises in line with the rate of inflation and would agree to the temporary arrangement of paying the newly hired long-term unemployed below the collectively agreed rate if the employers of the metal industry, first, would not lay off employers for managerial reasons in the following three years; second, committed themselves to the creation of 300,000 additional jobs; and, finally, hired 30,000 long-term unemployed. Furthermore, the government was expected to withdraw the proposed reduction in unemployment benefits and social welfare. This spectacular offer, which was anything but noncontroversial within the unions, was received quite positively at first by the employers, especially since it indirectly implied the recognition of an interdependence between the wages and the level of employment, which, until then, the unions had always denied.

Even though there have been many signs that the employers are increasingly prepared to embark on a collision course in collective bargaining policy, the majority in their associations still keep to the principle of social partnership. Strategies for refusing cooperation have been raised for discussion by some of the representatives of the employers' associations, but none have been adopted as official association policy by any of the associations affiliated to the BDA. Such mind games, which usually have a more demonstrative character, are primarily designed to serve the purpose of increasing the unions' willingness to make concessions with regard to the employers' strategy of cutting cost. The complete abandonment of social partnership, however, is perceived by the employers to be much too risky, because the unions, despite the weakening of their organizational structure, still possess a significant capacity to mobilize themselves, as was most evident in the 1993 collective bargaining dispute in the east German metal industry. However, because of both their drop in membership and crisis in employment, the unions themselves are much weakened and must act broadly from a defensive position. At the moment, any adversarial tendencies from within the ranks of the unions—which could, nonetheless, represent a possible response to the challenges of the employers' position—hardly play a role at all. Instead, there conviction prevails that the formalization of collective bargaining policy through juridification and the informal relations of social partnership have proven to be important instruments for the preservation of unions' bargaining power especially in times of economic crises. Therefore, union representatives have, at present, adopted the strategy of restricting their loss of power by insisting on the tradition of social partnership and by putting the employers on the spot through pointed offers of cooperation.

Conclusion

The network of institutions and practices which had guaranteed a comparatively high degree of stability to industrial relations in the old Federal Republic, has been severely put to the test by the economic, social, and political turbulences since the 1980s and, to a greater extent, since German unification. The processes of deconcentration, decentralization, deregulation, and the rejection of cooperation, which were triggered by the rapidly changing underlying situation, are signs of a change in industrial relations, which touches not only the form and content of established institutions and practices, but also their organizational, legal, and cultural basis. The established institutions, therefore, cannot survive unless they prove to be adaptable and, so, change in keeping with new requirements. This, in turn, necessarily presupposes that the corporate actors involved—the unions, the employers, and the state—are prepared to maintain these institutions and, so, act accordingly.

Viewed from these perspectives, the current situation in the Federal Republic is characterized by continuity in principle, but, at the same time, by a partial loss in efficiency of the established institutions and courses of action. The traditional patterns of industrial relations continue to provide the framework for the interaction between the actors involved. However, they have lost part of their previous relevance because of the various processes of insidious erosion and mainly the employers', but also the state's, deliberate retreat.

The consequences of the structural changes in society are especially clear in the system of associations. The heterogenization of the social and economic reality has brought about an erosion of the memberships and an increase in internal conflicts for both the unions and the employers' associations, which even changes to the policy on organization have not been able to lessen yet. Where the employers are concerned, this means that the unions are meeting ever more with individual companies and, in the future, possibly even with several employers' associations as negotiating partners. In contrast, where the workers are concerned, there is a growing number of employees whose interests are either only indirectly represented by a union, in that they profit from the results of bargaining while being nonmembers, or who are trying to realize their market opportunities as individuals face to face with management. As far as the degree of the breaking up of the former quasimonopolies of representation are concerned, there has been a change from collective representation to that of individual interests.

Just as with the development of the corporate actors, so too can, in the field of collective bargaining policy, a change be detected from the previously greatly standardized relations of interaction to more pluralized ones. The change in the basic conditions manifests itself in a tension between the increased heterogeneity of interest positions and the traditional collective bargaining system based on centralization and standardization. It seems that, in the long run, the traditional procedure of trade-wide negotiations and, the setting of trade-wide standards as regards their content, can hardly be reconciled with the increasingly varied conditions at plant level and the increasing individualization of demands in employer-employee relationships. Whereas, from the employers' perspective, these conditions speak for both a rejection of traditional area-wide collective bargaining as well as greater flexibility and decentralization of a collective bargaining policy, the centralism to which the actors have become well-accustomed still has so many advantages in principle that to replace it by a fragmented collective bargaining policy would hardly seem an attractive alternative. Moreover, because the unions continue to be interested in a comprehensive standardization of wages and working conditions, it has seemed reasonable to adopt a compromise by maintaining the centralized system of negotiations in principle, while at the same time limiting the obligations and scope of the collective agreements. Thus, the partial rejection of regulation has proven to be a necessary prerequisite to the preservation of the practice of the trade-wide collective agreements. Moreover, the centralized system of collective bargaining has been used by the social partners to control the processes of change and channel them properly. However, the unions in particular risk losing the initiative in this process in direct proportion to the degree of "insidious" decentralization outside their sphere of influence. Indeed, should the negotiated trade-wide collective agreements actually no longer have any validity, then this would mean not only a change in function, but also, eventually, the death of centralized collective bargaining policy.

The still rather high degree of juridification may very well account for the fact that the shift in collective bargaining policy from a more centralized level to that of the firm has not led to a greater disagreement between the social partners. Even though the so-called "regulations discussion" gives a different impression, the legal framework is still proving to be an important factor in stabilizing industrial relations. At company level, the relationship between the employees and the employers is far more formalized and much less adversarial today than it has ever been. The various codetermination regulations have developed into cooperative mechanisms with a high degree of institutional weight, now that both sides have accepted them and tried them out in practice. They have proven to be highly efficient as instruments for the regulation of conflicts they have, particularly under crisis conditions. Consequently, neither legislators nor the social partners are seriously making any attempt at present to abandon this set of regulations or, for that matter, modify part of the regulations to the detriment of the other side. In the most part, this is similarly true for the other sectors of collective labour law. Despite the protests especially from the academic world, legislators have refused to modify the law pertaining to strikes and collective bargaining, and have thus contributed to securing the continuation of collective bargaining relations. The amendment to Article 116 of the *Arbeitsförderungsgesetz* in this respect is the only serious exception so far. A process of incremental deregulation that clearly disfavours the employees is taking place in the area of individual labour law. Under the pressure of international competition, legislators have systematically reduced juridification in this area, and, thus, have assisted the erosion of one of the basic institution of industrial relations.

The culture of industrial relations grounded on the principle of social partnership has always been among the guarantors of institutional stability. However, it would mean an overestimation of the social partners' consensus if one failed to notice that the willingness to solve conflicts peacefully has always been subject to larger or smaller fluctuations, depending on the economic and political situation, and that there have always been groups both within the unions' and the employers' ranks that have favoured a more adversarial strategy. Nonetheless, where it has come to open conflict in the form of industrial disputes, this has always led to an escalation limited by duration and not a rejection of the principle of social partnership. Moreover, threats to terminate the consensus have often been symbolic in character, because they serve more to mobilize the membership than to signal a fundamental change in the attitude towards the social partner. In this light, it would also be inappropriate to judge the more aggressive stand the employers have taken in collective bargaining policy in the 1990s as an indication of the total abandonment of social partnership. At most, this represents an attempt to convert the growth of their power, which they have experienced during economic crisis, into an advantage in collective bargaining. The unions, in turn, have discovered that cooperative behaviour can be a means of putting pressure on the other side and, thus, can help them to reach partial results which otherwise, under crisis conditions, they would never have been powerful enough to obtain. Furthermore, it has also been shown that strikes are most successful when they are forceful and well-targeted and used only rarely.

Thus, the economic crisis and the manifestations of social and political upheaval have not led to the end of social partnership, but, instead, the social partners' consensus has contributed considerably to the often productive ability to cope with these new challenges. It is likely that there will be more centres of conflict as the social partners' scope for concessions continues to become ever smaller and decentralization of collective bargaining systems continues to grow. The actual test for social partnership is still to come. However, on the basis of the general positive experience the practice of social dialogue in the Federal Republic, especially in comparison with other European countries, it ought to be expected that the actors will in future continue to gear their actions towards reaching agreement. This would be a much desired course of action in view of the continuing high level of unemployment and the many other problems that have to be dealt with in the framework of industrial relations.

NOTES

1. See Leo Kißler and Rene Laserre, *Tarifpolitik. Ein deutsch-französischer Vergleich*. (Frankfurt/Main: Campus, 1987).
2. Otto Jacobi, "Neues technologisches System, lange Wellen und Gewerkschaften," in *Arbeitsmarkt, Arbeitsbeziehungen und Politik in den 80er Jahren*, ed. Heidrun Abromeit and Bernhard Blanke (Opladen: Westdeutscher Verlag, 1987), pp. 194–207; 206; Pete Burgess, "Was tut sich bei den Nachbarn? Tarifpolitik im europäischen Vergleich," in *Tarifpolitik der Zukunft*, ed. Reinhard Bispinck (Hamburg: VSA, 1995), pp. 111–36; 116f.

3. Gerhard Himmelmann, "Diffusionstendenzen und Stabilitätsfaktoren im Tarifvertragssystem der Bundesrepublik Deutschland," in *Arbeitsmarkt*, ed. Abromeit and Blanke, pp. 105–17; 105–7.

4. Himmelmann, "Diffusionstendenzen," p. 109.

5. Peter Ellguth, Markus Promberger, and Rainer Trinczek, "Neue Branchen und neue Unternehmensstrukturen. Eine Herausforderung an die gewerkschaftliche Tarifpolitik," in *Tarifpolitik*, ed. Bispinck, pp. 173–94.

6. Walter Müller-Jentsch, *Soziologie der industriellen Beziehungen. Eine Einführung* (Frankfurt/Main: Campus, 1986), p. 269.

7. Another aspect is also important in this context. Unions and associations of employers are forced to adapt themselves to the federal state losing sovereignty to supranational actors and their being confronted with new partners when formulating their political demands. The European Union here plays the key role. Since already more than 50 to 60 per cent of laws with economic and social character are passed on this level the decisive institutions of the European Union have become almost equally important partners for interest groups as their national governments and parliaments. Thus, effective representation in Brussels and a supranational coordination of the policies of associations is more and more the prerequisite for the chance of influencing laws concerning industrial relations.

8. Elmar Altvater and Birgit Mahnkopf, *Gewerkschaften vor der europäischen Herausforderung. Tarifpolitik nach Mauer und Maastricht* (Münster: Verlag Westphälisches Dampfboot, 1993), p. 185.

9. Berndt Keller, *Einführung in die Arbeitspolitik. Arbeitsbeziehungen und Arbeitsmarkt in sozialwissenschaftlicher Perspektive* (Munich and Vienna: Oldenbourg, 1995), p. 330.

10. Hans-Peter Ullmann, *Interessenverbände in Deutschland* (Frankfurt/Main: Suhrkamp, 1988), pp. 134ff.

11. Kißler and Lasserre, *Tarifpolitik*, p. 91.

12. Müller-Jentsch, *Soziologie*, p. 141.

13. Ullmann, *Interessenverbände*, p. 241.

14. Ronald F. Bunn, "Employers Associations in the Federal Republic of Germany," in *Employers Associations and Industrial Relations: A Comparative Study*, ed. John P. Windmuller and Alan Gladstone (Oxford: Clarendon Press, 1984), pp. 169–201; 174.

15. Klaus Schönhoven, *Die deutschen Gewerkschaften* (Frankfurt/Main: Suhrkamp, 1987), pp. 136f.

16. Schönhoven, *Gewerkschaften*, pp. 199, 204.

17. Schönhoven, *Gewerkschaften*, p. 206.

18. Klaus Armingeon, *Die Entwicklung der westdeutschen Gewerkschaften 1950–1985* (Frankfurt/Main: Campus, 1988), p. 133.

19. Walter Müller-Jentsch, *Basisdaten der industriellen Beziehungen* (Frankfurt/Main: Campus, 1989), pp. 72, 130, 133.

20. Kißler and Lasserre, *Tarifpolitik*, pp. 95f., 99f.

21. Schönhoven, *Gewerkschaften*, pp. 224, 226.

22. Walter Müller-Jentsch, "Streiks und Streikbewegungen in der Bundesrepublik 1950–1978," in *Beiträge zur Soziologie der Gewerkschaften*, ed. Joachim Bergmann (Frankfurt/Main: Campus, 1979), p. 38.

23. Kißler and Lasserre, *Tarifpolitik*, pp. 83, 99.

24. Kißler and Lasserre, *Tarifpolitik*, pp. 106ff.

25. Keller, *Arbeitspolitik*, p. 193.

26. Müller-Jentsch, *Soziologie*, pp. 157, 238–42.

27. Reinhard Bahnmüller and Reinhard Bispinck, "Vom Vorzeige- zum Auslaufmodell? Das deutsche Tarifsystem zwischen kollektiver Regulierung, betrieblicher Flexibilisierung und individuellen Interessen," in *Tarifpolitik*, ed. Bispinck, pp. 137–72; 138.

28. Joachim Kreimer-de-Fries, "Die Allgemeinverbindlicherklärung von Tarifverträgen. Ein unzeitgemäßes Instrument?" in *Tarifpolitik*, ed. Bispinck, pp. 205–29; 212, 214.

29. Keller, *Arbeitspolitik*, pp. 189, 193.

30. Müller-Jentsch, *Soziologie*, pp. 157, 251; Kißler and Lasserre, *Tarifpolitik*, pp. 139f.

31. Kißler and Lasserre, *Tarifpolitik*, pp. 83, 99.

32. Kreimer-de Fries, "Die Allgemeinverbindlicherklärung," pp. 209f., 214.

33. Keller, *Arbeitspolitik*, pp. 164ff.

34. Klaus von Beyme, *Gewerkschaften und Arbeitsbeziehungen in kapitalistischen Ländern* (Munich: Piper, 1977), pp. 194, 196; Keller, *Arbeitspolitik*, pp. 167, 172.

35. Werner Milert and Rudolf Tschirbs, *Von den Arbeiterausschüssen zum Betriebsverfassungsgesetz. Geschichte der betrieblichen Interessenvertretung in Deutschland* (Cologne: Bund Verlag, 1991).

36. Milert and Tschirbs, *Von den Arbeiterausschüssen zum Betriebsverfassungsgesetz*, pp. 73–81.

37. Leo Kißler, *Die Mitbestimmung in der Bundesrepublik Deutschland. Modell und Wirklichkeit* (Marburg: Schüren, 1992), pp. 46ff.; Keller, *Arbeitspolitik*, pp. 95ff.

38. Schönhoven, *Gewerkschaften*, 209; Werner Müller, "Die Gründung des DGB, der Kampf um die Mitbestimmung, programmatisches Scheitern und der Übergang zum gewerkschaftlichen Pragmatismus," in *Geschichte der Gewerkschaften in der Bundesrepublik Deutschland*, ed. Hans-Otto Hemmer and Kurt Thomas Schmitz (Cologne: Bund Verlag, 1990), pp. 95f.

39. Siegfried Mielke, "Die Neugründung der Gewerkschaften in den westlichen Besatzungszonen 1945–1949," in Hemmer and Schmitz, *Geschichte der Gewerkschaften*, p. 82.

40. Müller, "Die Gründung," p. 87.

41. Schönhoven, *Gewerkschaften*, pp. 219–24.

42. Müller-Jentsch, *Soziologie*, pp. 119f.

43. Müller-Jentsch, *Soziologie*, pp. 123–25.

44. Schönhoven, *Gewerkschaften*, pp. 224f.

45. von Beyme, *Gewerkschaften und Arbeitsbeziehungen*, p. 165.

46. Hans Kastendieck and Hella Kastendieck, "Konservative Wende und industrielle Beziehungen in Großbritannien und der Bundesrepublik," in *Arbeitsmarkt*, ed. Abromeit and Blanke, pp. 179–93; 189.

47. Kißler and Lasserre, *Tarifpolitik*, p. 93.

48. Keller, *Arbeitspolitik*, p. 168.

49. Schönhoven, *Gewerkschaften*, pp. 237f.

50. Müller-Jentsch, *Basisdaten*, p. 68.

51. Thomas Leif, Ansgar Klein, and Hans-Josef Legrand, eds., *Reform des DGB* (Cologne: Bund Verlag, 1993), p. 16.

52. Jacobi, "Neues technologisches System," p. 203; Keller, *Arbeitspolitik*, p. 340.

53. *Frankfurter Allgemeine Zeitung*, 27 July 1994, p. 12.

54. Himmelmann, "Diffusionstendenzen," p. 112.

55. Walter Müller-Jentsch, "Eine neue Topographie der Arbeit. Organisationspolitische Herausforderugen für die Gewerkschaften," in *Arbeitsmarkt*, ed. Abromeit and Blanke, pp. 159–78; 167.

56. *Frankfurter Allgemeine Zeitung*, 27 July 1994.
57. Müller-Jentsch, *Soziologie*, pp. 270ff.
58. See also Müller-Jentsch, "Topographie," pp. 160ff.
59. Klaus Armingeon, "Ende einer Erfolgsstory? Gewerkschaften und Arbeitsbeziehungen im Einigungsprozeß," *Gegenwartskunde* 1 (1991): 29–42.
60. Altvater and Mahnkopf, *Gewerkschaften*, p. 205.
61. Altvater and Mahnkopf, *Gewerkschaften*, p.206.
62. Altvater and Mahnkopf, *Gewerkschaften*, pp. 208f.
63. Birgit Mahnkopf, "Gewerkschaften im Ost-West-Spagat," in Leif, Klein, and Legrand, *Reform*, pp. 145–65; 149ff.
64. Peter Seideneck, "Die soziale Einheit gestalten. Über die Schwierigkeit des Aufbaues gesamtdeutscher Gewerkschaften," *Aus Politik und Zeitgeschichte* B13 (1995): 3–11; 8.
65. Leif, Klein, and Legrand, *Reform*, pp. 23f.
66. Wolfgang Schröder, "Arbeitgeberverbände in der Klemme. Motivations- und Verpflichtungskrisen," in *Tarifpolitik*, ed. Bispinck, pp. 44–63; 48, 50.
67. Schröder, "Arbeitgeberverbände in der Klemme," pp. 45ff.
68. *Frankfurter Rundschau*, 7 December 1993, p. 4; *Frankfurter Allgemeine Zeitung*, 12 December 1993, p. 13.
69. *Frankfurter Allgemeine Zeitung*, 25 March 1995, p. 11.
70. Especially employers' associations in the engineering and electrical industries feel encouraged to take this step, since in their areas of organisation there already exists a majority of companies which are either not bound by a collective agreement or evade existing agreements anyway; see *Frankfurter Allgemeine Zeitung*, 31 May 1995, p. 15.
71. Altvater and Mahnkopf, *Gewerkschaften*, pp. 203f.
72. Gerhard Kleinhenz, "Tarifpartnerschaft im vereinten Deutschland," *Aus Politik und Zeitgeschichte* B12 (1992): 14–24; 19.
73. Fred Henneberger, "Transferart, Organisationsdynamik und Strukturkonservativismus westdeutscher Unternehmerverbände—Aktuelle Entwicklungen unter besonderer Berücksichtigung in Sachsen und Thüringen," *Politische Vierteljahresschrift* 34, no. 4 (1993): 661ff.
74. Altvater and Mahnkopf, *Gewerkschaften*, passim.
75. Wolfgang Schröder, "Arbeitgeber- und Wirtschaftsverbände: Strategie und Politik," in *Gewerkschaften heute. Jahrbuch für Arbeitnehmerfragen 1995*, ed. Michael Kittner (Cologne: Bund Verlag, 1995), pp. 577–96; 591ff.
76. Schröder, "Arbeitsgeberverände in der Klemme," pp. 57f.
77. Schröder, "Arbeitsgeberverände in der Klemme," pp. 55ff.
78. *Die Zeit* (29 March 1996): 17.
79. Also Altvater and Mahnkopf, *Gewerkschaften*, p. 33.
80. Kißler and Lasserre, *Tarifpolitik*, pp. 128f., 167ff.
81. Müller-Jentsch, *Soziologie*, pp. 273, 277.
82. Kißler, *Mitbestimmung*, p. 35.
83. Karl Hinrichs and Helmut Wiesenthal, "Bestandsrationalität versus Kollektivinteresse. Gewerkschaftliche Handlungsprobleme im Arbeitszeitkonflikt 1984," in *Arbeitsmarkt*, ed. Abromeit and Blanke, pp. 118–32; 118ff.
84. Hajo Weber, "Desynchronisation, Dezentralisierung und Dekomposition? Die Wirkungsdynamik des Tarifkonflikts '84 und ihre Effekte auf das System industrieller Beziehungen," in *Arbeitsmarkt*, ed. Abromeit and Blanke, pp. 133–46; 134, 139.

85. Reinhard Bispinck and WSI-Tarifarchiv, "Zwischen Beschäftigungssicherung und Tarifabsenkung. Eine Bilanz der Tarifpolitik im Jahr 1994," *WSI-Mitteilungen* 1995, no. 3, pp. 145–63; 155.

86. Bahnmüller and Bispinck, "Vom Vorzeige- zum Auslaufmodell?" pp. 148ff.

87. Reinhard Bispinck and WSI-Tarifarchiv, "Der Tarifkonflikt um den Stufenplan in der ostdeutschen Metallindustrie," *WSI-Mitteilungen* 1993, no. 8, pp. 469–81; 469ff.

88. Helmut Schauer, "Erosion und 'Reform' des Flächentarifvertrages," in *Tarifpolitik*, ed. Bispinck, pp. 28–43; 33.

89. Ellguth et al., "Neue Branchen," pp. 186f.

90. Bahnmüller and Bispinck, "Vom Vorzeige- zum Auslaufmodell?" p. 140.

91. Bahnmüller and Bispinck, "Vom Vorzeige- zum Auslaufmodell?" p. 138.

92. Keller, *Arbeitspolitik*, p. 140.

93. Bahnmüller and Bispinck, "Vom Vorzeige- zum Auslaufmodell?" p. 145.

94. Altvater and Mahnkopf, *Gewerkschaften*, pp. 201f.

95. Walter Müller-Jentsch, "Das (Des-)Interesse der Arbeitgeber am Tarifvertragssystem," *WSI-Mitteilungen* 1993, no. 8, pp. 496–502; 496, 500.

96. *Die Zeit* (29 September 1995): 27.

97. Schröder, "Arbeitsgeber- und Wirtschaftsverbände," p. 585.

98. Bahnmüller and Bispinck, "Vom Vorzeige- zum Auslaufmodell?" p. 137.

99. *Frankfurter Rundschau*, 24 October 1995.

100. *Frankfurter Rundschau*, 26 March 1996, p. 4.

101. Müller-Jentsch, "Das (Des-)Interesse," p. 502.

102. Berthold Huber and Klaus Lang, "Tarifreform 2000—Förderungskonzepte und Verhandlungsstände im Bereich der Metallindustrie," *WSI-Mitteilungen* 1993, no. 12, pp. 789–97; 792f.

103. Keller, *Arbeitspolitik*, p. 375.

104. Keller, *Arbeitspolitik*, pp. 334f.

105. Wolfgang Däubler, "Immer wieder und immer öfter: Eingriffe in die Tarifautonomie," in *Tarifpolitik*, ed. Bispinck, pp. 64–77; 70.

106. von Beyme, *Gewerkschaften*, p. 193.

107. Däubler, "Immer wieder," p. 66.

108. Keller, *Arbeitspolitik*, pp. 376f.

109. Däubler, "Immer wieder," pp. 66f.

110. Altvater and Mahnkopf, *Gewerkschaften*, pp. 196f.

111. Altvater and Mahnkopf, *Gewerkschaften*, p. 196.

112. Kißler, *Mitbestimmung*, pp. 38f.

113. Hermann Kotthoff, *Betriebsräte und Bürgerstatus—Wandel und Kontinuität betrieblicher Mitbestimmung* (München-Mehring: Rainer Hamp Verlag, 1994).

114. Kotthoff, pp. 41ff.

115. Kißler, *Mitbestimmung*, pp. 71ff.

116. Kißler, *Mitbestimmung*, pp. 48ff.

117. Kißler, *Mitbestimmung*, p. 92.

118. Kißler, *Mitbestimmung*, pp. 93f.

119. Müller-Jentsch, "Das (Des-)Interesse," p. 497.

120. Kleinhenz , "Tarifpartnerschaft," pp. 20ff.

121. Müller-Jentsch, "Das (Des-)Interesse," p. 499.

122. Bispinck, "Tarifpolitik," p. 22.

123. Wieland Stützel, "Kein Abschied vom Arbeitskampf. Formen und Funktionswandel des Streiks," in *Tarifpolitik*, ed. Bispinck, pp. 95–110; 99ff., 109.

124. Bispinck and WSI-Tarifarchiv, "Tarifkonflikt," pp. 469ff.

125. Bispinck and WSI-Tarifarchiv, "Beschäftigungssicherung," p. 146.

126. Bispinck and WSI-Tarifarchiv, "Beschäftigungssicherung," pp. 155f.

127. Bahnmüller and Bispinck, "Vom Vorzeige- zum Auslaufmodell?" pp. 167f.

9 Youth, Education and Work in Germany

WALTER R. HEINZ

Today, youth has become a more or less independent phase of the life course in all industrialized service societies. Its onset, duration, and end depend on society's economic and cultural development. Thus, the age range of youth as the transition stage between childhood and adulthood varies from society to society and with historical periods. As a socially defined developmental agenda, the transition to adulthood is linked to a progression of social rights and duties, for instance entering secondary school, driving, voting, and drinking. Whereas in Germany drinking and voting is linked to ages 16 and 18, respectively, in the US and Canada the voting age is 18 but the drinking age varies from 18 to 21.

In the industrialized service societies of Europe, North America, and Asia the youth phase is primarily defined by the student role that extends from secondary school to leaving postsecondary education. Young men and women are members of formal institutions of socialization in the education and training systems that require more independent and responsible learning compared to childhood.

Youths are expected to develop intellectual and social competence and to test their limits in various social arenas, like school attainment, sports, and cultural activities, and to acquire skills and resources for making a living and to participate in community life. This is not a simple task; many young men and women do not manage to cope with the expectation of developing a personal identity and of becoming a responsible citizen at the same time. Many conflicts with the agencies of social control—parents, teachers, police, social workers, and judges—are caused by the lack of individual resources, like a high school diploma, and social opportunities, like jobs.

In Germany a minority of young people (approx. ten percent, more of them in east Germany) live in insecure social and economic conditions, which reinforce their marginalized position at school and in the labour market. Living in circumstances of welfare dependency and just above the poverty line distracts from educational and occupational aspirations and tends to harm psychological well-being. The group of marginalized young people is much smaller in Germany than it is in Canada and the US, where school dropouts, underemployed and unemployed youth are a very serious social problem. The Grant Commission estimates that almost half of the youth population are at risk in the US; the Canadian Youth Foundation reports that the rates of joblessness and underemployment among the young have increased to levels between 15 percent and 30 percent in the mid 1990s in Canada.[1]

In social research, education, and labour force statistics, youth in general is differentiated by the phases of adolescence and young adulthood and covers the age range from 14 and 25. Today, it has become more difficult to mark off youth from adulthood; because of the time spent in higher education and searching for jobs, the transition to full adult status may extend to the age of 30.

The entire transition to adulthood is a prominent field of political concern and educational, psychological, and sociological research in Germany.[2] In Canada and the US, less attention is given to the entire transition and to general questions concerning youths' personality and social development, but policy making and research tend to focus on adolescents at risk. The "youth question" has a long tradition in Germany,[3] which started with the youth movements in the 1920s, the forced participation in youth organizations in Nazi Germany, the socialistic youth organizations in the German Democratic Republic (GDR), and the apprentices' and students' protest movements in the second half of the 1960s. Germany has a Federal Ministry for Youth, Family and Seniors, a federally supported Youth Research Institute (*Deutsches Jugend-Institut* (DJI)), and it publishes Federal Reports on Youth and on Vocational Education and Training. Youth support and counseling are core areas of Germany's social policy, which created a youth welfare legislation as early as 1922. This legislation was most recently reformed to become a Children and Youth Welfare Law in 1991.

Not very different from the two North American societies, German youth has become incorporated into the global youth entertainment and fashion culture. International pop and rock stars like Michael Jackson, Madonna, Bryan Adams, or Alanis Morissette are as well known to German as they are to North American teenagers; and the same holds for consumer labels such as Levis and Nike. While most young people are well integrated in the areas of consumption, media, and computers by the age of 15, and many have had their first sexual experiences around that age, their status passage through education, training, and labour market entry may extend from the age of 18, when compulsory schooling ends in Germany, and the age of 27, when the average student is graduating from university with a Master's degree. The increased duration of education and the delay of labour market integration are also reflected in the process of family formation. Marriage and having children have been postponed in Germany from generation to generation. In the 1990s the average age of marriage is 26 for women, and 28 for men. In the German Democratic Republic this transition occurred at least four years earlier, but has adapted to the West German pattern since unification in 1989/90.[4]

The transition from education to employment in Germany differs from Canada and the US in the structure and duration of this crucial process of becoming an adult. Though family support and social class background still play an important role in the social placement of young people in Germany, the family now shares the responsibility for its offspring's future with other social institutions, namely schools, companies which train apprentices, universities, labour and manpower agencies, and—in phases of risk—with counseling and welfare agencies. Hence, there is not one but many social organizations that form the fabric of youth's transition to adulthood. Therefore, young people have to become more responsible, and accountable, in coping with divergent social expectations and requirements.[5] Their position in society is ambivalent, because they are torn between the demands of the student and employee role and the claim of participating in semi-autonomous youth cultures.[6] And, another important aspect is the social differentiation of youth—youths differ by social and ethnic origin (12 percent of Germany's school population are children of foreign workers, mainly from Turkey), gender, and social position in the school and employment systems (student, apprentice, worker). In Germany, this social differentiation is interrelated with the three-tier school structure and the two main pathways to employment: apprenticeship and university education.

The Changing Economy and Qualifications

In the last decade economic turbulence and major labour market changes have not only affected the labour force, but also school-to-work transitions and their outcomes in Canada, the US, and Germany. Sociologists and labour market researchers in these countries have documented similar trends:

- a shift of jobs from the manufacturing to the public and private service sector;
- an upgrading of skill requirements at the workplace;

- a restructuring and downsizing of private companies, public services and administration;
- an increase of women's labour market participation;
- a deregulation of employment standards,
- the integration into supranational economic organizations: European Union (EU) and North American Free Trade Agreement (NAFTA).

These global modernization processes have been met with different sets of public policy and private sector adjustments. Germany has reformed its apprenticeship system and expanded its tuition-free universities, while in Canada and the US decentralized on-the-job training and Human Resources Management co-exist with an increasing enrollment at colleges and universities.

These trends have not only created a growing mismatch between academic credentials and employment opportunities, but society is also confronted with the social issue of how to stabilize the transition of the majority of its youth who are not college-bound or drop out of the education system.

Though having a comprehensive and open school system, Canada and the US are not providing institutions that would prepare, train, and socialize young people who either do not want or fail to enter higher education. Thus, in North America and also in Great Britain, there are much weaker organized ties between schools and business compared to the dual system of apprenticeship in Germany.[7]

In the US and to a lesser degree in Canada, educators and progressive policy makers are now debating and promoting a system of vocational education and training (VET), crafted according to the German dual system or apprenticeship.[8] This institution is regarded as a very successful learning and training arrangement for noncollege bound youth, because it provides a solid base of certified portable skills and work habits, and for lifelong learning. Furthermore, because it combines public vocational education with firm-based training, this "dual system" also establishes pathways to employment. This is not only important for generating a well trained labour force, but also for stabilizing adolescents and young adults in a life-course transition that confronts them with new social roles and expectations to become independent from their parents.

As these debates go on in North America, government, unions, business, and crafts associations in Germany, however, are looking for ways to increase the attractiveness of the apprenticeship. This concern is caused by the growing number of youths who stay in school for attaining the university entrance credentials (*Abitur*) in order to prepare for a better paid professional career. Nevertheless, an apprenticeship in one of the 380 skilled trades, business, technical, and service occupations is still the most popular way of preparing for the world of work in Germany: more than two-thirds of all school leavers in Germany graduate as journeymen/women, skilled blue- and white-collar workers.[9]

Increased participation in postsecondary education is influenced by the shift to skilled service sector and professional jobs, the deregulation of labour standards, and the trend towards more occupational flexibility and self-employment. Staying in the education system longer is a response of young adults to employers' more selective criteria for hiring and promotion. Thus, the relative duration of the life phases of adolescence and young adulthood have become contingent on educational and training pathways and their connections with the labour market. Societies that recognize and reward vocational and academic skills in very different ways have established various hierarchies of education to employment routes whose accessibility varies by social class, gender, and race. These pathways and structural variations influence young people's activities and goals in their education and employment careers, and they inform employers' expectations and perceptions of young job applicants. These differences in educational and career planning and life course orientations can be explained by the influence of the unequal distribution of employment rewards on young people's educational attainments. Those who do not plan to get a college degree do not have an incentive to study, because a high school diploma is not regarded as a signal of employability.[10]

The declining value of high school credentials for employment corresponds with the collapse of a youth labour market and informs the hiring decisions of US and Canadian employers who, quite in contrast to Germany, instead of training workers under 25, do not trust them to be responsible enough to be offered full-time jobs. Thus, if they are considered at all, they will only get part-time or temporary jobs. More recently, nonstandard job entry processes have become a dominant pattern for both high school and college graduates in Canada in the 1990s.[11] This development underscores the fact that North American employers and public alike take youths' high job turnover for granted—as the "floundering period"—whereas in Germany nonuniversity bound adolescents are expected to move through an apprenticeship and on to full-time employment.

The life-course perspective,[12] when applied to economic change and qualifications, conceives of transitions as being determined neither by social origin nor by labour market dynamics. Transitions from school to work are constructed by individuals in the context of educational selection, work experiences, and employment options. Young people tend to make reasonable choices under very different circumstances, that is, adequate to the more or less limited range of education and employment options available to them.[13]

The kind of institutional linkage between school and work is crucial for promoting skill profiles, work habits, and career resources, as well as the readiness for lifelong learning. Such competence is not only essential for the wealth of nations, which compete in a global economy, but also for a person's economic independence, social identity, and adaptability to changing labour markets. Countries that provide institutionalized passages and occupational credentials for noncollege bound young people, like Germany, Austria, Switzerland and Denmark, not only have lower youth unemployment rates than Canada and the US, but they also have a labour force with flexible intermediate occupational skills. According to their economic development and cultural traditions these societies not only reward the college route, but promote and reform vocational education and training as a major transition pathway to employment. In contrast to such a two-route transition system, in North America those youths who do not go to college do not find any organized pathway that would train and socialize them to cope with a volatile labour market and flexible careers. Thus, we find higher youth unemployment, more fragmented transitions, and uncertain destinations in Canada and the US than in Germany.[14]

The Institutional Structure of Education to Employment Transitions

Youth and transition systems to adulthood are embedded in the social class structure and culture of society. The way they operate, their outcomes, and their balance between efficiency and equity, can be understood in the framework of the tradition and structure of both the education and employment system. The preparation for employment can be organized in very different ways: by the general school system with different tracks, in vocational schools and community colleges; by an apprenticeship or by on-the-job training or by no provision whatsoever; and, of course, in colleges and universities. The labour market and employment efficiency of different institutional arrangements and their contribution to the stabilization of young persons' transition to adulthood can be compared using four dimensions:

- the fit between education and employment, or the match between skills acquired and competence required;
- the standardization of vocational education and training (VET);
- the stratification of VET credentials and employment prospects;
- the short-term and long-term outcomes of transition pathways.

The Fit Between Education and Employment

There are two contrasting arrangements for job preparation. Secondary schools, vocational schools, and community colleges provide vocational education mainly by offering theoretical instruction. The world of work, shop floors, offices, and craft shops, is simulated or only partly integrated. Such an arrangement is quite popular in North America, though only in the vocational tracks of high school and community colleges with co-op programs. Vocational schools and community colleges can in principle promote a comprehensive knowledge base for understanding work tasks and forms of team work. Such an education may facilitate the adaptation to changing job requirements and is a platform for further education. But, the exclusion of the workplace and of a real business environment creates the necessity for extended adjustment processes to the reality of work and substantial organizational socialization at job entry.

In contrast, there is on-the-job training without much theoretical instruction that tends to be offered to high school graduates who do not attend college in Canada and the US. The disadvantages of this type of VET are the lack of occupational standards and its low individual skill flexibility, because skills are tied to the workplace. Changing technology and work environments will require substantial effort for retraining the labour force.

The apprenticeship in Germany combines the two approaches into one well structured VET arrangement. It coordinates school-based theoretical with firm-based job related learning. This improves the match between qualification and employment substantially, but does not guarantee it. Trainees get the theoretical background for practical in-the-firm training and general education at the public vocational school which they have to attend twice a week. The duration of an apprenticeship is three years on the average and it is completed with a specific occupational title. Government (vocational schools) and business (systematic training-on-the-job) share the costs of training: an apprentice costs DM 18,000 (CAN$ 17,000) a year, the average training allowance is less than DM 1,000 (CAN$ 900) a month. Apprentices are put to work in a productive way in the course of training. After graduating from apprenticeship, the former trainees do not have to work for the company, though the majority will be offered a full- or part-time job.

Since many companies train apprentices the problem of poaching does not exist. There is rather a tradition that small firms train young people who will move on to larger companies as skilled or semiskilled workers. Recent labour market data document the importance of VET for job entry.[15] Three-fourths of the jobs offered in western Germany in 1994 required either a completed apprenticeship, a polytechnic or university degree; only 12 percent of the jobs were advertised for unskilled or semi-skilled workers.

The dual system, furthermore, can be a safeguard against downward mobility; but it is also a ceiling limiting upward mobility into the professions that require a university degree. Therefore, there is growing pressure on policy makers today to open polytechnic colleges and universities for VET graduates. This is one way to increase the attractiveness of the apprenticeship in view of the steady rise of university enrollment from 14 percent in 1970 to 25 percent in 1990 and almost 30 percent in 1995. Making the two German transition routes more permeable to working class and foreign workers' children, however, will require a massive effort of government and business for creating high quality apprenticeships in occupations that are competitive and flexible and can be combined with continuous education. However, in today's world of downsizing, one out of three German companies does not see a demand for young skilled employees in the near future. This documents that the restructuring of the work organization and the workplace may endanger the supply of a well-trained workforce in Germany in the long run.

Standardization of Vocational Education and Training

Having standards for content, duration, and examination as well as certification of VET are essential transition signals for both employers and young workers. Vocational schools and the dual system in Germany are under public control, that is, employers, unions, and government share responsibility for quality and supply of training places. This framework of social partnership is sensitive to the economy and thus not always free of conflicts.[16]

The German system has created a close link between vocational credentials, university degrees, and job entry levels as well as career progression. Journeywomen and -men expect to enter permanent skilled blue- or white-collar jobs, university graduates claim to enter professional jobs and management positions in the private and public sector. This *Normalarbeitsverhältnis* or employment relations standard pertains also to job conditions, job security, promotion, and income level. In combination with the German labour codes there is a high standard of worker's protection.

At first glance, unregulated on-the-job training, which is favoured in North American societies, seems to have the advantage that workers are not tied to an occupation but can move from one job assignment to another. However, there are no shared standards concerning training, work requirements, skill levels, and wages. Hence, the quality of training varies from firm to firm, and the individual skill profiles are much less comparable then in a standardized VET transition system. This restricts free mobility of workers—the American ideal—between employers and it increases the risk that companies hire the wrong person for a certain job. Thus, on-the-job training creates an inefficient "trial-and error" process for both job applicants and employers. This has the effect that the transition from school to work is more discontinuous for young people in the US and Canada than in Germany, because it is an extended period of job insecurity, where part-time employment, underemployment and job-loss take turns for years.

Stratification of Credentials and Employment Prospects

In North America there are very few alternatives for the noncollege bound besides entering the casual labour market with nonstandard employment after leaving school. The high school diploma is not recognized by employers as an entry qualification for skilled jobs. Thus, high school leavers have to move, often between firms, from unskilled to semiskilled employment before they get a chance, depending on their work experience, to advance to skilled adult jobs. The "choice" young people have after high school is between higher education and (un)employment. The postsecondary system in Canada and the US with its hierarchy of two- to four-year community colleges, four-year colleges, and universities refers the education and training for intermediate occupational skills to the community colleges. These colleges offer a variety of programs for trade, clerical, technical, service, and health occupations. In the past many of its graduates moved on to university. Nowadays, however, more and more university graduates turn to the community college in order to acquire practical skills for job applications.

Thus, it does not come as a surprise that only two percent of all high school leavers in the US were in an apprenticeship in the 1980s, concentrated in construction and manufacturing. This low proportion of vocational trainees is not only caused by a decline of these industries but also mirrors the lack of a vocational training culture with appropriate institutions. In Canada there are initiatives in various provinces to improve the school-to-work transition through co-op programs. For instance, there is the Ontario Youth Apprenticeship Program, introduced in 1988/89, that is modeled according to the German apprenticeship. However, this institutionalized pathway to a Certificate of Qualification is only taken by 600 students a year, which equals a mere one percent of the eligible student population.[17]

Thus, in North America young people who start their working life with only a high school diploma or less are correctly called "the forgotten half" in an influential US report of the Grant Commission. President Bill Clinton and Vice-President Al Gore based some of their political visions in "Putting People First: A National Economic Strategy for America" (1992) on this report, when they promised to improve the contribution of the education system to the transition from school to work and to promote the introduction of apprenticeships.

In contrast to Germany, where the participation rate in the apprentice-ship system has increased in the last 20 years, the apprenticeship has been declining in Canada from 14 percent of the adult labour force to three percent of the young generation. This decrease is partly compensated by an increase of participation in higher education. With more than 40 percent Canada has one of the highest proportions of postsecondary students.[18]

Since in Canada and the US formalized vocational training, technical and vocational credentials are regarded as much less important than a higher degree compared to Germany, many college graduates have to cope with the experience of dequalification when they enter the labour market. This reflects the effects of an implicit stratification of school-to-work path-ways in a culture that overemphasizes university education and neglects vocational education and training.

In Germany the social class structure is more visible in the stratification of education-to-labour market pathways, which reflect its three-tier school system and the separation between its vocational and academic routes.[19] Universities and four-year polytechnic colleges are still fairly elite institu-tions of postsecondary education, because they admit only *Gymnasium* graduates, that is, from the top of the school levels (35 percent, out of which two-thirds enroll in higher education, that is, 25 percent of the young generation overall in the mid 1990s). In contrast to Canada and the US, however, there is a middle layer of an elaborate institutionalized tran-sition network for the nonuniversity bound who come from all three tiers. This system consists of one- to four-year full-time vocational schools, mainly for girls who are prepared for social service and health occupations, and the dual system that combines three to three-and-a-half years of firm-based training with a coordinated attendance of a public vocational school.

The market value and social recognition of an apprenticeship is quite remarkable, with a participation rate of more than 60 percent of the school-leaving cohort in the first half of the 1990s. This transition route, however, privileges young men: 55 percent of them compared to 45 percent of the young women, who are restricted to a smaller range of mainly service and office occupations. Young people who do not manage to enter either the academic or apprenticeship route (15 percent of a cohort, with a declining trend) are kept from dropping out by being channeled into VET schemes, which are provided by federal and provincial governments and the Social Fund of the European Union. This lower segment of the stratified transition system, however, is much less than in Canada and the US, where dropout rates and chronic underemployment reach 30 percent in some regions.[20] The integrative capacity of Germany's transition pathways and provisions prevents a higher dropout rate, together with the federal government's active training and labour market policy that includes VET schemes for those who do not manage to attain an apprenticeship. This policy is embedded in the framework of social partnership between government, employers' associations, and labour unions.

In periods of economic decline or jobless growth, however, this pro-active training policy can only be successful as a bridging or temporary support device. In a declining job market, young people who were are trained in a government scheme are confronted with the problem of not having real job experiences. Their VET took place mainly in school-based contexts, and they have to compete for adult jobs with those who were trained in firms. To illustrate this problem, a look at the situation of young adults in East Germany—the former socialist German Democratic Republic—is instructive.[21] There an apprenticeship or university studies (for a minority of mainly party elite children) and a secure job were taken for granted. Unemployment was unheard of because state central planning coordinated education and job placement. In 1990, shortly after the wall came down, 75 percent of the males and 60 percent of the females were employed by their training firm after VET. Four years later, only 50 percent of the male and 45 percent of the female skilled workers were employed after training. Because of the slow reconstruction of the East German economy the federal government has established special VET schemes or subsidized business to train over capacity. Experts estimate that almost half of the apprentices in East Germany get their training in government programs with little employment prospects.

These data direct a more critical look at the transition institutions in Germany. Compared to North America the system is less flexible, though more protective and demanding for young people. It is much more difficult to enter and to advance in the German labour market without certificates. Those who cannot present at least a vocational credential are mostly stuck in the secondary labour market for their entire work lives, whereas until the 1980s two-thirds of the employees with a skilled worker's credential used to stay in the primary labour market with employment continuity and good income. The strong linkage between education and transition pathways in Germany is underscored moreover by the fact that almost all poly-technic or university graduates are employed in the primary labour market.[22]

In recent years, however, these linkages have become weaker and career opportunities for the journeymen and -women to move into positions of technicians or managers less certain. Firms have started to hire more college-trained technicians, business administrators, and engineers for middle-management positions. This development indicates that in the future the apprenticeship certificate will not be sufficient to advance in the job hierarchy. The more attractive and well paid jobs will become accessible only to university graduates.[23]

There are indicators that a growing number of young people respond to the changes in the skill requirements by opting for a strategy of double qualification by continuing on the higher education pathway after having completed an apprenticeship. From a life-course perspective, this strategy is an example for a realistic coping with an uncertain future by using institutions to optimize individual transition outcomes. Such a strategy would not be possible in North America, because institutional arrangements are lacking that could provide stimulating and protective environments for occupational training.

Short- and Long-term Outcomes of School-to-Work Transitions

Up to this point cross-sectional data had to be relied on to tell us only part of the transition histories of the young in the countries that are being compared. In order to fill the life-course framework, longitudinal or panel data is needed. In a recent study Büchtemann, Schupp, and Soloff use data from the German Socio-economic Panel and the US Panel Study of Income Dynamics for a comparison of transition outcomes in these two countries in the 1980s. Unfortunately, similar data sets for comparing Canada with Germany and the US do not exist.[24]

One year after leaving school only a very small proportion (five percent) of young people in Germany has started to work. The vast majority were engaged in formal postsecondary studies in the dual system, at vocational schools or the university. This contrasts with the US, where one year after school half of the school graduates were in the labour market, and ten percent were looking for a job. One third were enrolled in full-time post-secondary institutions; a rate somewhat higher than in Germany, but lower than in Canada.

The differences between the US and Germany still hold up five years later. Half of the young adults were employed or were looking for work in Germany, in contrast to three-fourths of their counterparts in the US; 40 percent of the Germans, but only 20 percent of the Americans were still attending universities. This reflects the extended duration of academic studies in Germany. Today it takes about seven years until graduation with the equivalent of a Master's degree. And where are the VET graduates after five years? Three-fourths had entered employment, mainly in their training firm; one out of ten went on to university; and a small proportion either were unemployed or had withdrawn from the labour market. Finally, after 12 years, we observe dramatic differences between the US and Germany in the distribution of recognized credentials. In the US, one-third of all school leavers never received any additional formal education or training whatsoever and almost half remained without a degree—one-third of them were college dropouts. In Germany more than three-fourths had acquired either a vocational certificate or a university degree.

Canada does better in regard to academic degrees than both Germany and the US. A longitudinal study by Anisef et al. of an Ontario school-leaving cohort of 1972/73 shows that in 1988, after 15 years in the workforce, 40 percent had a postsecondary degree, 25 percent had completed a community college program, but 30 percent did not acquire any creden-tial.[25]

Transition outcomes in terms of unemployment, matching, mobility, and wages show that the German system used to deliver better returns for both the young person and the employer. One year after leaving school ten percent of the cohort were unemployed in the US, four percent in Germany; after five years five percent were jobless in the US, and two percent in Germany. Though making comparative generalizations is limited because only school-leaving cohorts that experienced different labour market conditions are studied, more recent data for Canada show that by the mid 1990s youth unemployment rose to 18 percent. Canadian youth is confronted with one of the highest levels of repeated unemploy-ment in the Organization of Economic Cooperation and Development (OECD). Furthermore, there is an increasing trend of social marginaliza-tion for young women without postsecondary education who either withdraw from the labour market (only 40 percent participate in the labour force) or are employed in the casual segment of the labour market with temporary, low skill, low paid part-time jobs.[26]

For young adults, part-time work has become the dominant form of employment for young adults under 25 years. There is also an increasing mismatch between individual educational investments and labour market position. Studies by Livingstone (1993) and Anisef et al. (1994) document that in Ontario one-third of all young adults under 25 are underemployed. According to a recent survey of Human Resources and Development Canada (1994) not even a third of university Bachelor's degree holders report that they had work they had been educated for.[27]

These results contrast with the transition histories in Germany. In the 1980s, one year after graduation from the apprenticeship, 85 percent of the craftsmen, skilled white- and blue-collar workers and 70 percent of the university graduates were employed in their respective occupational fields. This occupational stability continued for at least ten years in the labour market. This differs from the US, where five years after leaving high school three out of four young adults were employed in jobs that did not require any formal postsecondary education; two out of ten worked in jobs that required nothing but on-the-job training. Only for those who had acquired a Bachelor's degree is a better match found; two out of three were employed in jobs adequate to their skill level.

What about career mobility? In Germany three out of four young adults were in stable employment during the first five years after entering the labour market; 80 percent of the men, but only 66.6 percent of the women. This reflects the gender structure of the labour market and career pattern in German society. A decade after labour market entry career patterns become more dynamic in Germany. This results from moving to other employers, without leaving the trained occupation. This is evidence for the importance of the principle of "portable skills," which is constitutive for the German transition arrangements. In contrast to this pattern of high job continuity (for men) even college graduates in the US and Canada start their employment life in lower skilled jobs and gradually move into skilled, adequate positions. No improvement, however, is experienced by the large group of college dropouts. They could have started to look for a job right after leaving high school.[28]

It seems that in the US and Canada the mismatch between individual educational investment and economic returns acts as a signal for lower class parents and youths not to invest in postsecondary education. Another rationality motivates German school graduates to invest at least in an apprenticeship because those who do do not suffer a decline in their relative wage position over the life course.

Conclusions

There is a trend in Canada and the US, and to a lesser degree in Germany, of a decoupling between education and employment. In contrast to the school-leaving cohorts entering the labour market in the 1960s and 1970s, who went from full-time education to full-time entry jobs, today's cohorts have to cope with a discontinuous and prolonged, quite often stormy voyage to the entry ports of the employment system. Private and public sector employers offer a smaller number of training and entry level jobs on all skill levels. The uncertain employment future requires unusual individual determination and transition flexibility, demands that are shaking the confidence of many young people.

In view of such circumstances more and more young adults make a reasonable life-course decision by enrolling in a college or university. They start with the belief that a Bachelor's or Master's degree will be the entrance ticket for career jobs at a time when the number of good jobs is decreasing and part-time as well temporary employment is becoming the "standard" for entry jobs also for college graduates.

In Canada this situation has led to a growing number of young people who work part-time while still studying for a degree. And an increasing proportion of young Canadians will continue their education part-time after having entered employment. This behavior corresponds to the emergence of a deregulated labour market with growing temporary or contract employment.

In Germany the apprenticeship system has managed to adapt to the changes of job requirements and still offers quite a continuous transition to the labour market for the majority of youth. There is, however, a steady shift from the vocational to the academic pathway as the number of young people is increasing who acquire the *Abitur*. Hence, the number of applicants for apprenticeships in blue-collar, crafts, sales, and commerce occupations is declining, while there is a growing demand for apprenticeships in managerial, technical, social, and personal service occupations.

In order to summarize the main ideas of this comparative discussion of the relationship between education and work, a concise typology of the countries studied will suggest that there is no general convergence in the noncollege bound transition systems in North America and Germany.

- The United States is a country with an egalitarian school system and individualized transitions into the labour market in a training-on-the-job culture.
- Canada is a country with an egalitarian school system and discontinuous transitions in a postsecondary education culture.
- Germany provides continuous transitions based on a stratified education system and a vocational training culture.

This typology points to the contrasting cultural traditions, ideologies, and perceptions of the role that general education, vocational training, and university education should play in creating equal opportunities, social stability, and economic success in the global economy. It follows that transplanting the German dual system into Canada will not work. However, the high regard for postsecondary education and the need for a "high-performance workplace model"[29] in Canadian society should be used as a platform for promoting a commitment to train young people who do not enter or who drop out of university. Considering the German experience, training in the workplace should build on training for the workplace. Why? Sequences of ad hoc training-on-the-job reproduce a limited concept of portable skills that may very well be more expensive for business compared to a VET system that lays the foundation for pro-active and self-responsible work and learning behaviour in the workplace. Furthermore, team work and flexible work habits require a stable and coordinated training environment, monitored by expert tutors, modeled on the master craftsmen.

Canada has relied on immigration as a reservoir of skilled workers for most of its history; this has prevented government and business from establishing a VET system for the intermediate technical, communication, and service skills. Such skills are vital for the public and private sector, where high tech innovations are to be applied, equipment to be assembled, maintained and repaired, and the infrastructure for the quality of city life has to be improved. Moreover, in a period of rapid technological change further training in the workplace must build on a well-educated and generally skilled workforce. This may be more cost-efficient in the long run than ad hoc upgrading by further training.

The majority of Canada's young population does not acquire a university degree. This puts them in a transition at risk which is a lifelong disadvantage compared to university graduates. From a life-course perspective they are at risk of becoming locked in a transient job history. The future of work requires a solid intellectual and practical preparation for various forms of paid jobs, self-employment and continuing learning. Though the creation of more entry jobs is very urgent, it will not solve the problem of youth unemployment and will not improve career prospects of young people who do not have the chance to acquire a certified profile of portable skills. Chronic youth unemployment and a lack of skills training undermine not only Canada's economy but also contribute to the growth of a social underclass of young people.

A possible solution for some of these problems would be to invest in a community college-based pathway of occupational education and training which is linked systematically to in-company work experience by a coordinated curriculum of theoretical knowledge and skill acquisition. This pathway should be open to all nonuniversity bound youth who have participated in co-op programs in high school. This transition arrangement, when institutionalized, would signal young people that there is a socially accepted transition alternative to a university education. Community colleges as cornerstones of occupational education should create joint ventures with industries and business to create programs for education and training in occupations that require intermediate technical, commercial, managerial, and communication skills.

As we know from the German example, however, creating and managing such a transition system presupposes the collaboration of employers, government, and unions,[30] and a social consensus that promotes equality and efficiency for the occupational training pathway from school to work.

NOTES

1. *The Forgotten Half: Non-College Youth in America* (Washington, D.C.: W.T. Grant Foundation, 1988); Canadian Youth Foundation, *Canada's Hidden Deficit* (Ottawa: 1995).
2. Cf. Klaus Hurrelmann, *Lebensphase Jugend* (Weinheim: Juventa, 1994).
3. Cf. John R. Gillis, *Geschichte der Jugend* (Weinheim: Beltz, 1980).

4. See Artur Fischer and Jürgen Zinnecker, eds., *Jugend '92*, 5 vols. (Opladen: Leske and Budrich, 1992).

5. Hurrelmann, *Lebensphase Jugend*; Fischer and Zinnecker, *Jugend '92.*

6. Dieter Baacke, *Jugend und Jugendkulturen* (Weinheim: Juventa, 1987); Wilfried Heitmeyer and Thomas Olk, eds., *Individualisierung von Jugend* (Weinheim: Juventa, 1990).

7. Cf. Alan C. Kerckhoff, *Getting Started: Transition to Adulthood in Great Britain* (Boulder, CO: Westview Press, 1990); John Brynner and Ken Roberts, eds., *Youth and Work: Transition to Employment in England and Germany* (London: Anglo-German Foundation, 1992); Karen Evans and Walter R. Heinz, eds., *Becoming Adults in England and Germany* (London: Anglo-German Foundation, 1994).

8. Cf. Stephen F. Hamilton, *Apprenticeship for Adulthood* (New York: Basic Books, 1990); Thomas Bailey, "Can Youth Apprenticeship Thrive in the United States?" *Educational Researcher* (April 1993): 4–10.

9. Cf. Walter R. Heinz, "Youth Transitions in Cross-Cultural Perspective: School-to-Work in Germany," in *Youth and Transition to Adulthood: Research and Policy Implications*, ed. B. Galaway and J. Hudson (Toronto: Thompson, 1996), pp. 1–13.

10. Cf. James E. Rosenbaum, "Are Adolescent Problems Caused By School or Society?" *Journal of Research on Adolescence* (1991): 301–22.

11. Cf. Graham S. Lowe and Harvey Krahn, *Job Related Education and Training Among Young Workers* (Kingston, Ontario: IRC, Queens University, 1994).

12. See Walter R. Heinz, ed., *Theoretical Advances in Life Course Research* (Weinheim: Deutscher Studien-Verlag, 1991).

13. Heinz, "Youth Transitions in Cross-Cultural Perspective."

14. David Stern et al., *Research on School-to-Work Transition Programs in the United States* (Berkeley, CA: National Centre for Research in Vocational Education, 1994); Julian Tanner, Harvey Krahn, and Timothy F. Hartnagel, *Fractured Transitions from School to Work* (Toronto: Oxford University Press, 1995).

15. Institut für Arbeits- und Berufsforschung, *Kurzbericht 77* (Nürnberg: IAB, 1995).

16. See the annual *Berufsbildungsbericht* by the Bundesministerium für Bildung und Wissenschaft (Federal Minister of Education and Science).

17. *Toronto Star*, 31 December 1995.

18. David Ashton and Graham Lowe, eds., *Making Their Way: Education, Training and the Labour Market in Canada and Britain* (Milton Keynes: Open University Press, 1991).

19. Cf. Ludwig von Friedeburg, "Gatekeeping for Bildungsbürger: On the Development of the German Education System," in *Institutions and Gatekeeping in the Life Course*, ed. Walter R. Heinz (Weinheim: Deutscher Studien-Verlag, 1992), pp. 31–48.

20. Tanner, Krahn, and Hartnagel, *Fractured Transitions*; Jeylan T. Mortimer, "U.S. Research on School-to-Work Transitions," in *Youth and Transition to Adulthood*, ed. B. Galaway and J. Hudson, pp. 32–45.

21. See Gisela Westhoff, ed., *Übergänge von der Ausbildung in den Beruf* (Berlin: BIBB, 1995).

22. Hans P. Blossfeld and Karl U. Mayer, "Labor Market Segmentation in the Federal Republic of Germany: An Empirical Study of Segmentation Theories From a Life Course Perspective," *European Sociological Review* 4 (1989): 123–40.

23. Jean P. Gehin and Philippe Méhaut, "The German Dual System: A Model for Europe?" in *Industrielle Beziehungen* 2 (1995), pp. 64–81.

24. Christoph Büchtemann, Jürgen Schupp, and Dana Soloff, "From School to Work: Patterns in Germany and the United States," in *Labour Market Dynamics in Present Day Germany*, ed. J. Schwarze, F. Buttler, and G. Wagner (Boulder, CO: Westview Press, 1994), pp. 112–41.

25. Paul Anisef et al., "The Causes and Consequences of Underemployment Among University Graduates in Ontario," paper presented at the CSAA Meetings in Calgary, 1994.

26. Cf. Jane Gaskell, *Gender Matters From School to Work* (Buckingham: Open University Press, 1992).

27. Anisef, "The Causes and Consequences"; David W. Livingstone, "Lifelong Education and Chronic Underemployment: Exploring the Contradictions," in *Transitions: Schooling and Employment in Canada*, ed. P. Anisef and P. Axelrod (Toronto: Thompson, 1993); Human Resources Development Canada, *Social Security in Canada—Background Facts* (Ottawa: HRDC, 1994), pp. 89–101.

28. Cf. Mortimer, "U.S. Research on School-to-Work Transitions."

29. Gordon Betcherman, Kathryn McMullen, Norm Leckie, and Christina Caron, *The Canadian Workplace in Transition* (Kingston, Ontario: IRC, Queen's University, 1994).

30. Cf. Wolfgang Streeck, "Skills and the Limits of Neoliberalism: The Enterprise of the Future as a Place of Learning," *Work, Employment and Society* 3 (1989): 89–104.

10 Women and Social Policy in a Divided and Unified Germany

KATHERINE NASH

The merging together of the German Democratic Republic (GDR) with the Federal Republic of Germany (FRG) on 3 October 1990 rapidly brought about sweeping changes in the social, economic, and political conditions for all citizens living in the GDR. For those of us concerned with the role of women in society, and the issue of gender equality, it is particularly important to examine the impact of unification on east German women. Have they lost ground in terms of social and economic equality with men? Or as some writers disparagingly pose the question, are GDR-women the "losers" of unification? And what are the implications of unification for the work and family roles of east German women today?

After World War II, the two Germanys developed divergent social policies and expectations concerning women's labour force participation and childrearing. In the GDR paid employment had become a central part of women's lives, while the housewife role was frowned upon and considered boring. Low-cost comprehensive childcare provided by the government enabled mothers to engage in the labour force full-time. GDR-women were able to pursue both their goals—career and family—simultaneously.

In contrast, FRG-women tended to pursue their career and family desires sequentially, working full-time for awhile, but then leaving the labour force to raise a family; being a mother was considered an important full-time responsibility. Childcare was viewed, at best, as a supplementary activity for children and, at worst, as undermining the family. Limited childcare services rendered it difficult for mothers of young children to be employed in the labour force.

The differences between the GDR and FRG in terms of ideology, childcare services, and family and labour market policies resulted in markedly different employment patterns for women in the two Germanys. By the late 1980s, roughly

50 percent of FRG-women were employed in the labour force, whereas GDR-women had, with 90 percent, one of the highest female labour force participation rates in the industrialized world.[1]

When the two countries were unified, basically the legal, political, and economic system from the FRG was adopted by the old GDR territories, and so it is really the east Germans who have to adjust. Not much changed in the daily lives of west German women, but much was different for GDR-women living in a newly unified Germany. For instance, as a result of economic restructuring in response to the newly introduced market economy, east Germans experienced massive layoffs; for women the outcome was particularly grave: slightly more than 60 percent of all the unemployed were women.[2] In order to better understand the changes in life circumstances confronting east German women as a result of unification, it is important to first review some of the prior differences between the two Germanys with regard to women's roles and social policy. The chapter then examines how East German women have been affected by the unification process.

The History of GDR-Women in Social Policy

The GDR had as one of its official objectives the social and economic equality of men and women, which was formally granted in the constitution.[3] This goal of equality between the sexes was tied to employment, and official GDR ideology operated on the premise that women's labour force participation would eliminate inequality between men and women.[4] In the GDR, work was considered both a duty and right of each socialist citizen;[5] both men and women were expected to be active members of the labour force. In this official ideology promoting women's labour force participation, housewives were devalued and those people who did not work in the labour force were stigmatized and considered *asozial* (asocial).[6]

During the early history of the GDR (in the 1950s), the government set up policies to try and promote women's labour force participation.[7] This objective, however, was not motivated solely by the issue of gender equality, but also because the GDR government faced a severe labour shortage.[8] At the end of World War II there was a high demand for labour to rebuild the country and to cover the reparations extracted by the USSR. Demand for labour was also intensified by the exodus of people leaving for the west, which continued up until 1961 when the Wall was built, effectively sealing shut the national borders of the GDR and preventing any further exodus. In need of labour during this period, the government set up policies to encourage women to enter the labour force.

During the 1960s, but especially in the 1970s and 1980s, the GDR government began to focus on women's role in the family.[9] One of the main obstacles to increasing women's labour force participation had been women's responsibilities within the family. Over the years, the government developed a series of policy measures and programs to help women combine paid employment with motherhood.[10] By the end of the GDR era, the following supports for women had been instituted: (a) women were granted a one-year paid maternity leave with a job-return guarantee at the end of the leave (the *Babyjahr*); (b) mothers were given a generous number of paid days off from work when their children were sick; (c) mothers of two or more children were allowed to work a reduced work week of 40 hours (instead of the normal 43 hours) and; (d) mothers were given one day off a month from work to attend to housework.

The comprehensive, low-cost, state-subsidized childcare system in the GDR was a key program that enabled mothers to be employed in the labour force. The government initially established childcare services during the 1960s and over the next two decades the system expanded to be able to care for more and more children. The government provided three types of services for children from infancy up until the fourth grade of elementary school: *Krippe* (or nursery care) was for infants and toddlers up until the age of three years; *Kindergarten* (or preschool) was for children between the ages of three and six (until they reached school-age) and *Hort* (or after school care) was for children in grades one to four. By the end of the GDR era 80 percent of children under the age of three were in *Krippe* (nursery care), 95 percent of children between the ages of three to six were in *Kindergarten* (pre-school), and roughly 80 percent of elementary school children visited *Hort*. The GDR reported that any parent who wanted to send their child to *Kindergarten* or *Hort* could do so.[11]

There are some key aspects about childcare in the GDR that made it possible for mothers to be employed. The daycare centres were open long hours, from 6 a.m. until 6 p.m., which enabled mothers to work full-time in the labour force.[12] Cost was not an issue for women since the state covered most of the childcare expenses and parents paid only a minimal fee for meals (e.g., 35 and 55 Pfennig per day for *Kindergarten* and *Hort*.[13]

The policies aimed at increasing women's labour force participation appeared to have been effective. At the close of the GDR period in 1989, the country had one of the highest rates of female labour force participation in the industrialized world: approximately 90 percent of all women of employment age (i.e., between the ages of 15 and 65) were either employed in the labour force or they were in some form of educational or job training outside the home.[14] For most GDR-women, having a job or career had become an accepted way of life, and a large part of their self-identity. One woman's reflection about returning to work after the one-year maternity leave during the GDR period indicates this:[15]

> I studied and I enjoyed my career and I wanted to practice my profession. I didn't want to stay at home and be a housewife. I hadn't imagined my life like that. I had a child and I wanted to continue with my job, to continue working. I wanted to somehow combine the two.

Having a job or pursuing a career had become important to GDR-women for a variety of reasons: it gave them the chance to have some economic independence and to be autonomous; they felt needed and useful outside the home; the women liked being recognized for their own work and achievements in the workplace; they valued the chance to prove themselves through work-related tasks; and they enjoyed the social contacts of colleagues and opportunities for communication outside the family.[16] Overall, paid employment had become an important aspect of GDR-women's lives, and it is reflected in the words of east German women today:

> I needed to work—*for me*, to be with my co-workers, to simply get out of the house. It [the job] was interesting for me. They had modernized the machinery at work, and when I came back [from maternity leave] I had to learn it all, and I was able to do it. I enjoy it, I mean sometimes, I complain too, like today, it was a long workday. But still when you are out of work, you miss it.
>
> *employed laundress, mother of two children*

> I wanted to put to use what I had studied. I liked the contact with colleagues and the exchange of ideas. For me, work means independence, financial independence and recognition in one's field. And that you develop yourself further, that you don't just stagnate.
>
> *employed teacher, mother of two children*

The Persistence of Gender Inequality in the GDR

Given all the policies and programs insti-
tuted by the GDR to promote women's labour force participation, how
successful was the government in actually achieving gender equality? On
the surface, the GDR appeared to have done quite well in this respect: it
had one of the highest female labour force participation rates in the industrialized world; the fact that mothers were able to combine both work and
family was also considered to be a sign of achieving gender equality; and
women had made great strides in education, reaching the qualification
levels of men in a number of areas.[17]

Despite these successes, there were still areas where women had not
achieved equality with men. Although the GDR mandated "equal pay for
equal work" there was still a considerable gender gap in wages, with
women earning on average 70 to 75 percent of what men earned. The
income disparity between men and women has been attributed to occupational sex-segregation: women were concentrated in certain fields that
were lower-paying, such as health-care, social services, education, and in
postal and communication jobs; and they were under-represented in
managerial positions, occupying just barely one-third of all management
positions.[18]

Another obstacle to the achievement of gender equality in the GDR was
that an open examination and critique of continued gender discrimination
was not possible. In the absence of a democratic political system, it was
taboo to challenge the government and argue that, despite its policies,
inequality between the sexes still existed.[19] Researchers in the GDR did
not address the problem and women in GDR-society did not discuss it, or
even see women's inequality as an issue. The government perpetuated a
myth of equality between the sexes and this myth made many women blind
to actual disadvantages they encountered (for example, lower wages or the
double burden of employment and household duties). As a result, gender
inequality was simply not an issue for many GDR-women; they worked
just like men, and did not see themselves as being discriminated against.
As some authors describe it, GDR-women and the government were
"gender blind" when it came to issues of inequality between men and
women.[20]

A common criticism of the GDR mother-centred social policies is that
the problem of balancing employment and family responsibilities was

faced only by the women; it was not viewed as a dilemma for both mothers and fathers.[21] The division of household labour was still largely traditional,[22] with women responsible for cleaning, cooking, laundry, shopping, and childcare, while men did the household repairs and played with the children.[23] Because of the lack of available consumer goods in the GDR, homemaking was often a time-consuming task; women developed a number of improvisational strategies to compensate for limited consumer goods, such as sewing, knitting, gardening, canning, and developing an informal bartering network for the exchange of goods. Shopping for basic food items (e.g., meat or fruit) could be a major undertaking with people waiting in line for hours to purchase whatever happened to be available that day. Since most of the domestic labour was still women's responsibility, a large proportion of employed GDR-women ended up putting in a "second shift" of housework at the end of an already long workday.

Ilona Ostner[24] points out the ambiguous outcomes of the mother-centred policies for GDR-women. The policies enabled women to participate in the labour force, but mothers paid a high price for employment—they worked long hours and spent little time with their children who were in daycare all day. The GDR provided low-cost, full-time childcare services to working mothers, but at the same time, this system of daycare could be criticized for its regimented mass treatment of children. In a severe critique of GDR childcare, Susanne Rothmaler states:

> According to the rigid socialist ideal, the aim of education was to produce clean, well-behaved, adjusted, uncreative children…The most important rule was to take one's place in a group and to adjust to collective norms, which led to a ruthless leveling of individual characteristics and talents…[25]

Because labour and family policies in the GDR emphasized women's full-time labour force participation, mothers did not have a choice regarding whether they would work in the labour force or stay at home with their children; they had to work. In the end, policies that were intended to emancipate women actually reinforced the notion that women—and not both men and women—were responsible for raising children and maintaining a household, and this left women with the double burden of meeting employment and family obligations.

| Women and Social Policy in the FRG

Unlike the situation in the GDR, when women in the FRG have children, they often do not remain employed in the labour force. Differences in the availability of childcare services make it more difficult for FRG-women to combine paid employment with motherhood, and other family policies provide incentives for mothers to remain at home with their children. While the GDR implemented measures that enabled women to *simultaneously* engage in full-time employment and motherhood, the FRG developed policies that encourage women to organize employment and childrearing *sequentially*, that is, women engage in paid labour for a time, and then with the arrival of children, they remain at home, returning to work (either on a part-time or full-time basis) once their children are older (known as the three-phase model, paid employment—family—return to wage work). This sequential or three-phase model for balancing work and family life requires a set of government measures based on the notion of difference rather than equality; instead of emphasizing full-time labour force participation for both men and women, the policies of the FRG recognize unpaid, domestic labour (housework, but especially childrearing) as a form of work that is just as important as wage labour to the maintenance and operation of a household.[26] Let us now turn to a closer look at FRG family policy, in order to better understand these differences between the GDR and FRG regarding women's role in society.

Even though Article 3 of the FRG constitution established equal rights between men and women in 1949, there is a history of political thought in Germany that views men and women as playing different roles in society, with an emphasis on women's position in the family.[27] During the 1950s the CDU/CSU coalition government under the Adenauer administration promoted conservative marriage and family policies that served to buttress the nuclear family with its traditional gender division of labour (the male breadwinner and female homemaker model). For instance, a law was passed stipulating that a wife could only work outside the home if it did not interfere with her primary obligation as wife and mother.

It should be remembered that the 1950s in the FRG was a period of postwar reconstruction, a time of rebuilding after the ravages of World War II. Although large numbers of German women were doing men's work during the war and cleaning up the rubble in the aftermath, a positive image of the working woman did not emerge; most women experienced work outside the home under harsh conditions, which had worn them out, and they simply desired to return home and care for their children. After the war, people yearned to return to a "normal" life, and the nuclear family became the symbolic representation of that desire. During the 1950s most politicians believed that stable, nuclear families would be the way to rebuild social order and create a democratic society.[28]

In the 1960s the FRG experienced a wave of economic prosperity and growth, and along with this economic boom came an increase in the demand for labour. Government policy makers at this time started to view married women's employment in positive terms, as one way to help meet this increased demand for labour. Still, policies in the FRG discouraged mothers' labour force participation, favouring instead the sequential model of women's employment. For example, it was not until 1977, with the passage of the Reform of Marriage and Family Law, that the legally defined housewife marriage came to an end. Until that time the federal statute about marriage specified that it was the women's responsibility to run the household and care for the children. In the revised 1977 Marriage Law, the partners decide how they want to divide domestic responsibilities and paid work. What is significant about this change is that both paid work and the performance of domestic chores are considered to be equal contributions to the running of a household. The change in the marriage legislation illustrates the principle of "different but equal" treatment in family policy.

Keeping in line with the principle of different but equal, family policy during the 1980s and 1990s has moved in a direction that considers unpaid domestic labour (primarily childrearing) to be extremely important for society and something that should be recognized as a form of work, and as such financially compensated with public funds. This is best illustrated with the most recent government measures known in German as the policy of the four E's. These policies apply to either parent, mother or father, and are intended to acknowledge and reward the work of childrearing in the home:[29]

1. *Erziehungsgeld* (a childrearing allowance)—One parent has a right to receive DM 600 per month for the first two years of a child's life. The parent may work part-time, but no more than 19 hours per week;

2. *Erziehungsurlaub* (parental leave)—a three-year job protected parental leave is guaranteed to parents. Either the mother or father can take the leave, or it can be split between them. The parents do

not have a right to the exact same job when they return to the labour force, but they do have the right to return to a similar job;

3. *Erziehungszeiten* (childrearing time)—the time spent out of the labour force for childrearing is now actually included in calculations for social security benefits for retirement;

4. *Erwerbsarbeit*—measures to help a person re-enter the labour market after the family phase.

Although these policies are gender neutral and apply to both fathers and mothers, it is still mainly mothers who take the leave. On the positive side, these measures acknowledge the "work" that goes into raising children and provides families with some economic rewards for doing so. With such a policy focus, however, other forms of childcare outside the home are neglected or not given as much priority.

In contrast to the GDR, the FRG did not establish a comprehensive state-run system of childcare, and the shortage of childcare spaces in West Germany renders it difficult for West German mothers to work full-time or to pursue a professional career. There is a severe shortage of childcare facilities for infants and toddlers; just three percent of children between the ages of one and two were in nursery care in the West. The news-magazine *Der Spiegel* reported in 1991 that there were few after-school childcare programs for school-age children, and that in some areas in the West there were shortages of *Kindergarten* spaces for three to six year olds. This limited supply of childcare services in the FRG has made it very diffi-cult for mothers of infants and toddlers below the age of three to engage in any type of paid employment at all, or for mothers of children older than three to work more than part-time.[30] The German government, however, is taking steps to address the childcare shortage; in 1996, a federal law was scheduled to go into effect that makes each state responsible for guaran-teeing parents the right to send their children to *Kindergarten*, i.e., guaranteeing each child of *Kindergarten* age a daycare space.

Much of contemporary FRG social policy is still based on a traditional model of the family, and it assumes that there will be someone (usually the mother) at home with the children during the day. This becomes apparent when one looks at the hours of operation of daycares, *Kindergarten*, and schools in the FRG; most operate on half-day schedules, mainly during the morning hours. The school schedule is particularly problematic for mothers, finishing one day after two hours, another after four, and schools do not serve a hot midday meal. The FRG government also does not provide after-school childcare (although since unification the after-school *Hort* programs have remained in operation in the East, in the new federal states). As a result of this school schedule, someone—and it is usually the mother—has to be home to prepare the main midday meal and to supervise the children in the afternoon.

Like the GDR, the FRG government has sought through the development of particular family and social policies to address the dilemma of balancing work and family life. In contrast to the GDR, which aimed at getting mothers into the labour force, the current FRG measures acknowledge and reward the work of childrearing in the home. Contemporary FRG policies still favour the male-breadwinner family model by discouraging women's employment, at least when there are children, and encouraging a sequential model of women's labour force participation (wage work—family—return to work), and it is this model that is now being imposed upon east German women after unification. How east German women will ultimately fare under these new conditions for combining work and family remains to be seen.

The Impact of Unification on East German Women

The roles of women in work and family life were quite different in the two Germanys. When the countries were unified, the political and economic structures, the laws, and social services from the old FRG were adopted by the former GDR territories, or the new federal states. Thus, it is really the east Germans who are adjusting, adapting, and reacting to the sweeping social, economic, and political changes brought about by unification. Not much changed in the daily lives of west German women, but much was different for GDR-women living in a newly unified Germany.

What is the impact of unification on east German women? How are they managing following unification? Have they lost ground in terms of social and economic equality with men? Are east German women the "losers" of unification, as some writers have decried? What are the implications of unification for the work and family roles of east German women today?

Looking at the employment situation, it appears that east German women lost considerable ground in comparison to the gains made during the GDR period. Women have been especially hard hit by unemployment; statistics for the spring of 1992 indicate that slightly more than 60 percent of all the unemployed were women.[31] East German women have also been harder hit by unemployment than their male counterparts; in 1992 unemployment rates for women (at 18.6 percent) were almost double that of men (9.7 percent).[32]

Bohnenkamp and Eisbach[33] point out that the reason for this gender difference in unemployment patterns is *not* that more women than men were being laid off from jobs, but rather that women have a harder time finding a job again and remain unemployed longer than men. They identify two possible reasons for women's poorer chances of getting a job placement: (1) employers are more likely to give jobs to men and; (2) women are more restricted in their job search because of family responsibilities, and so cannot look for work outside of their immediate area.

For east German women, who are accustomed to working in the labour force, and who derive some of their identity and sense of self-worth from employment, the experience of unemployment can be discouraging, disheartening, and frustrating. The comments of two mothers who experienced bouts of unemployment for a few months, but then fortunately found jobs, reflect how discouraging the experience of unemployment can be:

> I was unemployed for about a quarter of a year. I had done a job-retraining for nine months and afterwards I tried to get a job. I filled out a lot of job applications and every day I waited for a response. Rejection after rejection. I started to think, "no one needs me." I cried, I felt terrible, I was depressed. I mean, I had the household…I mean, housework is work, but one gets no sense of success or achievement from it…it didn't bring me any satisfaction to just be at home all day.

> It's hard to describe. You know that you can do things, that you have skills, and you want to work, but despite that you can't get a job. You hope with each application that you put in, that it will work, that you will land the job, but when you get another rejection you feel pretty disappointed. You don't know why you have been rejected. You sit at home feeling useless…it's a little depressing.

It was thought at first that east German women might gladly return to the hearth and home simply because they carried the double burden of work and family for so long under the GDR regime. This expectation, however, has not come to fruition; there has been no voluntary retreat from the labour force by east German women; surveys indicate that over 95 percent of east German women prefer to be employed in the labour force, while only three percent desire the role of a full-time homemaker; contrast this to west German women, 25 percent of whom think the housewife-marriage is a desirable way of life.[34] East German women's strong desire to be employed is reflected in their active participation in employment and job-retraining programs currently offered by the government.

The problem of unemployment does not affect all East German women in the same way. For particular groups labour market chances are not that bad; e.g., young, single, childless women, with a good education stand a decent chance of finding employment. However, two groups of women— the middle-aged and mothers of young children—are particularly vulnerable to long-term unemployment. The prospect of middle-aged women (in their 50s) finding re-employment does not look good; in the competition for jobs, they learn that they are "too old," and that their education and qualifications have no value in today's job market. Many of the women over 50 have been forced into early retirement and are collecting a meager social security pension.[35]

Women with small children also face considerable difficulties finding employment. Employers often do not consider these mothers to be reliable workers, but instead suspect them of being at a higher risk of absenteeism (because younger children tend to be sick more often, and because of the possibility that unexpected problems with childcare arrangements might arise). It should be pointed out that in Germany it is legal to ask a female applicant in a job interview about her children, and what types of childcare arrangements she has made for them. Some single mothers felt that they were being viewed as deficient labour power in job interviews because they were single parents with primary responsibility for their children.[36] Similarly, some east German mothers with young children report a similar feeling about the job search process, i.e., they believe they are not considered for jobs by employers because they have young children:

...I had no possibility of finding a job because of my two kids. No firm would hire me. I applied for a lot of jobs but I just kept getting rejections. They never said outright that is was because of the kids, but at that time they were pretty young, she was 1 1/2 and he was 4 years old....

On my job applications I had to fill out that I was married and had two children. I assume that many of those employers saw that and just skipped over my application, without even checking if I had childcare for my kids. They (the employers) didn't care about that sort of thing— it could be that your kids would be sick and that you would miss work. There was no chance of me getting a job on the free market.

Single mothers, like east German women in general, are at a greater risk of unemployment than east German men. But, surprisingly, single mothers fare better in the labour market in comparison to other east German women; in fact, the unemployment rate for single mothers (13.7 percent) in the new federal states is actually lower than the overall unemployment rate for east German women (19.3 percent).[37] The reason for the lower rate could be that these women are strongly oriented toward work because they are the sole economic providers for their families.

Still, unification has been difficult for single mothers because they have lost the net of social and economic security that they once had during the GDR era. Even though the standard of living of single parents in the GDR was lower than that of married couples with children, single parents received considerable support from the state and their economic existence was secure: childcare was provided at a very low cost by the government; there was generous paid leave time for mothers when a child was sick; and there was no worry about losing one's job because of a child's illness. In addition, state subsidies for food, housing, and electricity made the basic cost of living low (e.g., people spent, on average, only 2.8 percent of income on rent). All in all, a single mother's basic existence with regard to employment, housing, childcare, clothing, and food was secure under the GDR system. That sense of economic security vanished after unification; single mothers worried about the rising cost of childcare, their employment situation, and the rise in the general cost of living.[38]

For east German mothers unification has made balancing work and family more problematic. The competitive labour market with its unemployment has heightened people's sense of economic insecurity. As a result, mothers are more fearful of losing their jobs (if they have one), and try not to miss work because of childcare responsibilities (e.g., when a child is sick, or leaving work early to pick up a child before the daycare closes). Even though FRG family policy entitles working parents to ten paid days off from work per year to care for sick children at home (20 for single parents), some east German mothers try to minimize the use of this because they fear that their employer will view the absence disfavourably.

Childcare is also much more expensive now than it was during the GDR era, which poses problems for both employed as well as unemployed mothers. Even though there are sliding fees based on income, childcare can still be expensive. For example, in Neubrandenburg, for a family whose income falls below the poverty line, a full-time daycare space (in *Krippe*) for a toddler costs DM 295 per month, for Kindergarten DM 135, and these fees do not include the extra DM 60 per month for food.[39] Employed mothers have to weigh the expense of childcare against their earnings and consider whether it is economically feasible to remain in the labour force, especially if a large proportion of their paycheck goes to child-care. Unemployed mothers face a particular quandary because of certain government regulations related to childcare: in order for a mother to receive unemployment benefits or get assistance from the employment office in finding a job, she has to demonstrate that she has adequate child-care arrangements; if she cannot prove this, the employment office will not consider her "available" for paid employment. If the mother does not have her child in daycare (or have other arrangements), she will not officially be considered unemployed and is then not eligible for unemployment bene-fits.

In addition to the cost, mothers had to worry about whether or not their childcare centre would remain open after unification, and if they would still have a daycare space. The new federal states closed numerous child-care centres partly on the grounds that the supply of spaces exceeded demand. For example, in Neubrandenburg, the government reduced the number of childcare spaces by 5,000 in a span of three years, from 1989 to 1992.[40] There are three primary reasons for the current low demand for childcare services: (1) the dramatic decline in births after unification; (2) the high unemployment rates of women (women then pull their children from daycare since they are not working, or have unemployed relatives watch their child); and (3) the new parent fees, which render childcare unaffordable for some families. Kistler et al. argue that it is important for the eastern territories to retain the current level of childcare centres and spaces; if further cutbacks are made in this area, it will become difficult for women to maintain jobs or careers because daycare services will not be available.[41]

Despite the closings of childcare centres in the east, the new federal states have officially remained committed to providing childcare services for employed parents, and in most areas there are a sufficient number of childcare spaces, so that parents who wish to send their children to daycare (and can afford it) may do so. While changes have been made since unification in the funding of these centres, as well as the quality and manner in which services are provided, centres still provide full-day services for toddlers and preschool children, and the after-school *Hort* program for children in grades one to four from the GDR days has also been maintained (although in a modified form). Many east Germans consider the provision of childcare services to be very important, not only so that parents can work in the labour force, but they also view it as an important developmental resource for their children. Mothers commonly give these reasons for sending their child to *Kindergarten*: social contact with other children; development of skills through *Kindergarten* activities; and preparation for school.

When assessing the impact of unification, it is important to keep in mind that not all east German women are alike; depending upon their age, education, marital and family status, as well as other social factors, they will have different experiences (some positive, some negative) surrounding the unification process. The slogan that women are the "losers" of unification, which was popularized not only in the press but also in academic writings shortly after unification, is too general and vague; instead, it is better to examine which particular groups of women have suffered setbacks from unification, and which have experienced gains.

The slogan has also been criticized for being too simplistic because there have been both losses and gains in the unification process.[42] Amongst the losses are the following: (1) conditions of high unemployment for women; and (2) a general sense of economic insecurity, which includes worries about getting and/or keeping one's job, about being able to pay the rent and other bills, and coming to terms with the dramatic price increases. Despite this seemingly bleak economic picture, there have also been considerable gains, which former GDR citizens find positive, such as the increase in the amount and quality of consumer goods, the expanded opportunities of consumption, and the freedom to travel. I would add to the list of gains the opportunity for women to have an input in changing the quality of childcare services; an increased freedom to develop one's own, as well as one's child's, potential and talents; greater cultural and political freedom; and the opportunity for democratic political participation.

The Abortion Issue

A woman's decision (and subsequent action) about an unplanned pregnancy—whether to terminate or continue it—is in many countries a controversial political topic. At issue in these debates are two sets of interests: the protection of the life of the unborn fetus versus a woman's right to self-determination. The laws about abortion were quite different in the two Germanys, with the GDR having a more liberalized version than the FRG. Three years after unification, east German women lost the right to self-determination in matters of reproduction.[43]

The GDR permitted unconditional, free, and legal abortion within the first three months of a pregnancy (referred to in German as *Fristenlösung*, the periodic model). Even though the GDR had established numerous policies and incentives to encourage women to have children, it also took the position that every child should be a wanted child (*Wunschkind*). In the event of an unplanned pregnancy, women could make their own decision about whether to continue a pregnancy or have an abortion.

In the FRG, by contrast, abortion was a criminal offense under Section 218 of the criminal codes, with certain exceptions made for specific medical, ethical, or social reasons. The 1976 law established an Indication or Conditional Model (*Indikationsmodell*): abortion was considered a criminal offense, punishable by fine or up to three years imprisonment; however, under certain medical, ethical, or social grounds, an exception could be made and an abortion legally permitted. In the FRG, if a woman wanted an abortion, she was required to speak with a counselor and then her case needed to be approved by a committee. An abortion could be permitted if the health of the mother was severely in danger (medical condition); if the child was expected to be born with severe physical or mental handicaps (eugenic reason); if the pregnancy resulted from rape or incest (ethical grounds); or if the mother was going to face some other serious distress that would make it difficult to continue with the pregnancy (social condition, e.g., a pregnant women may claim she is too young or too poor, i.e., emotionally or financially not ready to take on the responsibility of parenthood at this time in her life).

There seems to be broad room for interpretation of acceptable social indications or grounds for abortion, and as a result, whether or not a woman is granted permission actually varies from state to state, with catholic states (e.g., Bavaria and Baden-Württemberg) being more strict about granting exceptions. This variation is in part due to the federal structure of the government which gives the individual states (*Länder*) latitude in the implementation of the law. For example, it is within the states domain to create and approve the counseling agencies. In more politically liberal areas, agencies have been set up to counsel women in a nondirective way; in the more conservative and catholic states, however, counselors predominate who are obligated to urge women to continue their pregnancies. Because of such differences between the conservative catholic and the more liberal states, what Ursula Nelles describes as an "abortion-tourism" developed in the FRG, with women from conservative areas going to a more liberal state for their abortion, or even going to another country, like the Netherlands, where abortion laws are less restrictive.[44]

The unification treaty deferred any resolution on the differences in the abortion legislation between the GDR and the FRG for two years. During that period, two contradictory laws were in existence: for the new federal states the old GDR law applied, whereas the west was still under the more restrictive FRG abortion law. The German Parliament was called upon to resolve the situation by the end of 1992. Many west German feminists and activists hoped that when the issue was finally addressed that a more liberalized abortion law would be enacted. In 1992 the German Parliament did liberalize the law, decriminalizing abortion within the first 12 weeks of pregnancy, essentially adopting the law on abortion that had existed in the GDR. This, however, was challenged by the conservative catholic Bavarian State government and some Christian Democratic parliamentarians, and as a result, in 1993, the Federal Constitutional Court overturned the new law legalizing abortion, declaring it unconstitutional; in the end the original FRG legislation, which criminalized abortion except under certain circumstances (the *Indikationsmodell*) prevailed.[45]

For GDR-women, the personal decision to terminate a pregnancy had become a right. In a united Germany, the Federal Constitutional Court's 1993 ruling took it away from them; it was a step backward for east German women, who lost control of their reproductive rights and their right to self-determination.

Conclusion

There is no doubt that east German women have been adversely affected by the unification process: they have been especially hard hit by unemployment; there is a general sense of economic insecurity among many; and their right to self-determination in reproductive matters has been restricted. But they have also experienced gains: like an increase in the availability of consumer goods; freedom to travel; and greater cultural and political freedom. When examining the impact of unification, it is important to keep in mind that east German women are a diverse group and that their experiences and expectations surrounding the unification process will vary depending upon their social background characteristics (e.g., their age, education, and marital and family status).

The process of unification rekindles old questions about women's economic and familial roles in society and about how to best achieve social and economic equality between men and women. Unification brought to the foreground a problem that is common to both east and west German women: the dilemma of combining work with family life. The two Germanys had devised different models to address this: GDR policies focused on enabling women to simultaneously combine motherhood with full-time employment; whereas FRG policies promoted a sequential model where women first work and then leave the labour force to raise children. One of the outcomes of German unification is that the sequential model, which tends to favour a traditional family form with a male breadwinner, is being imposed upon east German women. But how east German women will respond to this and how they will fare under conditions of a unified Germany remain important questions that require further investigation by social scientists.

ACKNOWLEDGEMENT

I would like to thank Barbara Laslett for comments on an earlier version of this paper.

NOTES

1.   See Ute Gerhard, "German Women and the Social Costs of Unification," *German Politics and Society* 24/25 (Winter 1991/92): 34–52; Gunnar Winkler, "Social Policies at a

Crossroad," in *German Unification: Process and Outcomes*, ed. M. Donald Hancock and Helga A. Welsh (Oxford: Westview Press, 1994), pp. 223–43.

2. Winkler, "Social Policies," p. 232.

3. Eva Kolinsky, *Women in Contemporary Germany: Life, Work and Politics* (Oxford: Berg Publishers, 1993).

4. Kolinsky, *Women in Contemporary Germany*; Kerstin Bast and Illona Ostner, "Ehe und Familie in der Sozialpolitik der DDR und BRD—ein Vergleich," in *Schriften des Zentrums für Sozialpolitik*, vol. 1, *Sozialpolitik im Prozeß der deutschen Vereinigung*, ed. W. Schmaehl (Frankfurt/Main: Campus Verlag, 1992), pp. 228–70.

5. Hildegard Maria Nickel, "Women in the GDR: Will Renewal Pass Them By?" *Women in German Yearbook* (1991): 99–107.

6. Kolinsky, *Women in Contemporary Germany*, p. 259.

7. Ursula Schröter, "Ostdeutsche Frauen im Transformationsprozeß: Eine soziologische Analyse zur sozialen Situation ostdeutscher Frauen (1990–1994)," *Aus Politik und Zeitgeschichte* B20 (1995): 31–42.

8. Christiane Lemke, "Women and Politics: The New Federal Republic of Germany," in *Women and Politics Worldwide*, ed. Barbara J. Nelson and Naima Chowdhury (New Haven: Yale University Press, 1994), pp. 263–84.

9. Schröter, "Ostdeutsche Frauen im Transformationsprozeß."

10. See Jacqueline Heinen, "The Impact of Social Policy on the Behaviour of Women Workers in Poland and East Germany," *Critical Social Policy* 10 (Fall 1990): 79–91; Dorothy Rosenberg, "Shock Therapy: GDR Women in Transition from Socialist Welfare State to Social Market Economy," *SIGNS* 17, no. 1 (1991): 129–51; Marilyn Rueschemeyer and Hanna Schissler, "Women in the Two Germanys," *German Studies Review* (DAAD special issue, 1990): 71–85.

11. Gunnar Winkler, *Frauenreport '90* (Berlin: Verlag Die Wirtschaft GmbH, 1990), pp. 141–44; for similar figures also see Bundesministerium für Frauen und Jugend, *Frauen in der Bundesrepublik Deutschland* (Bonn: Bundesministerium für Frauen, Jugend und Gesundheit, 1992), p. 80.

12. Hedwig Rudolph, Eileen Apfelbaum, and Friderike Maier, "After German Unity: A Cloudier Outlook for Women," *Challenge* (1990): 33–40.

13. Winkler, *Frauenreport '90*, p. 145.

14. Irene Dölling, "Alte und neue Dilemmata: Frauen in der ehemaligen DDR," *Women in German Yearbook* (1991): 121–36; Nickel, "Women in the GDR," pp. 99–107.

15. The quotes from East German mothers selected for this chapter are from an ongoing dissertation research project by Katherine Nash, "Motherhood and Childcare in Pre- and Post-Unification Germany" (ongoing dissertation research, University of Minnesota, Dept. of Sociology).

16. Bast and Ostner, "Ehe und Familie," p. 244; Barbara Bertram, "Zur Entwicklung der sozialen Geschlechterverhältnisse in den neuen Bundesländern," *Aus Politik und Zeitgeschichte* B6 (1993): 27–38.

17. For an excellent review of the situation of East German women at the close of the GDR era see Winkler, *Frauenreport '90*.

18. Nickel, "Women in the GDR," pp. 100–101.

19. See Lemke, "Women and Politics," p. 270; Nickel, "Women in the GDR," p. 100.

20. Lemke, "Women and Politics"; Nickel, "Women in the GDR."

21. Bast and Ostner, "Ehe und Familie"; Rueschemeyer and Schissler, "Women in the Two Germanies."

22. See Kolinsky, *Women in Contemporary Germany*; Nickel, "Women in the GDR."

23. Clemens Dannenbeck, "Einstellung zur Vereinbarkeit von Familie und Beruf," in *Die Familie in den neuen Bundesländern: Stabilität und Wandel in der gesellschaftlichen Umbruchsituation*, ed. Hans Bertram (Opladen: Leske und Budrich, 1992), pp. 239–60; Sarina Keiser, "Zusammenfassende Darstellung zentraler Ergebnisse des Familiensurveys—Ost," in *Die Familie in den neuen Bundesländern*, ed. Bertram, pp. 19–38.

24. Ilona Ostner, "Slow Motion: Women, Work and the Family in Germany," in *Women and Social Policies in Europe: Work, Family and the State*, ed. J. Lewis (Aldershot, England: Edward Elgar, 1993), pp. 92–115.

25. Susanne Rothmaler, "The Impact on Childcare," *German Politics and Society* 24/25 (1991/92): 106–10, 107f.

26. Ostner, "Slow Motion," p. 94.

27. Christiane Lemke, "Women and Politics," pp. 271–72. See also Robert Moeller, *Protecting Motherhood: Women and the Family in the Politics of Postwar West Germany* (Berkeley: University of California Press, 1993).

28. Ostner, "Slow Motion," pp. 96–100.

29. Ilona Ostner, "Ideas, Institutions, Traditions: The Experience of West German Women, 1945–1990," *German Politics and Society* 24/25 (1991/92): 87–99. See also Bundesministerium für Frauen und Jugend, *Frauen in der Bundesrepublik Deutschland*.

30. Ursula Müller, "The Family: Space for Self-Development or Privatization of Social Problems?" in *The Life Course and Social Change: Comparative Perspectives*, vol. 2, ed. Walter R. Heinz (Weinheim: Deutscher Studien-Verlag, 1991), pp. 159–68; Rosemarie Nave-Herz, "Historical Developments in Family Events and Employment of Women," in *Theoretical Advances in Life Course Research*, vol. 1, ed. Walter R. Heinz (Weinheim: Deutscher Studien-Verlag, 1991), pp. 130–43.

31. Winkler, "Social Policies at a Crossroad," p. 232.

32. Ernst Kistler, Dieter Jaufmann, and Anita B. Pfaff, "'Die Wiedervereinigung der deutschen Männer braucht keine Frauen…' Frauen als Wendeverliererinnen?" *Aus Politik und Zeitgeschichte* B6 (1993): 39–52; 41.

33. Ulrike Bohnenkamp and Joachim Eisbach, "Frauen als arbeitsmarktpolitische Zielgröße in Rostock" (Bremen: PIW, 1992).

34. Ute Gerhard, "German Women and the Social Costs of Unification," p. 22.

35. See Barbara Bertram, "Zur Entwicklung der sozialen Geschlechterverhältnisse in den neuen Bundesländern," pp. 29–31; Kolinsky, "Women in Contemporary Germany," pp. 283–85.

36. Tatjana Böhm, "Allein mit Kindern—eine Familienform," in *Alleinerziehende in den neuen Bundesländern: Immer noch eine Lebensform wie jede andere?* (Bonn: Friedrich-Ebert-Stiftung, 1993).

37. Petra Drauschke, Eva Mädje, Claudia Neusüß, and Margit Stolzenburg, "Ausdauernd, selbstbewußt und (noch) optimistisch?!" in *Alleinerziehende in den neuen Bundesländern*, pp. 21–42.

38. Monika Langkau-Herrmann, "Vorwort," *Frauen in den neuen Bundesländern: Rückzug in die Familie oder Aufbruch zur Gleichstellung in Beruf und Familie?* (Bonn: Friedrich-Ebert-Stiftung, 1991).

39. Kistler, Jaufmann, and Pfaff, "'Die Wiedervereinigung der deutschen Männer braucht keine Frauen…,'" p. 50.

40. Kistler, Jaufmann, and Pfaff, "'Die Wiedervereinigung der deutschen Männer braucht keine Frauen…,'" p. 48f.

41. Kistler, Jaufmann, and Pfaff, "'Die Wiedervereinigung der deutschen Männer braucht keine Frauen….'"

42. See Ursula Schroeter, "Ostdeutsche Frauen im Transformationsprozeß."

43. For a more detailed discussion, see the following articles in *German Politics and Society* 24/25 (1991/92): Daniela Birkenfeld-Pfeiffer, "Abortion and the Necessity for Compromise," pp. 122–27; Tatjana Böhm, "The Abortion Question: A New Solution in Unified Germany?" pp. 135–41; Ursula Nelles, "Abortion, the Special Case: A Constitutional Perspective," pp. 111–21; Margarethe Nimsch, "Abortion as Politic," pp. 128–34; see also Katharina von Ankum, "Political Bodies: Women and Re/Production in the GDR," *Women in German Yearbook* (1993): 127–43.

44. Nelles, "Abortion: the Special Case."

45. Winkler, "Social Policies at a Crossroad," p. 235.

Selected Bibliography

Altenhof, Ralf and Eckhard Jesse, eds. *Das wiedervereinigte Deutschland. Zwischenbilanz und Perspektiven.* Düsseldorf: Droste, 1994.

Andersen, Uwe and Wichard Woyke. *Handwörterbuch des politischen Systems der Bundesrepublik Deutschland.* Opladen: Leske & Budrich, 1992.

Bade, Klaus J. *Ausländer, Aussiedler, Asyl. Eine Bestandsaufnahme.* Munich: Beck, 1994.

Baring, Arnulf, ed. *Germany's New Position in Europe: Problems and Perspectives.* Oxford: Berg, 1994.

Bark, Dennis L. and David R. Gress. *A History of West Germany.* 2nd ed. 2 vols. Oxford and New York: Blackwell, 1993.

Berg-Schlosser, Dirk and Ralf Rytlewsky, eds. *Political Culture in Germany.* New Haven: Yale University Press, 1992.

Betz, Hans-Georg. *Postmodern Politics in Germany: The Politics of Resentment.* New York: Macmillan, 1991.

———. *Radical Right Wing Populism in Western Europe.* New York: St. Martin's Press, 1994.

Beyme, Klaus von. *Der Gesetzgeber. Der Bundestag als Entscheidungsorgan.* Wiesbaden: Westdeutscher Verlag, 1997.

Braunthal, Gerard. *The German Social Democrats in Power and Opposition.* Boulder, CO: Westview, 1994.

———. *Parties and Politics in Modern Germany.* Boulder, CO: Westview, 1996.

Brückner, Herbert. *Privatization in East Germany: A Neo Institutional Analysis.* London: Frank Cass, 1997.

Cafruny, Alan W. and Glenda G. Rosenthal. *The State of the European Community: The Maastricht Debates and Beyond.* Boulder, CO: Lynne Rienner Publ., 1993.

Carrington-Windo, Tristam. *A Dictionary of Contemporary Germany.* London: Hodder & Stoughton, 1996.

Childs, David. *The Stasi: The East German Intelligence and Security Service.* New York: New York University Press, 1996.

Clasen, Jochen and Richard Freeman, eds. *Social Policy in Germany.* London and New York: Harvester Wheatsheaf, 1994.

Conradt, David P. *The German Polity.* 6th ed. New York and London: Longman, 1996.

Conradt, David P. et al., eds. *Germany's New Politics: Parties and Issues in the 1990s.* Providence, RI: Berghahn, 1995.

Currie, David P. *The Constitution of the Federal Republic of Germany*. Chicago: University of Chicago Press, 1994.

Dalton, Russell J. *Politics in Germany*. 2nd ed. New York: HarperCollins, 1993.

———. *Germans Divided: The 1994 Bundestagswahl and the Evolution of the German Party System*. Oxford: Berg, 1996.

———, ed. *The New Germany Votes: Reunification and the Creation of a New Party System*. Oxford: Berg, 1993.

Dyson, Kenneth, ed. *The Politics of German Regulation*. Aldershot: Dartmouth & The Association for the Study of German Politics, 1992.

Eppelmann, Rainer, Horst Möller, and Günther Nooke et al., eds. *Lexikon des DDR-Sozialismus: Das Staats- und Gesellschaftssystem der Deutschen Demokratischen Republik*. Schöningh: Paderborn, 1996.

Frankland, E. Gene and Donald Schoomaker. *Between Power & Protest: The Green Party in Germany*. Boulder, CO: Westview, 1992.

Frevert, Ute. *Women in German History: From Bourgeois Emancipation to Sexual Liberation*. Oxford: Berg, 1989.

Fritsch-Bournazel, Renata. *Europe and German Unification*. New York and Oxford: Berg, 1992.

Fulbrook, Mary. *Anatomy of a Dictatorship: Inside the GDR, 1949–1989*. Oxford and New York: Oxford University Press, 1995.

Gabriel, Oscar W., and Everhard Holtmann, eds. *Handbuch des politischen Systems der Bundesrepublik Deutschland*. Munich: Oldenbourg, 1997.

Gabriel, Oscar W., ed. *Politische Orientierungen und Verhaltensweisen im vereinten Deutschland*. Opladen: Leske & Budrich, 1997.

Garton Ash, Timothy. *In Europe's Name: Germany and the Divided Continent*. London: Jonathan Cape, 1993.

Geissler, Rainer. *Die Sozialstruktur Deutschlands: Ein Studienbuch zur sozialstrukturellen Entwicklung im geteilten und vereinten Deutschland*. Bonn: Bundeszentrale für politische Bildung, 1992.

George, Stephen. *Politics and Policy in the European Union*. 3rd ed. Oxford: Oxford University Press, 1996.

Ghaussy, A. Ghanie and Wolf Schäfer, eds. *The Economics of German Unification*. London and New York: Routledge, 1993.

Giersch, Herbert, Karl-Heinz Paqué, and Holger Schmieding. *The Fading Miracle: Four Decades of Market Economy in Germany*. Cambridge: Cambridge University Press, 1992.

Glaeßner, Gert-Joachim, ed. *Germany After Unification: Coming to Terms with the Recent Past*. Amsterdam and Atlanta: Rodopi, 1996.

Goodhart, David. *The Reshaping of the German Social Market*. London: Institute for Public Policy Research, 1994.

Grosser, Dieter. *Soziale Marktwirtschaft—Soziale Sicherheit: Erfahrungen in der Bundesrepublik, Perspektiven im wiedervereinigten Deutschland*. Melle: Ernst Knoth, 1993.

Hacke, Christian. *Weltmacht wider Willen. Die Außenpolitik der Bundesrepublik Deutschland*. 3rd rev. ed. Frankfurt/Main and Berlin: Ullstein Verlag, 1997.

Haftendorn, Helga and Christian Tuschhoff, eds. *America and Europe in an Era of Change*. Boulder, CO: Westview Press, 1993.

Hancock, M. Donald and Helga Welsh, eds. *German Unification: Process and Outcomes*. Boulder, CO: Westview, 1994.

Hanrieder, Wolfram F. *Germany, America, Europe: Forty Years of German Foreign Policy.* New Haven: Yale University Press, 1989.

Herrigel, Gary. *Industrial Constructions: The Sources of German Industrial Power.* Cambridge: Cambridge University Press, 1996.

Hettlage, Robert and Karl Lenz. *Deutschland nach der Wende. Eine Bilanz.* Munich: Beck, 1995.

Horrocks, David and Eva Kolinsky, eds. *Turkish Culture in German Society Today.* Providence, RI: Berghahn Books, 1996.

Huelshoff, Michael G., Andrei Markovits, and Simon Reich, eds. *From Bundesrepublik to Deutschland: German Politics after Unification.* Ann Arbor: University of Michigan Press, 1993.

Hyman, Richard and Anthony Ferner, eds. *New Frontiers in European Industrial Relations.* Oxford, UK and Cambridge, MA: Blackwell, 1994.

James, Harold. *A German Identity: 1770 to Present.* London: Phoenix, 1994.

Kilper, Heiderose and Roland Lhotta. *Föderalismus in der Bundesrepublik Deutschland. Eine Einführung.* Opladen: Leske & Budrich, 1996.

Kolinsky, Eva, ed. *Everyday Life in Postunification Germany: A Case Study of Leipzig.* Keele: Keele University Press, 1995.

Kommers, Donald P. *The Constitutional Jurisprudence of the Federal Republic of Germany.* 2nd ed. Durham, NC: Duke University Press, 1997.

Lampert, Heinz. *Die Wirtschafts- und Sozialordnung der Bundesrepublik Deutschland.* 12th ed. Munich: Verlag Vahlen, 1995.

Larres, Klaus and Panikos Panayi, eds. *The Federal Republic Since 1949: Politics, Society and Economics Before and After Unification.* London and New York: Longman, 1996.

Lewis, Derek and John R.P. McKenzie. *The New Germany: Social, Political and Cultural Challenges of Unification.* Exeter: University of Exeter Press, 1995.

Lewis, Rand C. *The Neo-Nazis and German Unification.* Westport, CT: Praeger, 1996.

Markovits, Andrei S. and Philip S. Gorski. *The German Left: Red, Green and Beyond.* New York: Oxford University Press, 1993.

Marsh, David. *Germany and Europe: The Crisis of Unity.* London: Heinemann, 1994.

McAdams, A. James. *Germany Divided: From the Wall to Reunification.* Princeton, NJ: Princeton University Press, 1993.

McFalls, Laurence H. *Communism's Collapse, Democracy's Demise? The Cultural Context and Consequences of the East German Revolution.* Houndmills, Basingstoke: Macmillan, 1995.

Merkl, Peter H. *German Unification in the European Context.* University Park: University of Pennsylvania Press, 1993.

————, ed. *The Federal Republic of Germany at Forty-Five: Union without Unity.* New York: New York University Press, 1994.

Niedermayer, Oskar and Klaus von Beyme, eds. *Politische Kultur in Ost- und Westdeutschland.* Opladen: Leske & Budrich, 1996.

Opp, Karl-Dieter, Peter Voss and Christiane Gern. *Origins of a Spontaneous Revolution: East Germany 1989.* Ann Arbor: University of Michigan Press, 1995.

Padgett, Stephen, ed. *Parties and Party Systems in the New Germany.* Aldershot/UK: Dartmouth Publishing Company, 1993.

Parkes, K. Stuart. *Understanding Contemporary Germany.* London: Routledge, 1997.

Parness, Diane L. *The SPD and the Challenge of Mass Politics: The Dilemma of the German Volkspartei.* Boulder, CO: Westview Press, 1991.

Poguntke, Thomas. *Alternative Politics: The German Green Party*. Edinburgh: Edinburgh University Press, 1993.

Pommerin, Rainer, ed. *Culture in the Federal Republic of Germany, 1945–1995*. Oxford and Washington, D.C.: Berg, 1996.

Pulzer, Peter. *German Politics, 1945–1995*. New York: Oxford University Press, 1995.

Quint, Peter E. *The Imperfect Union: Constitutional Structures of German Unification*. Lawrenceville, NJ: Princeton University Press, 1997.

Rohe, Karl, ed. *Elections, Parties and Political Traditions: Social Foundations of German Parties and Party Systems, 1867–1987*. New York: Berg, 1991.

Scharf, Thomas. *The German Greens: Challenging the Consensus*. Oxford and Providence, RI: Berg, 1994.

Schlecht, Otto, ed. *Transition to a Market Economy*. Krefeld: Sinus Verlag, 1993.

Schoenbaum, David and Elizabeth Pond. *The German Question and Other German Questions*. New York: St. Martin's Press, 1996.

Schweitzer, Carl-Christoph and Detlev Karsten. *The Federal Republic of Germany and EC Membership Evaluated*. New York: St. Martin's Press, 1990.

Schweitzer, Carl-Christoph et al., eds. *Politics and Government in Germany, 1944-1994: Basic Documents*. Providence, RI and Oxford, UK: Berghahn, 1995.

Sinn, Gerlinde and Hans Werner Sinn. *Jumpstart: The Economic Unification of Germany*. Cambridge, MA: MIT Press, 1992.

Smith, Gordon, William E. Paterson and Stephen Padgett. *Developments in German Politics 2*. Durham, N.C.: Duke University Press, 1996.

Sontheimer, Kurt, and Wilhelm Bleek. *Grundzüge des politischen Systems der Bundesrepublik Deutschland*. Rev. ed. Munich: Piper, 1997.

Swann, Dennis. *The Economics of the Common Market*. London: Penguin Books, 1995.

Veen, Hans-Joachim, Norbert Lepszy, and Peter Mnich. *The Republikaner Party in Germany: Right-Wing Menace or Protest Catchall?* Westport: CT: Praeger/Greenwood Publ., 1993.

Verheyen, Dirk and Christian Soe. *The Germans and Their Neighbors*. Boulder, CO: Westview, 1993.

Wallace, Helen and William Wallace. *Policy-Making in the European Union*. Oxford: Oxford University Press, 1996.

Weidenfeld, Werner and Karl-Rudolf Korte, eds. *Handbuch zur deutschen Einheit*. Bonn: Bundeszentrale für politische Bildung, 1993.

Welfens, Paul J.J., ed. *Economic Aspects of German Unification*. 2nd ed. Berlin: Springer, 1996.

Windolf, Paul. *Expansion and Structural Change: Higher Education in Germany, the United States, and Japan, 1870–1990*. Boulder, CO: Westview, 1997.

Index